DISASTERS AND HEROES

Disasters and Heroes

On War, Memory and Representation

ANGUS CALDER

UNIVERSITY OF WALES PRESS
CARDIFF
2004

British Library Cataloguing-in-Publication Data.
A catalogue record for this book is available from the British Library.

ISBN 0–7083–1867–3 paperback
      0–7083–1868–1 hardback

The right of Angus Calder to be identified as author of this work has been asserted by him in accordance with Sections 77 and 78 of the Copyright, Designs and Patents Act 1988.

Typeset by Bryan Turnbull
Printed in Great Britain by Cromwell Press Ltd, Trowbridge

Contents

Introduction

One

On 22 February 1944, during the so-called 'Little Blitz' of London, a German bomb fell on a detached house in the southernmost suburban fringe of London. The crew of the Luftwaffe plane from which it fell had presumably decided to retreat from AA flak and nightfighters over the city. It would have been unwise to return to base with bombs undropped.

Under a Morrison 'table' shelter downstairs in the house in question were my mother, elder brother aged twelve, younger brother just seven weeks old, myself aged two years and two and a half weeks, and Betty who helped Mother look after us. My elder sister, sleeping upstairs, had not joined us, nor had Auntie Margie, widow of my father's brother, recently dead in his prime due to over-exertion as an executive in the aircraft industry. Fiona escaped unscathed but doctors would spend months picking 156 pieces of glass out of Margie's back – after which, with pleasing irony, she would marry a German POW twelve years younger than herself.

All my life I have been constructing and reconstructing memories of an event which I could not have remembered. (Every two or three months I dream of broken glass underfoot or in my mouth.) For a very long time I believed that I could recall the white head of baby Allan carried by an adult into an Anderson shelter, which would have been underground and out of doors. My sister Fiona disabused me of this, just as she has now relieved me of a much more recent misunderstanding, that we were 'buried alive' for an hour under rubble in our Morrison shelter before rescue workers arrived. But my little life was certainly transformed. Furniture, books, domestic goods and treasures were destroyed. My parents had to start home-making all over again, after a spell when we lived as evacuees in a big house in Bedfordshire, then shared with a family of German Jews a small house back in Surrey.

It is not surprising that throughout my writing life I have returned, though sometimes reluctantly, to stories and themes of war.

Two

Construction of memory begins with the wartime event itself. A diarist or letter-writer selects detail – and may find later that phenomena which nag the memory went unrecorded at the time. Non-scribblers adjust their memories to what they hear on radio, see in newsreels and movies and photos and perhaps works of art. Though Fiona corrects me, I can correct her. Despite her insistent recall of fighter planes crossing ever-clear skies, the weather over southern England in August 1940 was not exceptionally fine, but often cloudy, *pace* Paul Nash's fine painting of vapour trails forming an abstract pattern evocative of heroism and death.

As time goes on, memories form and reform. Books about the war appear in profusion. Old soldiers pick and mix them and adjust their memories. In the British Legion club, at reunions, they homogenize these with those of old comrades. They are irritated yet beguiled by sanitized accounts in movies of action on fronts where they participated. They find it very hard to talk to anyone except former comrades about horrors they saw and traumas they experienced.

Meanwhile, historians have been at work since the beginning. The UK Civil series of Histories of the Second World War were written by scholars conscripted to judge and observe actually within relevant ministries, from early in the conflict. They avoid naming individuals, but are candid about bureaucratic bungling, so that I am perfectly sure that very little significant muck on the direction of the Home Front remained unraked when, using the Civil Histories, I concocted my book *The People's War* in the mid to late 1960s. But with the notable exception of R. M. Titmuss's *Problems of Social Policy,* these rarely make vivid reading. TV representations of the war have again and again sought to make it vivid by splicing 'talking heads' – increasingly old witnesses with increasingly unreliable memories – with newsreel and other film from the period. Humphrey Jennings's wonderful dramatized documentary about the London Blitz, *Fires Were Started,* involved reconstruction many months after heavy raiding had ceased. Yet clips of it have turned up, as if 'true', in TV evocations of the raids. The most veridical documentation we have on the Home Front is provided by the diaries kept for Mass-Observation, a unique, not to say eccentric, social survey. Filed month by month, these were subject neither to official censorship nor to retrospective self-censorship. Here one can find immediate representation of experience and the earliest stages of memory-formation.

'Popular memory' of the Home Front has been adjusted, like that of old soldiers, to what has been published and screened since, and to overviews, from *parti pris* positions, of what the war in general 'meant'. Of course, one's morale was 'high' under aerial bombardment. Of course – many on the left insisted – there was wild enthusiasm for Labour's 'landslide' victory in the 1945 general election (when the party in fact got less than half the national vote). Of course, the brave but modest British displayed qualities during the war and after their deserved victory which were superior to those of brainwashed Germans, panicky French, pusillanimous Italians – and brash Yanks . . .

The second part of this collection of essays is concerned with issues I have just raised, regarding Memory. These essays refer in passing to Commemoration, which is central to the first part and Representation more widely, discussed in Part 3.

Three

The idea of such a gathering of essays came to me in 1993 when I was asked to give one of a series of lectures on Representation of War at Anglia Polytechnic University, and decided to begin with Homer. I had been professionally engaged for fifteen years with teams of academics at the Open University which created and taught two very popular courses on the Enlightenment, and had latterly had the privilege of tutoring a splendid new course on 'Homer and Society'. I was (and remain) fascinated by eighteenth-century Classicism. Since my first book, co-authored with my then wife, was on Walter Scott, the interfaces between Enlightenment and Romanticism have been a still more enduring preoccupation.

After 1993, I began to be seriously involved in military history, encouraged by my friends Paul Addison and Jeremy Crang who set up the Centre for Second World War Studies at Edinburgh University, and to take a lively interest in the deathly subject of Commemorations and Memorials. I cannot claim to have constructed a general theory, or theories, about representations of war. Movies and poetry, painting and fiction, theatre and prose memoirs, sculpture and ceremonial go about representation in different though related ways. But I will conclude this introduction with one general observation.

What we have to call 'fact', assumed to have had 'real' manifestation, is rapidly translated into myth by incorporation into pre-existent discourses and narrative structures. From the Renaissance on, facts arising in warfare were commonly represented in ways suggested by the ancient epics, though by the age of Scott medieval and later Romances were coming on stream as well. The horrendous melding of Classicism with Wagnerian Romanticism in Nazi official culture met its Waterloo, so to speak, at Stalingrad. The related perversities of Soviet 'Socialist Realism' fell with the Berlin Wall. But these apparently aberrant discourses were extreme and belated examples of tendencies formerly present in all Western cultures.

Quotations from two of the famous soldier poets of 1914–1918 demonstrate how reaction against heroic and chivalric conceptions of war began in the trenches of Flanders and France. Wilfred Owen, in a letter *(Collected Letters,* 1967, p. 482) wrote: 'Tennyson, it seems, was always a great child. So should I have been, but for Beaumont Hamel.' Sassoon, in a poem, 'Conscripts', remarked: 'Rapture and pale Enchantment and Romance/ . . . Went home because they couldn't stand the din.'

Homeric, Virgilian, Romantic and Wagnerian conceptions of heroism, conditioning representations of war, have lost their glamour in both old and current senses of that word – strong magic and surface prettiness. And in June 2003 it is a notable fact that after the victory of US–UK forces over Saddam Hussein's Iraq, in a war opposed before it began by astonishing, huge demonstrations in every continent, the undermanned British Army reported, with dismay, that there was no upsurge in recruiting such as had followed the Falklands War of 1982 and the Gulf War of 1991. There is abundant sad evidence that young males between seventeen and twenty-four are prone, in Britain, to gang violence. But it seems that the idea which Owen debunked, that it is sweet and decorous to die for one's country, may have lost some of its potency.

Edinburgh, February 2004

STOP PRESS
Thanks to Donat Gallagher of James Cook University, Townsville, Queensland, I have recognized errors in my essay on Crete, 1941, and have striven to correct them. Otherwise, I have not changed any of these essays since their previous publication – that way would lie infinite regress. But I am minded now to annotate 'Meditation on Memorials'.

On p. 18, I refer to the war memorial in Wick as incomprehensible. On my latest visit to the town (October 2003), I decided to dive into the library and settle matters. The *John O'Groats Journal* for 2 November 1923 made all clear at last.

The memorial was unveiled on 31 October by General Lord Horne. Distinguished persons and representatives of public institutions were in attendance. Large crowds filled the thoroughfares in all directions.

The memorial cost about £2,600 – a six-figure sum in today's currency. The sculptor, Percy Portsmouth of Edinburgh, had also designed memorials for Thurso and Elgin. Bronze panels set in the pedestal (of Creetown granite) commemorated by name nearly 300 men of the Burgh of Wick who had fallen in the Great War. The message conveyed by the 8 ft 9 in figure on top would then have been understood at least by the platform party. Others would receive it from the newspaper.

This robed male represents Victory and Peace.

A sheathed sword is held in the right hand with the point resting on the palm of the left hand and with an olive branch outstretched. This constitutes an interesting symbolism, stimulating as it does the idea that the sword has been used so that peace may be established and not merely for military glory and conquest. Broken implements of war beneath and behind the feet serve to express the fact that war is alien to the higher instincts of humanity, having served their purpose in subduing and chastizing the arrogance and aims of a military race raised to a pitch previously unknown in the history of the world.

The 'fine, heroic, firm, noble and purposeful countenance' of the robed male is devoid of the 'arrogance of militarism in the German sense', and the whole figure expresses 'the desire to achieve noble ends in conflict with the grosser elements that stimulate war'.

This made sense in 1923. The Great War had been fought, men said, to end all wars. But after 1945 the monument had added to it the names of casualties in another Great War. It is for this reason that it is now incomprehensible.

Acknowledgements

The idea of this book began when Anglia Polytechnic University asked me in 1993 to give a paper in a series on representations of war. This became 'The Hero From Homer Till Now'. The essay on *Seven Pillars of Wisdom* introduces the Wordsworth Classics edition (1997). 'Writing in the Sky' and 'Mr Wu and the Colonials' were first presented as papers at conferences at Edinburgh University – the latter appears in *Time to Kill: The Soldier's Experience of War in the West, 1939–1945*, edited by Paul Addison and Angus Calder (1997), the former differently titled in *The Burning Blue: A New History of the Battle of Britain*, edited by Jeremy Crang (2000), both published by Pimlico. 'Scottish Poets in the Desert' was written for *South fields*. 'Art and War' was commissioned by *Alba*. 'The New Zimbabwe Writing and Chimurenga' originated with a British Academy grant which enabled me to revisit east and central Africa in 1991 – it was first presented as a paper at the Universities of Cambridge and York, then published in *Wasafiri*. 'Just a Nasty Kid' was an Edinburgh Festival review for *New Statesman*.

'Meditation on Memorials' began with invitations to speak from Glasgow Philosophical Society and the University of Edinburgh Scottish History Society. 'D Day 1994' appeared in *New Times*.

'The Wars of Ian Hamilton Finlay and 'Verse and Bosnia' were published in *Chapman*.

'Campaign Honours' appeared in Anne Smith's *Literary Review*. My review *of Civil War Soldiers* was commissioned by *London Review of Books* in anticipation of a British publication of the book which never occurred. 'Britain's Good War' was in *History Today*, which had previously published a review of Juliet Gardiner's book on GIs. My review of David Reynolds's *Rich Relations*, coupled with that here appeared in the *Sunday Times*.

'Mass-Observation's War' appeared under a different title in the *Independent* magazine, 'New Zealand Women at War' in *British Review of New Zealand Studies*, and 'The People's Peace' in *Scotland on Sunday*. The essay on Rattigan was prompted by queries from Muriel Romanes when she was directing *The Deep Blue Sea* for the Royal Lyceum Theatre, Edinburgh, incorporates parts of a note written for the programme, and was finished after watching the production.

For help with my Coda I must thank Karen McPherson and Peter Arnott. My thanks also to editors, and others, implied or mentioned by name above. I must thank, too, Ceinwen Jones, Editorial Manager, and other staff at University of Wales Press. It is a great pleasure to be published in Cardiff, where two of my children live and where I have often gathered with Welsh friends to watch Rugby Union internationals at the wonderful old Arms Park and the still-more-wonderful Millennium Stadium which has replaced it. However, a lot of material here was written for Scottish publications where it was natural for one to use words employed every day by people around me, but not current south of the Tweed (or perhaps the Wear?). I therefore gloss a few words here:

kenspeckle (p. 19)	conspicuous
wally dugs (p. 36)	ornamental porcelain dogs displayed in pairs on mantelpieces
stushie (p. 37)	uproar, quarrel
keelie (p. 42)	low-class person
doitered (p. 66)	witless, confused

To gloss all the Scots used by Robert Garioch (pp. 212–14) would be cumbersome. *The Concise Scottish National Dictionary* is invaluable.

1

COMMEMORATIONS

Meditation on Memorials

1

The handsome young Kosovo Liberation Army rifleman, interviewed early in February 1999 by BBC TV, says that he keeps one bullet aside, for himself. However he may actually behave in whatever conflict may follow, he clearly intends just now that BBC viewers should understand that he will fight to the death for his small country's complete independence from Yugoslavia. If the Serbs corner him, he will kill himself rather than surrender. We may be prepared to believe him because we know that many men and women in various times and places have sacrificed their lives for what they conceived to be the cause of their people. Thus, in 480 BC Leonidas, king of the Spartans, faced Xerxes' Persian Host, numbered by some absurd accounts at five million, with a bare three hundred of his fellow countrymen, in the small pass leading from Thessaly into Locris, only twenty-five feet wide at its narrowest part, named 'Thermopylae', 'hot gates', after certain hot baths nearby. All but one of the Spartans died, but Greece was saved. Memorial columns were erected on the battlefield.

It had seemed obvious in ancient times that the victories of kings and emperors were worthy of monumental commemoration. Egyptian pharoahs memorialized their military triumphs with obelisks – that is, blocks of stone pointed at the top. Ultimately, future conquerors of Egypt looted them, so that more ancient obelisks stand in Rome than anywhere else and Cleopatra's Needle is a landmark beside the Thames. Ironically, this symbol of triumphalist hierarchy was adopted by the people who in 1793 erected the Martyrs' Monument in Edinburgh to commemorate those who were banished for advocating parliamentary reform, and another obelisk at Drumclog, near Strathaven, marks the only victory of the Covenanters over Royalist troops, in a skirmish there in 1679.

That ordinary persons might perform so heroically that their deeds should be celebrated in words and stone was clear to the ancient Greeks who bequeathed to the West a legacy of political ideas which included a prototype of democracy, as well as a range of literary and artistic forms. The niche devoted to commemorating nearly six thousand men of the Royal Scots Fusiliers who died in the First World War, in the Scottish National War Memorial at Edinburgh Castle, displays a passage from Pericles' oration, as presented by Thucydides, over the Athenian dead of the Peloponnesian War: 'The whole earth is a tomb of heroic men, and their story is not graven in stone over their clay, but abides everywhere without visible symbol, woven into the stuff of men's lives.' However, the Greeks created visible symbols. As well as columns for the 300 Spartans, there was the column erected by the government of Samos to honour Samian sailors who fought at the battle of Lade, and this might be seen as a distant forerunner of, for instance, the column outside Westminster Abbey erected in 1861 to commemorate old boys of Westminster School who had died in the Crimean War. But Nelson's Column in the centre of London followed the ancient precedent of the Emperor Constantine, who erected a great column in the centre of his new city Constantinople on which a figure of himself stood in the form of a sun-god, and the more recent one of Napoleon's column in the Place Vendôme in Paris to commemorate his victory at Austerlitz. 'The commonest use of memorial columns', writes Alan Borg, to whose book *War Memorials* I am indebted for much of the preceding information, 'has been as pedestals for hero statues.' He goes on to remark that we may find it 'surprising that crosses were not widely used as war memorials in Europe before the twentieth century, but this reflects the fact that individual or communal war memorials were not themselves common in medieval or early modem Europe.' This began to change, like so many things, with the French Revolution and Napoleon's subsequent onslaught on the rest of the continent. As early as 1793 a monument, the *Hessendenkmal,* was erected in Frankfurt to commemorate the city's liberation from French occupation, where the names of the fallen were listed without regard to military rank. The German Wars of Liberation in 1813–14 were fought by citizen armies, and by the mid-nineteenth century there were monuments in Germany to the volunteers – and poets – of that struggle. In 1818–21 the Prussian king erected a monument in Berlin commemorating all who had died for Prussia. In the wave of memorials in Germany following the Franco–Prussian War of 1870–1, the common soldier was still given equal honour with his officers.[1]

However, only generals were named on the Arc de Triomphe in Paris. Individual warriors with high social status or considerable military rank had of course long been memorialized by tombstones and monumental entries inside churches. We are startled to find a crusader commemorated at Rodel in the south of Harris. I cannot forget the tomb of a tough Elizabethan landowner from sixteenth-century Sussex, whose ebullient effigy was adorned with verses including:

> When that the French did come to sack Seaford
> This Pelham did repel 'em back aboard.

Memorable indeed, though perhaps I do not remember it exactly. The crypt of St Paul's Cathedral in London offers a frightful mass of monumental statuary idolizing successful British commanders. More modestly, St John's, the episcopalian church across Princes Street at the West End of Edinburgh's New Town, now a centre of Christian activity on behalf of the world's poorest countries, is garnished within with plaques commemorating communicants who died in nineteenth-century wars, notably those sustaining British conquest in India, which speak of the genteel imperialism of the people who originally worshipped there. But these are not 'war memorials'. These men merely died, like coalminers and cranesmen, performing an intrinsically dangerous job.

Samuel Hines in his book *The Soldier's Tale,* a survey of memoirs of twentieth-century war, has remarked of the cavalry units in the British Expeditionary Force of professionals who went to France in 1914 that 'The officers of those regiments were soldiers in the tradition of the European officer caste, sons of the aristocracy and gentry, for whom the army was a career, a vocation, and often the ultimate field sport.'[2] They included the leaders of the Royal Scots Greys, Scotland's only cavalry regiment. Its charge at Waterloo was commemorated long after by Lady Butler in a very famous painting probably known to most people in Britain in 1914. Napoleon is credited with a surreal and surely apocryphal comment – 'Those terrible grey horses – how they fight' – in Ian Hay's reverent account of the Scottish National War Memorial, published in 1931, four years after it was opened. But during the First World War these heirs of a great tradition found themselves, Hay has to admit, 'practically immobilized'. Mounted on fragile and conspicuous animals, they were almost always useless in the new conditions of mechanized warfare. Hence they lost only 144 dead, mostly, Hay suggests, when they were dismounted and dug in or fought on foot.[3] With the cavalry tradition died the long era in which the entire British Navy, for instance, might consider its losses adequately commemorated by a column erected in honour of dashing Lord

Nelson. Mechanization made the very notion of representative individual heroism problematic, since generals did not direct complex operations involving observation from aircraft, wireless telegraphy, artillery directed to fire at long range, tanks, and poison gas, at the front, or anywhere near it. The heroism of Lawrence leading Arabian irregulars on camels, or von Richthofen directing his 'flying circus' in person was now exceptional and anachronistic. Because European leaders now answered to mass electorates, ways had to be found to commemorate dead volunteers and conscripts from the great national aggregations of European population, who had died in their millions. Nine million is a frequently cited figure. Thirteen million is equally plausible. But all statistics of casualties are suspect when so many missing men were never found and when deaths caused by war wounds years after were not necessarily noted. Certainly, the total of dead exceeded the present-day population of Sweden. Ian Hay accepted the figure of 100,000 fatal Scottish casualties, out of a total population of 4,760,904 recorded in the 1911 census, but by one estimate 20 per cent of the 800,000 odd British and Irish dead and missing were Scots. Whichever figure is accepted, Scottish losses were proportionately larger than those of the rest of the UK, though persons interested in the way in which demography seems to make nonsense of folk history may note that the 1921 census, after such carnage, showed a small increase in Scotland's population. It fell back slightly by 1931 after a decade of economic recession and consequent emigration. Incidentally, what might be called the Myth of Miss Jean Brodie's Felled Fiancé – the idea that a generation of young British women were largely deprived of husbands – is also queried by statistics, which show that among women in England and Wales aged 20 to 44 the proportion unmarried fell, from 41.6 to 40.7 per cent, between 1911 and 1921.[4]

However, whether casualties were 2 or 3 per cent of overall Scottish population, the Great War, as it was then known, seemed cataclysmic in relation to small Scottish communities. The 8,432 lives of Seaforth Highlanders lost were, bar those of the battalion of Canadian Seaforths, mostly drawn from Ross and Lewis. On the monument at Lochinver, the names Mackenzie and Macleod preponderate to an extent which remains poignant. My father was a boy of eight when the Fife and Forfar Yeomanry rode out of his home town, Forfar, on their way to France. A cavalryman stooped from his saddle, picked him up and gave him a ride to the town boundary. 'I never knew his name', my father used to say, 'and I cannot remember his face. I know just one thing about him. He never came back. None of them ever came back.' I used as a child to believe that he meant that they were all killed. But life was more complex than that. In the British forces were my father's elder brothers, both of whom survived the war as mechanics behind the lines specializing in petrol-driven vehicles, and both of whom rose afterwards, via Clydeside engineering, far from Forfar, to high positions in the new aircraft industry. Detaching men from the lives of sleepy localities, war also gave some of them opportunities which, as much as their deaths, would leave gaps at home.

Hence what is perhaps the most moving passage in the whole of Scottish prose fiction resounds far beyond the location of the small imagined community which it evokes. In the Kinraddie of Lewis Grassic Gibbon's *Sunset Song*, the profits of wartime lumbering and agriculture have done more enduring damage to the culture of the independent crofters than the deaths of men in the war. The Munros have made a small fortune by abandoning farming and raising hens. The Trustees in charge of the land decide to sell it at last, so that crofters with enough cash can buy their own places. Long Rob Duncan of the mill, despite his pacifism, finally enlists and is killed in France. Gordon of Upperhill, who has already acquired one croft which its occupants cannot pay for, buys the mill land for almost nothing, and he and his family convert themselves to gentry, except for his lively daughter Maggie Jean who joins the Labour Party and becomes a trade unionist organizing farm servants. (But this too marks nemesis for the crofting tradition.) Chris Guthrie, Gibbon's heroine, the brave woman crofter, whose husband Ewan Tavendale has died in France, has taken up with the new minister, a Great War veteran himself, Robert Colquhoun. After the banns of their marriage have been announced, the minister, now inducted by Chris, as it were, into the immemorial Mearns community, makes his decision about commemoration.

> He'd been handed the money, the minister, to raise a memorial for Kinraddie's bit men that the War had killed. Folk thought he'd have a fine stone angel, with a night-gown on, raised up at Kinraddie cross-roads. But he sent for a mason instead and had the old stone circle by Blawearie loch raised up and cleaned and set all in place, real heathen-like, and a paling set round it.

The inscription is unveiled on a January Saturday before the local population, with snow shining on the Grampians:

> The minister said, *Let us pray*, and folk took off their hats, it smote cold on your pow. The sun was fleeing up in the clouds, it was quiet on the hill, you

saw young Chris stand looking down on Kinraddie with her bairn's hand in hers. And then the Lord's Prayer was finished, the minister was speaking just ordinary, he said they had come to honour the folk whom the War had taken, and that the clearing of this ancient site was maybe the memory that best they'd have liked. And he gave a nod to old Brigson and the strings were pulled and off came the clout and there on the Standing Stone the words shone out in their dark grey lettering, plain and short:

> FOR: THE: MEMORY: OF: CHA
> RLES: STRACHAN: JAMES:
> LESLIE: ROBERT: DUNCAN:
> EWAN: TAVENDALE: WHO:
> WERE: OF: THIS: LAND: AND:
> FELL: IN: THE: GREAT: WAR:
> IN   FRANCE: REVELATION:
> II CH: 28 VERSE

And then, with the night waiting out by on Blawearie brae, and the sun just verging the coarse hills, the minister began to speak again, his short hair blowing in the wind that had come, his voice not decent and a kirk-like bumble, but ringing out over the loch:

FOR I WILL GIVE YOU THE MORNING STAR

In the sunset of an age and an epoch we may write that for epitaph of the men who were of it. They went quiet and brave from the lands they loved, though seldom of that love might they speak, it was not in them to tell in words of the earth that moved and lived and abided, their life and enduring love. And who knows at the last what memories of it were with them, the springs and the winters of this land and all the sounds and scents of it that had once been theirs, deep, and a passion of their blood and spirit, those four who died in France? With them we may say there died a thing older than themselves, these were the Last of the Peasants, the last of the Old Scots folk . . . It was the old Scotland that perished then, and we may believe that never again will the old speech and the old songs, the old curses and the old benedictions, rise but with alien effort to our lips. The last of the peasants, those four that you knew, took that with them to the darkness and the quietness of the places where they sleep. And the land changes, their parks and their steadings are a desolation where the sheep are pastured, we are told that great machines come soon to till the land, and the great herds come to feed on it, the crofter is gone, the man with the house and the steading of his own and the land closer to his heart than the flesh of his body. Nothing, it has been said, is true but change, nothing abides, and here in Kinraddie where we watch the building of those little prides and those little fortunes on the ruins of the little farms we must give heed that these also do not abide, that a new spirit shall come to the land with the greater herd and the great machines. For greed of place and possession and great estate those four had little heed, the kindness of friends and the warmth of toil and the peace of rest – they asked no more from God or man, and no less would they endure. So, lest we shame them, let us believe that the new oppressions and foolish greeds are no more than mists that pass. They died for a world that is past, these men, but they did not die for this that we seem to inherit. Beyond it and us there shines a greater hope and a newer world, undreamt when these four died. But need we doubt which side of the battle they would range themselves did they live to-day, need we doubt the answer they cry to us even now the four of them, from the places of the sunset?

And then, as folk stood dumbfounded, this was just sheer politics, plain what he meant, the Highlandman McIvor tuned up his pipes and began to step slow round the stone circle by Blawearie Loch, slow and quiet, and folk watched him, the dark was near, it lifted your hair and was eerie and uncanny, the *Flowers of the Forest* as he played it . . .

It rose and rose and wept and cried, that crying for the men that fell in battle, and there was Kirsty Strachan weeping quietly and others with her, and the young ploughmen they stood with glum, white faces, they'd no understanding or caring, it was something that vexed and tore at them, it belonged to times they had no knowing of.[5]

Of course, this is wholly fictional in detail. As Scott had fictionalized his own Border ancestors, and Tolstoy his own forebears in the year 1812, so Gibbon finds symbolic means to express what he thought had happened to the Mearns of his own actual childhood. A reader coming fresh to this passage out of context might find it sentimental. In the context of the entire *Scots Quair*, where *Sunset Song* is the first part of a trilogy, it is deeply moving because it is deeply ironic. The minister himself, gassed in France, will die a young man, a belated war casualty. His Christian Socialism, present in his oration, will be seen as a sentimental and inadequate prescription for Scotland's ills. Above all it is ironic that apart from James Leslie, of whom we know nothing, Kinraddie's casualties are Chae Strachan the crofter socialist, Long Rob the freethinking miller – and Ewan Tavendale, shot for desertion after court martial in France.

In 1998 there was much agitation in the media to secure long-posthumous pardons for all the victims of court martial in the British Army of the Great War. Haig personally signed warrants for the deaths of well over 200 men, most if not all of them victims of shellshock, an involuntary reaction to the strains of mechanized warfare. It is to the credit of the British Army that in the Second World War a man might deliberately desert more than once and live to tell the tale, whereas the Wehrmacht executed soldiers in their thousands, and Stalin's evil Order 227, of 28 July 1942, 'Not a Step Back' – an Order officially revealed to the Soviet public at large only in 1988 – authorized summary execution of 'panickers' and 'cowards'.[6] Such facts do not fully exonerate Haig. The notion of executions *pour encourager les autres* was an intrinsically odious one, even though mutinies had actually occurred and their prevention was a serious worry. However, some of the men executed must have committed crimes punishable in any community. Dr John Reid, then junior Minister of Defence, was sensible to refuse a blanket pardon. As a distinguished alumnus of Stirling University, he must have read Grassic Gibbon. His suggestion was that all those executed should be listed and commemorated along with the other war dead, as, though he did not add this, at 'Kinraddie'.

Colquhoun's attempt to merge the recent war dead with the landscape of Scotland and its ancient human associations was far from eccentric at the time in question. Again, it was the French Revolution which had propelled forward a movement to take burial grounds away from town centres – and thus outside the domination of the church. There was a sensible fear of pestilence connected with the stench of death. Père Lachaise, the garden cemetery of Paris, set an example copied all over Europe. Americans, from 1830, developed the still more radical idea of the 'park cemetery', placed in untouched woodland. After the First World War, the victorious but saddened French created *jardins funèbres* on these lines, the defeated Germans *Heldenhaine* – 'heroes' groves'. These, officially approved in 1915, were, George L. Mosse tells us, 'surrogate military cemeteries (without any graves) enclosed and separate from their surroundings. A *Heldenhain* was a space within nature specifically for the cult of the fallen, the trees taking the place of rows of actual graves.' Sometimes each dead man had his own tree. Usually, there was a semicircle of trees with an 'oak of peace' in the middle, or a rock or boulder which unlike the Stones of Remembrance favoured in Britain would retain its natural contours.[7] The symbolism involved was non-Christian, like Colquohoun's assimilation of the newly dead crofters with the unknown ancient pagans who had erected the standing stones.

As for 'The Flowers of the Forest', Colquhoun's idea occurred to many. The classic lament for Flodden represented grief of national proportions, commensurate with the scale of the new carnage. John Boyd Orr (later Lord Boyd Orr) recalled in his memoirs the Somme of 1916. 'My officer friends were nearly all dead. While what was left of a first class battalion travelled back, I heard the piper of a Highland regiment which had suffered a similar fate, playing "The Flowers of the Forest". I have never in my life felt so unutterably sad. My friends and comrades were nearly all gone.'[8]

2

Following Jay Winter's masterly analysis in *Sites of Memory, Sites of Mourning* (1995), we may consider European grieving and memorialization in and after 1914–18 as a series of which some of the parts may be engaged simultaneously. There is the shock of loss, most immediate on the battlefield, at the airbase or on shipboard where the young warrior sees his best mate slain beside him or learns that he is missing, presumed dead. Then there is the telegram, for relatives of officers, letter to those of other ranks. It is presumed by the authorities that they will grieve, and this is probably justified, since the wife relieved of an oppressive husband, or revelling in joyful adultery, will most likely be afflicted with guilt, that constant and intolerable companion of grief. It is further presumed that they will want to know that the loved one died creditably. He might have been picked off at random by a sniper's bullet, blown up by a mine, killed in an accident behind the lines, been shot himself at the very moment when he aimed his rifle at the back of an unpopular officer, left dead and putrefying for weeks in No Man's Land, or even, perhaps, cut down heroically at the moment of storming a German trench. In all cases equally he was presumed to be a brave man who had sacrificed his life for his country, rather than, let us say, perishing in a knife-fight in Glasgow after closing time, being buried under a fall of coal in a Fife mine, or losing his life at sea fishing out of Aberdeen. Because he had died serving the nation, the nation took a paternal responsibility for his death.

It could have been worse if he had died when home on leave. In Geoffrey Moorhouse's remarkable book *Hell's Foundations: A Town, Its Myths and Gallipoli* (1992), he discusses grieving in Bury, a cotton town home to the Royal Lancashire Fusiliers. This regiment set an unbreakable record when the men of its First Battalion won six VCs before breakfast, plus one DSO, two MCs and four Mentions in Despatches, landing on West Beach at Cape Hellas in the first dawn of the doomed Gallipoli campaign in April 1915. Altogether 1,816 Lancashire Fusiliers died at Gallipoli, a very significant component of the Allied total. The entire New Zealand contingent lost only half as many more (2,701). French losses at nearly 10,000 exceeded those of the Australians (8,709) for whom Gallipoli was a sacred turning point in their national consciousness. The Indian army, mostly non-white, lost 7,594. The British dead numbered 21,255. Turkish losses, opposing the allies, are probably underestimated at 86,692. The total killed and wounded at Gallipoli in thirty-seven weeks exceeded the total present-day population of Edinburgh. Australians relayed to people at home, and the legend persists to this day, that the Poms at Gallipoli were cowards. New Zealand culture, by contrast, was still Anglophile. Even so, one New Zealander wrote, 'A Lancashire battalion took over from us. Little kids they seemed, about sixteen. And they were blubbing, crying their eyes out.' Some men who came home to Bury on leave from this and other hells found their own ways out of active service:

> Corporal Billington, who had been an insurance agent before joining up, returned to Bury complaining of pains in the head and suffering the after-effects of acute bronchitis . . . He stayed in bed one morning after locking the door, and there gassed himself through a rubber tube connected to the lamp bracket on the wall . . . Private Elliott had almost finished his leave, having appeared quite normal, cheerful even, since the day he came home. His wife and three children had noticed nothing untoward and she had just come down after taking him breakfast in bed as a treat because that morning he was due to return to the war. She heard a loud bang and rushed back upstairs, where she screamed. A neighbour ran in and found Elliott on his hands and knees, with his rifle on the floor . . . His jaw was shattered and the bullet had gone through the back of his head . . . Private Schofield, a dentist, told a friend he would rather sweep streets than go back to the front. Sent his wife to bed, stayed below, and overdosed on cocaine in his fireside chair.

Private Schofield's widow would therefore not receive the anti-grief kit supplied by the British state. This consisted of: (a) a tribute from the Mayor, Aldermen and Burgesses of the County Borough of Bury to the Honoured Memory of [blank] who 'died for King and Country in the Great War. Greater Love Hath No Man Than This, That a Man Lay Down His Life For His Friends. *Pro Patria Mori*.' (b) A brass plaque arrived from the government with the dead man's name between Britannia's raised arm and a lion, above the legend, 'He Died for Freedom and Honour.' (c) Also, there was a scroll, not illuminated, with the Royal Arms above the following: 'He whom this scroll commemorates was numbered among those men who, at the call of King and Country, left all that was dear to them, endured hardness, faced danger, and finally passed out of the sight of men by the path of duty and self-sacrifice, giving up their own lives that others might live in freedom. Let those who come after see to it that his name is not forgotten.' Rolled inside the scroll was a slip of paper headed, 'Buckingham Palace', with a reproduction of George V's signature.[9]

At this and later stages of grief, patriotic poetry might provide for some the effect of instant commemoration in noble language. Clever young men in the 1930s derided the sentiments of Rupert Brooke, who fell sick and died on his way to Gallipoli, and Laurence Binyon, who never served at all. But a widow might find genuine consolation in believing that through her man's death there was, as Brooke put it, a 'corner of a foreign field / That is forever England', a father's agony might be assuaged by that statement of Binyon, so often recited even now on Armistice Day: 'They shall grow not old as we that are left grow old.'

There either was, or was not, a corpse. Recoveries of those killed at Verdun had a macabre outcome. Skulls and bones of supposedly French soldiers were collected and interred in an ossuary built at the military cemetery at Douaumont by a private organization led by the bishop of Verdun. Here, like holy relics, they could be seen through glass. Remains adjudged to be German were simply covered with earth. In France, attempts to reclaim corpses for traditional burial at home became a major administrative problem for the authorities. With the Channel to cross, British parents and widows were less of a nuisance. The Imperial War Graves Commission, long since renamed 'Commonwealth', created cemeteries overseas. Over time, pilgrimages to these were organized for parents and widows. Demand endured. In 1931, 140,000 took part and in 1939, 160,000. Though temporary wooden crosses erected above British graves were retrieved in numbers, were ceremonially interred in churchyards, were hung on walls, were placed in porches, few British corpses came home. Apart from the formidable logistics, 'bringing back only identified bodies would discriminate against about half of the population'. The body of an 'unknown soldier' was selected from among six dug out from different battlefields of the Western Front by a blindfolded officer so that no one could possibly find out who the dead man was, to be interred in 1920 in Westminster Abbey. He was intended to provide a focus for the grief of those whose loved ones, if not blown to excessively small pieces, lay in

unmarked graves. A similar interment was made under the Arc de
Triomphe in Paris. The following year, equivalent ceremonies were
mounted in the USA, Italy, Belgium and Portugal. Canada, Australia
and New Zealand accepted the Westminster tomb as a memorial to
their own dead, and it was a symptom of mounting republican nationalism when, in 1993, the Australians at last insisted on digging up an
unidentified corpse from a Commonwealth War Grave Commission
cemetery and reinterring it after a full military funeral in the 'Hall of
Memory' at the Australian National War Memorial in Canberra.[10]

3

With the commemoration of death in battle having thus been dem-
ocratized, memorials in stone or bronze listing the names of all the
dead from particular regiments or places were psychologically
essential. Throughout the 1920s, work on these proceeded. Never did
ambitious sculptors have a more propitious market. They could draw
on traditional symbolism, or create new forms. Naturally, the taste of
their clients impelled most towards the former option.

In some parts of Europe commemoration was complicated by re-
drawings of national boundaries. William Kidd has researched
minutely into war memorials in Lorraine. Much of this province, along
with Alsace, was lost to France through the Franco–Prussian War of
1870–1. When Lorraine was liberated in 1918, 'the province's sons were
more likely to have fought in the armies of the Wilhelmine Reich than
those of the Third Republic with which it was reunited'. So the icons
adopted for memorials elsewhere in France were not suitable. Hundreds
of French communes adopted the image of a helmeted *poilu* with fixed
bayonet, often treading a German underfoot. The patriotic cockerel,
gallus gallus, was another favourite symbol which was inappropriate in
Lorraine where the dedication 'aux enfants de (. . .) morts pour la
France' would not serve. Choice of imagery was further complicated
because in Alsace-Lorraine, which had escaped the separation,
deplored by the Catholic faithful, of Church and state in France in
1903–5, wording and imagery celebrating the French Republic were not
acceptable. But 'that quintessential warrior *Lorraine*', Joan of Arc, was
conveniently canonized in 1920. Factory-produced Joans were soon
available to stand on memorials for undifferentiated 'victimes de la
guerre'. Angels, crucifixes, sacred hearts and *pietàs* featured widely. In
Metz, a *pietà*, commemorating lost father or lost child, impartially

featured in an imposing monument inaugurated by the French president as late as 1935. This was dedicated to *victimes* generally, but two bas-relief side panels represented unmistakeably French soldiers. When the Germans reconquered the town in the summer of 1940, they stripped these away and rededicated the memorial, 'Sie sterben fur das Reich.' Along with other readjustments, this was changed to 'Aux Morts de la Guerre' after 1945.[11]

In Britain, never invaded since the eighteenth century, an increasingly secularized society with boundaries stable for centuries, problems were primarily ethical and aesthetic and only in a very broad sense 'political'. In some few cases existing monuments might suffice. Monuments listing the dead of the Boer War of 1899–1902 had been erected in some British towns. The busbied cavalryman on horseback in Princes Street Gardens, Edinburgh, sculpted by Birnie Rhind and erected in 1906 above the names of the seventy-six Royal Scots Greys dead in the Boer War, now, thanks to the regiment's relatively light Great War mortality, mentioned earlier, stands over full lists of 1914–18 victims and those of the Second World War, when, perhaps uniquely, losses (159) were heavier. Wholly new memorials were required by every settlement of any size above a hamlet, along with suitable monuments on the Continent where the dead lay.

The master-artist involved in supplying them was Sir Edwin Lutyens. The great work which he had in hand was the building of New Delhi. Paradoxical though it may seem, the mystification of the British Raj was wholly compatible with Lutyens's many services to the democratization of death. A utopian, paternalistic patriotism operated in both cases. The Raj, by now certain to be modified by native self-government within the Empire, represented an ideal of impartial justice, secularist toleration and general economic progress for India's teeming millions. In creating a metropolitan monument without religious symbolism to commemorate the British and imperial dead of all classes, Lutyens found himself in alliance with Lord Curzon, given special responsibility for commemoration in Lloyd George's post-war Cabinet. As viceroy of India, Curzon had been notorious for the grandiosity of his official pageantry. This hereditary aristocrat was widely detested for his arrogance. But he was a very clever man, and the Great War, in which men of his own class had suffered disproportionately heavy losses, must have chastened him. By 1920, he had created a format for annual mourning accepted down to the present day.

The idea of the two minutes' silence at 11 a.m. on 11 November – the day of the 1918 Armistice, and the eleventh day of the eleventh month –

originated in South Africa but was a great success in the mother country when it was first observed in 1919. Cities became awesomely quiet as bells, sirens or maroons or, as in Edinburgh, artillery, sounded. 'Great stations fell silent, travellers froze into immobility.'[12]

For this first anniversary of the Armistice, Lutyens had designed a cenotaph ('empty tomb') of plaster and wood. This extremely simple, plain, massive form, tapered gently by stages towards the top, was much applauded. For the Armistice Day of 1920 it was recreated in Portland stone. Over several days, 100,000 wreaths were laid beside it. Exotic blooms and magnificent roses mingled with humble bunches of chrysanthemums bought from wayside vendors. Its unveiling by King George V was followed by the burial of the Unknown Warrior. Leading commanders, Haig among them, were his pallbearers. But Curzon had realized that this event must not be dominated by social hierarchy. Only bereaved MPs were invited to the abbey. Fathers got no special consideration, the congregation was primarily composed of women, and at Curzon's insistence priority was given 'not to society ladies or the wives of dignitaries, but to the selected widows and mothers of those who had fallen, especially in the humbler ranks.' The coffin was interred at the foot of the statue of the Elder Pitt – 'the Great Commoner'. Future Armistice Day ceremonies, down to the present, likewise emphasized the equality of all citizens in grief – veterans, wounded, ex-servicewomen, marching and standing in an order not dictated by rank or class. BBC radio distributed silence for the first time in 1923, and broadcast the Cenotaph service live from 1928. So all the nation's people were potentially involved in one ceremony of grieving at exactly the same time. (By 1939, three-quarters of households would have radios.)[13]

Lutyens designed over ninety war memorials altogether, including an extremely chaste and beautiful obelisk for the Lancashire Fusiliers at Bury. No Christian himself, but a pantheist, with friends involved in theosophy and spiritualism, when he 'drew', as Jay Winter observes, 'on neo-classical forms, he tended to reduce them to simpler and simpler outline or notation'. His masterpiece in this field is judged to be his memorial to the missing of the Battle of the Somme at Thiepval. The names of 73,000 men whose bodies were never found are engraved on its inner walls. Lutyens's concept, extremely austere, is geometrical. Four triumphal arches 'describe the base of the memorial; their height is two-and-a-half times their width and they are superseded by a series of larger arches placed at right angles to the base'. These larger arches, enclosing larger areas of emphasis, are in the same 2½ to 1 ratio to the smaller ones. 'The progression extends upward . . . to a still larger arch at the centre of the monument, to nothing at all. Lutyens has brilliantly managed to create an embodiment of nothingness, an abstract space unique among memorials of the Great War.'[14]

At the other extreme there was at least one monument in Britain which, through expressive realistic sculpture, presented approvingly not only the details of Great War uniform and weapons, but a soldier busy at his work of killing. Near the Art Gallery in Kelvingrove Park, Glasgow, on the memorial to the fallen of the Cameronian Regiment, erected in 1924, we see, sculpted by P. Lindsey Clark, between a machine gunner and a fallen comrade, an infantryman surging forward, gun in hand and an expression of angry determination on his face which does not match very comfortably the conventional notions of 'tranquil' grace and 'knightly virtue' evoked in the inscription below. This monument exceeds in militancy the notorious memorial to the Machine Gun Corps on that most conspicuous site in London, Hyde Park Corner. The lethal potency of machine guns had been amply shown at the Somme and elsewhere. The contemplative bronze figure of the Boy David holding Goliath's huge sword point down is almost mournful, not fierce. But the inscription, taken from the Bible, reads 'SAUL HATH SLAIN HIS THOUSANDS BUT DAVID HIS TENS OF THOUSANDS.'

Much closer to the spirit of the actual soldiery was the monument which Alexander Carrick sculpted for Oban, where, on a base of rough boulders, two Highlanders are carrying a wounded comrade. A Celtic cross was sufficient for the Brooke family, who erected in Springbank Cemetery, Aberdeen, a stone recording the loss of three sons and a son-in-law in the Great War, and for Mr McLelland of Crossmichael in Galloway, who unveiled in 1921 a memorial to forty-one men of the village who had died, including four sons of his own. Eleven Heart of Midlothian footballers volunteered in 1914, and the clock tower in the form of an obelisk commemorating fallen players and associates of the club, which dominates the western approach to Edinburgh city centre at Haymarket, encourages the mournful myth that the club has never been as good since. The Scottish Rugby Union settled for a simple stone memorial arch at Murrayfield 'IN PROUD MEMORY OF THE SCOTTISH RUGBY MEN WHO GAVE THEIR LIVES IN THE GREAT WAR 1914–1918.'

Perhaps the commonest icon was a soldier in front-line dress, but with the rifle in his hand resting on the ground. Five life-size soldiers in line stand thus on the Guards Division Memorial (1926) by St James's Park in London, designed by H. C. Bradshaw. Over the high, cold, windy lead-mining village of Wanlockhead (sixteen dead) and Penpont, another Dumfriesshire village (forty-one dead), such figures keep eternal vigil. Kellock Brown sculpted a kilted Jock for St Margaret's Hope, South Ronaldsay, Orkney, and another for Inverary. Carrick provided effigies for Blairgowrie and Walkerburn, and a bronze for Dornoch where, in an interesting variant, the Jock, rifle grounded casually in his left hand, has his right raised to shield his eyes (from the sunrise of Resurrection) as he looks out towards the firth. An English sculptor, Henry Price, produced a bronze soldier for Annan, but the base was of Creetown granite, like that supporting a seven-foot-high bonneted stone Borderer in Dumfries. The Bon Accord-Granite Works of Aberdeen (Messrs Stewart & Co.) was kept very busy in the 1920s. In nearby Maxwelltown (over 200 war dead), home of Annie Laurie, Price devised a bronze figure to stand on a Bon-Accord granite base, but this man, it seems, has entered the light of Resurrection – without rifle, he holds out both arms, palms upward, towards the heaven at which he gazes.

For Frazerburgh, Carrick sculpted a seated female figure of Peace, with a helmeted medieval knight in attendance. Symbolic statues were often thus favoured, as at Kirkcudbright where G. H. Paulin of Edinburgh provided a primeval soldier (his sword seems Roman), seated with a child asleep against his knee. The spirit of Scottish Patriotism (1314 and All That) is represented at Paisley, where Sir Robert Lorimer designed the memorial. In a bronze group sculpted by Alice Meredith Williams, Tommies trudging through mud surround a mounted Bruce-like medieval knight. At Galashiels, unveiled in 1925 by Earl Haig himself, a bronze border reiver (sculptor Thomas J. Clapperton) prances on horseback in front of a massive memorial clock tower. Greenock went deeper into Scotland's past. The town had lost over 1,500 men. On a high site overlooking the Firth of Clyde, the architects Wright and Wylie of Glasgow and the sculptor Andrew Proudfoot commemorated ancient maritime traditions. A high base on a broad platform is surmounted by a tall obelisk, at the base of which is the prow of a Viking ship. On this, a bronze figure of Victory holds out a laurel wreath. A Celtic cross, a two-handed Scottish sword and many other Celtic ornaments are carved on the memorial. But for unionist Troon, Walter Gilbert sculpted a 10 ft 6 in bronze of Britannia, on a 13 ft granite pedestal. Wick, on the other hand, could not devise a clear message. The rather dumpy, androgynous, cloaked and helmeted classical figure, sword in one hand, olive sprig in the other, above the town's memorial might be Pallas Athene, but nobody nowadays seems to know.

A generalized simplicity, free of historic or mythological, let alone triumphalist, imagery was wisely favoured in places small and great. At Kilmartin in Argyll, the memorial is an arch into the churchyard, on which each stone bears the name of a fallen soldier. On a hill outside Stonehaven (small capital of Grassic Gibbon's Mearns), on the route along the cliffs towards Dunottar Castle, stands a bare temple-like structure, with eight massive columns linked in a circle, open to the wind, and recalling 'Scotland's Shame', the stark and now very moving colonnade on Calton Hill, Edinburgh, which was fortunately all that came, in the 1820s, of the grandiose project to produce a replica of the Parthenon in honour of Scotland's dead of the Napoleonic Wars, for which insufficient funds were subscribed by the people. Dundee (30,000 dead) erected – in Cornish granite, cheaper than Aberdeen's – a simple obelisk, surmounted by a bronze brazier, on the Law, a 570 ft hill above the city. Aberdeen, in contrast, employed the architects A. M. and A. G. Mackenzie to create a complex, though austere, memorial, opened by King George V in 1925, in the city centre. A lion sat in front of a concave group of six Corinthian pillars flanked by doors giving entry to a circular, domed 80-ft-high Memorial Court large enough to accommodate 700 people, and to an extension of the adjacent City Art Gallery. Aberdeen granite of course was used in this case. Nearly a third of the large sum required came from Lord and Lady Cowdray – 'for the advancement of learning and the encouragement of art and music among the citizens of Aberdeen'. Though the result of this project is literally chilling, even on a warm day, it represented a new attitude towards memorialization which prevailed after 1945.[15]

4

In a most suggestive essay (1981), David Cannadine has analysed British responses to death in the twentieth century. The commercialized ostentation of the Victorian funeral was increasingly rejected from the 1880s onward, while the death rate fell from 22 per 1000 to 13 per 1000 by 1910, and average life expectancy for men rose from forty in the mid-nineteenth century to fifty-two just before the Great War. The death of children and adolescents was much rarer. Now that dying was increasingly associated with old age, the gratuitous deaths of young men in war 'for the Empire' acquired the aura of 'sacrifice' and the glamour of sporting glory. Before 1914, such heroes were few and kenspeckle. A great fear among volunteers in that year was that the war would be over before they got to the Continent.

But as many British men were killed in the first day of the Battle of the Somme in 1916 as died in the whole of the Boer War. The ruling class was especially hard hit by losses, since officers died disproportionately. Six peers of the realm and ninety-four sons of peers died. Of twelve Eton scholars elected in 1906, only seven survived the war. Nearly a third of men matriculating at Oxford in 1913 perished. So the highest in the land were united with the lowest in the bewilderment and pain of loss. Ostentatious private mourning now finally disappeared. There had been thirteen crematoria in 1909 – eight more were built between 1922 and 1931. Emotional consent to incineration of cadavers went along with inevitable scepticism, generated by the Great War, about the Resurrection of the Body, 'when all that was left might be a few rat-bitten pieces of rotten flesh'. But those who had lost relatives, lovers and friends in 1914–18 were interested in large-scale public expressions of grief.[16]

The Scottish National War Memorial at Edinburgh Castle therefore represents a very particular moment in the history of death and grieving in Britain. Triumphalism was impossible. Christian dogma was no longer generally accepted. The society notionally united in grief was riven by 'class warfare' at a time when 'ex-serviceman' was virtually synonymous with 'unemployed'. The result of pressures to be truthful, decent and fair was a monument devised and executed with extraordinary thoughtfulness, sincerity and care.

The idea for such a memorial was first mooted as early as 1917. Its execution by a team of some two hundred artists, artisans and labourers under the architect-in-chief, Sir Robert Lorimer, was accomplished in 1927. The names of the major battlegrounds (killing fields) of the Great War are ranged as a frieze above stylized classical columns in the large but not grandiose Hall of Honour. The eyes are first struck by bays dedicated to Scotland's twelve famous regiments. Crests, arms and colours identify their traditions. In each, a book contains all the names of the fallen. The irony of these memorials is Wagnerian. A panel in each outlines the regiment's history. The Black Watch, for instance, is accorded its glory in campaigns from Guadaloupe in 1759, through the Napoleonic Wars, battles in India, the South African frontier wars of 1846–53, the march into Ashantiland in 1873, the Boer War – then, the debacle of surrender to the Turks at Kut-al-Amara in 1917, the shapeless Western Front battles of the Marne, Ypres, Loos, the Somme, Arras . . . In 1914–18, this regiment lost over 10,000 dead, as did the Royal Scots and the Highland Light Infantry (City of Glasgow Regiment). Such statistics dissolve the Valhalla of the kilted soldier in flames and ruin.

But the Empire endures. The curious visitor may already have noted that the very small equestrian statue of Earl Haig in the Castle Esplanade was presented 'in admiration' by Sir Dunjibhoy Bomanzi of Bombay. The inner side of the tall arch which gives entry from the Hall of Honour to the Shrine is encircled by the Tree of Empire which supports upon its branches the coats of arms of the Dominions and of India, and the Royal Arms of Scotland. This seems to give unobtrusive support to an idea popular in Scottish political circles at that time – even C. M. Grieve, 'Hugh MacDiarmid', surprisingly favoured it – that Scotland should acquire through Home Rule the status of a dominion within the Empire.

From the roof of the shrine hangs a sculpted St Michael, Captain of the Heavenly Host, sword raised to strike. Beneath him there is a Stone of Remembrance, green Carrara marble, supporting a steel casket, guarded by kneeling angels, which contains Rolls of Honour with names of Scotland's Great War dead. Seven stained-glass windows tell in symbol and allegory the history of Strife and its final defeat by Peace and the Power of the Spirit. At the centre we have a remarkably cheerful crucifix, symbolizing Triumph by way of Sacrifice. Christ is not nailed to his cross – he is free, upward-looking, ascending. Flanking windows display the glories of peace – philosophy, music, craftsmanship and science. Below these Galgacus stands beside Wallace, Alexander III and Bruce are shoulder to shoulder with a kilted modern Jock. This ensemble seems to look forward to a distinctively Scottish free commonwealth.

In a bronze frieze running right round the interior of the shrine shuffle, sometimes two or more deep, a hundred figures in uniform, with at least one representative of every rank and unit. These were superbly modelled by Alice Meredith Williams, who also sculpted St Michael above them. There are only three kilted soldiers among them. Nurses and navy men, sappers, mechanics and fliers throng with a Camel Corps trooper in shorts, a cowled and snowshoed soldier from the 1919 Russian Expeditionary Force and a full general. This indicates a feature of the memorial which emerges strongly when one returns to inspect the hall more closely. The aim of those who devised it is to include every creature which had served in the war.

Thus we not only find artworks and inscriptions specifically commemorating the work of the seven yeomanry regiments, men of the merchant marine, engineers and signallers, chaplains, doctors and stretcherbearers, WRNS and the Women's Forage Corps, landgirls and female munition-makers, there is a frieze of the heads of the 'Humble

Beasts that served and died' – horse, mule, camel, reindeer, elephant, dog – and a sculpted panel for 'The Tunnellers' Friends', canaries and mice, who, as in the coal mines whence sappers were commonly recruited, were at hand to give advance warning of gas. Stained-glass windows represent the seasons through images of the home front. In autumn the leave train arrives in a station complete with newsboy and coffee bar, in winter a uniformed figure guards the coast, in spring anti-aircraft gun and ambulance defy an air raid, and in summer a little boy dives into a pool while a troopship departs shepherded by a mine-sweeper and soldiers convalesce in hospital blue . . .

As one leaves, one sees above the exit the sculpted figure of Reveille, androgynous, rising in cape and tunic phoenix-like from flames, left hand grasping a broken sword-blade while the right holds the hilt, cross-shaped, up in triumph, with behind, over stylized land and sea, the far-pointing golden rays of the rising sun. C. d'O. Pilkington Jackson (1887–1973) contributed this, along with many other items – bosses, keystones, memorial bays with all the lettering in stone and bronze. Lorimer recruited fine collaborators. Beside Alice Meredith Wiliams (c.1870–1934) he employed Alexander Carrick (1882–1966) and Phyllis Bone (1894–1972) among his sculptors. Douglas Strachan (1875–1950) designed all the stained glass. The overall effect includes our sense that a distinguished generation of artists, affected by the Arts and Crafts Movement, lavished their skill proudly on a project en-nobling their whole society and the Scottish nation. It had to be the first and last memorial of its kind, because it was predicated upon the idea that men had sacrificed their lives in a Great War to end all wars.

The war of 1939–1945 which followed was longer and, though not for Britain, much bloodier. Its aftermath saw one new commemorative ritual – Battle of Britain Day – but this was less a national occasion than a regional event for south-east England. It was fun for small boys to see the famous fighter planes in the sky again. In January 1946, the government ordained that both wars would be remembered on one day – the Sunday immediately before 11 November. Since Sunday was quiet anyway, the two minutes' silence would now be less intense. Except for Lutyens and a few others, there was no enthusiasm for building new memorials. Instead, the shorter lists of the Second World War dead were appended to existing monuments. The idea pioneered in Aberdeen came to the fore. The dead would be best honoured by the dedication of libraries, parks, gardens which would be of use to the living. In 1946, the National Land Fund was set up as the principal English war memorial, to acquire for the nation country houses and areas of natural beauty. One might speak of a return to the idea attributed to Pericles – that the story of heroic men 'is not graven in stone over their clay, but abides everywhere without visible symbol, woven into the stuff of men's lives'.

It was now embarrassing that the one individual memorialized by a panel in Lorimer's Hall on Castle Rock was Earl Haig, regarded by many as the callous bonehead who had sent hundreds of thousands of soldiers to their deaths. But the old tradition that statues of commanders honoured those who had served under them gave one kick, probably its last, in the 1990s. Bomber Command had been ordered to pound German civilians nightly in the Second World War. Arthur Harris, in charge, did not institute the policy of 'area bombing', but it suited his somewhat brutal temperament. Public opinion recoiled from it. After victory, Harris was the only commander of such seniority not to be given a peerage. Bomber Command had suffered 60 per cent casualties. Now its surviving crewmen were denied honour. Veterans saw the erection of a statue to Harris in central London nearly half a century after the war as an overdue vindication. Germans, and many informed British people, thought the idea profoundly mistaken. But the traumatized survivors of Bomber Command, as much as their dead young friends, had been victims of war. Surely they deserved a different kind of memorial – a huge stark monolith in East Anglia, whence they flew, or a museum like the New Zealand army's at Waiouru, where a recording plays and replays the names of the slain, or a smaller counterpart to the low-lying, black Vietnam Wall in Washington, simply engraved with the names of lost men?

5

During the Kosovo refugee crisis of 1999, a British journalist was jolted when a senior aid worker remarked that she was reminded of *Schindler's List* – not of the Holocaust directly, not of the ethnic cleansing which brutally displaced *volksdeutscher* from their ancestral homes in eastern Europe in 1945, but of Steven Spielberg's successful film. No one under sixty now has direct first-hand memories of much import from the Second World War. Only a few centenarians remember the trenches of France and Flanders. For most adults and all children notions of war today derive from television news reports, conceptions of previous wars from historical documentaries and, more potently, from feature films.

Outside a big cinema in Edinburgh, in 1998, veterans of the Normandy landings, aiming to erect a memorial in Musselburgh, collected nearly £8,000 over just three weekends from filmgoers coming out after seeing Spielberg's three-hour epic, *Saving Private Ryan*. This gruesomely detailed fable about GIs in Normandy on D-Day and just afterwards had visibly, it was said, shaken its audiences. We have here a rare instance of an artwork producing a measurable effect. Proceeds far exceeded collections at the same cinema previously for good causes connected with films on show.[17]

In *Schindler's List* and *Empire of the Sun*, Spielberg had produced artistically successful war films based on strong stories provided by major novelists. With a flimsier narrative basis, *Ryan* is much less satisfactory. As a feat of production – reproduction of destruction – it is astounding. Direction is sensitive, acting is good, and the movie is unflaggingly serious. Blood swirling in the sea, a dying soldier with guts spilling out, another seizing his own severed arm, are not presented for ghoulish titillation. Horrors emphasize the heroism of the GIs who stormed the Nazis' Atlantic Wall from 'Omaha Beach'. They fought in a good cause, and the film makes no sentimental concession to notions that the Germans were not such bad guys after all.

But what for a long time seems to be the film's central question is smudged and finally fudged. Eight GIs are ordered to find Private Ryan, dropped by parachute inland, because his three brothers have just died in action and US Army Chief of Staff George C. Marshall is determined that their mother shall not lose her last son . . . Understandably, Private Ryan's designated saviours begin to wonder why his life is worth more than theirs. Five of the six who make it through to where Ryan is among troops preparing to defend a vital bridge against advancing German tanks die in the action which ensues. But they do not die 'for Ryan', who, fortuitously, survives. They reinforce the Allied side in a significant little battle. Had they not been searching for Ryan they might very well have died in action in the general thrust from Omaha Beach. Their quest for one man merely merges them in the overall struggle. Had the film stated this clearly, its sentimental allure might have diminished. The statements that the fighting in Normandy was tough, but was necessary, are stock truths, unchallengeable except in the counterfactual terms which bored historians sometimes like to play with – 'if x, y or z had been done by the Allies, then D-Day might not have been "necessary".' Spielberg creates dubiety and suspense by playing on our memories of screen westerns and previous war films. And he frames his film with shots of the aged Ryan visiting the cemetery where his designated saviours are buried. Thought about what is going on in these sequences brings us up against limitations, and even inanity, in the twentieth-century memorial tradition.

Remembrance Sunday in Britain proceeds on the unexamined assumption that our dead of the two world wars, and by extension of Korea, Malaya, Kenya, Cyprus, the Falklands, Bosnia – were brave young men deprived of long and happy lives by their 'sacrifice' for their fellow countrymen. Each might be said, in more pious days, to have imitated Christ's sacrifice, but now that society takes Christ less seriously some vague notion of the decorousness of laying down one's life for one's country, *pro patria mori,* is what we are left with. Armistice Day gathers the nation together, as whatever it is that its armed men have died for, either defending the motherland directly, or maintaining its commitments overseas. Until recently, these commitments were 'imperialistic'. Now we assume that, as in the Balkans in the 1990s, our armed forces' prime role is and should be to share the international tasks of 'peacekeeping' and 'humanitarian' intervention. There will be occasions when courage displayed in such causes should be duly honoured, but it will be hard to relate them to the grandiose concept of national remembrance.

The Nazis were defeated. Ryan survived. And then survived his own survival. He did not drink himself to an early grave as he struggled with traumatic memories of war, nor, we infer, did murderous reflexes make him brutal towards family or neighbours. His survival, blessed with progeny, may be taken sentimentally to imply that good American family values were saved with him. Hokum is truth, truth hokum – that is all ye know of World War II, if you are less than sixty years old, and all ye need to know.

The sombre truth is that in twentieth-century history war cannot be separated from everyday life in the countries which have enlisted vast conscript armies. In the eighteenth century young men died of smallpox, in the nineteenth century of tuberculosis. In the first half of the twentieth they killed each other in very large numbers. With the exception of the notorious 'Spanish Flu' of 1918–19, high explosive, machine guns, bayonets and torpedoes replaced germs and viruses as the Grim Reaper's chief means of attacking young men. What the societies where rulers promoted the slaughter presented later as 'heroic sacrifice' was in fact, for the time being, a normal way of dying.

The Thin Red Line, directed by Terence Mallick, contended with *Saving Private Ryan* for Oscars in 1999. Though not without flaws, it is a far more intelligent and profound work of art because it recognizes death as a permanent and wholly natural presence in life. It does not commit the solecism of working up a far-fetched Hollywood story. In 1942 US marines land on Guadalcanal, a steamy, rain-sodden, malaria-infested island in the 'Solomon' group in the South Pacific, where the first major land battle between US and Japanese forces develops. The marines go inland and fight for a while. They kill lots of Japanese, but the Japanese kill many of them. Then these particular marines leave the island, where others go on fighting. End of story. The closest the film comes to conventional narrative is when a popular officer, unwilling to sacrifice his men's lives in gung-ho attacks, is sent back to a desk job in the USA, and when a GI gets a 'Dear John' letter from the wife whom he adores telling him that she now loves another man. Otherwise, we might say that the film concerns itself with people living and dying in a tropical environment in which figure both heaven and hell – natural beauty, animal cruelty, human cruelty. We are forced to peer at liminalities – the border between advanced, technology-based 'civiliza-tion' and the easy-going life of peaceful islanders, the intersection of nostalgic memories of home with military actualities, the point where human consciousness confronts the otherness of 'nature', the moments which separate life from death.

In his great poem 'For the Union Dead', written in the 1950s, Robert Lowell presents us with images of Boston, Massachusetts, being torn apart by developers, so that

> . . . Colonel Shaw
> and his bell-cheeked Negro infantry
> on St Gaudens's shaking Civil War relief,
> [are] propped by a plank splint against the garage's earthquake.
>
> Two months after marching through Boston,
> half the regiment was dead;
> at the dedication,
> William James could almost hear the bronze Negroes breathe.

Shaw's story is now familiar to all who have seen the powerful film *Glory,* directed by Edward Zwick, released in 1989. Morgan Freeman and Denzil Washington star as recruits to the 54th Regiment of Massachussetts, which is officered by whites, but is otherwise the first aggregation of black soldiers committed by the North in combat against the South. Matthew Brodrick plays young Colonel Shaw very effectively – prim, limited, ultimately committed entirely to his regi-ment and its mission to prove that black men, even ex-slaves, can fight and die with discipline and courage. Lowell goes on to observe that Shaw 'is out of bounds now' and 'rejoices in man's lovely,/ peculiar power to choose life and die'. We can recognize that there were some men in both world wars who consciously made such a choice. We might even call them 'heroes'. Shaw's father, white New England puritan traditionalist, had

> . . . wanted no monument
> except the ditch,
> where his son's body was thrown
> and lost with his 'niggers'.

Now Lowell invokes the spirit of the Shaws as an ally against the current corruption of American values by militarism and industrialism – Boston is dominated by big cars and 'a savage servility/ slides by on grease'.

He could not make his point without Shaw's finely sculptored monument. Shaw's father clearly subscribed to a view like Pericles'. But the specific monument to an individual commander and his brave troops may have, as in this case, monitory and inspirational force for much later generations. We may wonder how fresh imaginations born into the twenty-first century will respond to, and perhaps make use of, the values projected in Great War memorials, and also whether Remembrance Day will reach its centenary, and if so, by what process of transformation.

References

[1] Alan Borg, *War Memorials* (London: Leo Cooper, 1991), p. 69; George L. Mosse, *Fallen Soldiers: Reshaping the Memory of the World Wars* (New York: Oxford University Press, 1990), pp. 16–21, 36, 46.

[2] Samuel Hynes, *The Soldier's Tale: Bearing Witness to Modern War* (London: Pimlico, 1998), p. 33.

[3] 'Ian Hay' (Major John Hay Beith), *Their Name Liveth: The Book of the Scottish National War Memorial* (London: Bodley Head, 1931), pp. 114–17.

[4] Ian Donnachie and George Hewitt, *A Companion to Scottish History* (London: Batsford, 1989), pp. 209, 229; David Cannadine, 'War and death, grief and mourning in modern Britain', in J. Whaley (ed.), *Mirrors of Mortality: Studies in the Social History of Death* (London: Europa, 1981), p. 200.

[5] Lewis Grassic Gibbon, *A Scots Quair* (Edinburgh: Canongate, 1995), pp. 253–7.

[6] Richard Overy, *Russia's War* (London: Viking, 1998), pp. 158–9.

[7] Mosse, *Fallen Soldiers*, p. 86–9.

[8] Cannadine, 'War and grief', p. 207.

[9] Geoffrey Moorhouse, *Hell's Foundations* (London: Hodder & Stoughton, 1992), pp. 10–11, 12, 79, 93, 104–5, 124ff.

[10] Cannadine, 'War and grief', p. 231; Jay Winter, *Sites of Memory, Sites of Mourning: The Great War in European Cultural History* (Cambridge: Canto, 1998), pp. 27–8.

[11] William Kidd, 'Memory, memorials and commemoration of war in Lorraine, 1908–1998', in M. Evans and K. Lunn (eds), *War and Memory in the Twentieth Century* (Oxford: Berg, 1997), pp. 143–59.

[12] Adrian Gregory, *The Silence of Memory: Armistice Day 1919–1946* (Oxford: Berg, 1994), pp. 8–17.

[13] Gregory, *Silence of Memory*, pp. 25–7, 136; David Gilmour, *Curzon* (London: John Murray, 1994), p. 495.

[14] Winter, *Sites of Memory*, p. 101.

[15] I have drawn on Borg, *War Memorials* and Derek Boorman, *At the Going Down of the Sun: British First World War Memorials* (York: Ebor Press, 1988), for information about almost all the monuments mentioned above; both are well and copiously illustrated.

[16] Cannadine, 'War and grief', pp. 191–200, 217–18, 231–2.

[17] *Herald*, 12 October 1998.

D-Day 1994

Major's government, now in accord with D-Day veterans, has quietly shifted its fiftieth anniversary 'family day' in Hyde Park from July to August. Awkward memories of the bomb dropped on Hiroshima in that month forty-nine years ago may or may not intrude to spoil whatever fun folk find there. During the recent fuss over D-Day commemoration it emerged that most people are now very hazy about the pattern of events in the Second World War, and still more so about the moral and political implications for the present time. Does D-Day, 6 June 1944, 'mean' anything now?

The youngest people who worked in 'war industry' or served in the forces are now in their late sixties. Their grandchildren receive only a patchy picture of the war. Dunkirk, the Battle of Britain and the Blitz survive in tabloid metaphor and much-shown film footage. The Desert War in North Africa prompted poetry – by Sorley Maclean, Hamish Henderson, Keith Douglas – which matches that of Owen and Rosenberg in quality, but it remains much less famous. In the centre of his war trilogy, Evelyn Waugh placed an unforgettable account of the British defeat in Crete in 1941. But, while there has been a great deal of pulp fiction about the 1944–5 campaigns in north-west Europe, there is no powerful novel or non-fiction narrative to make it vivid for new generations, only some indifferent US films. The Italian arena, thanks to fiction by Calvino, films by Rosselini and some notable memoirs (Stuart Hood, Norman Lewis), is far easier to imagine. Since the young have no vivid conception of their scale and character, one could say that D-Day and the campaigns which followed are becoming 'meaningless'. Even John Major, alive at the time, seems to have got June 1944 mixed up with May 1945 and the street parties on VE Day.

In June 1944, no one was celebrating. Most people had friends and relatives who were involved, or would soon be involved, in the carnage in France. They listened avidly to radio bulletins and flocked into cinemas to see the latest newsreels. Confidence in Allied victory was strong, but within a fortnight the Germans were sending over their 'secret weapons', V1 pilotless planes, bringing fear and death to southern England and fostering the apprehension that they might have even nastier tricks up their sleeves, confirmed when V2 flying bombs followed. Edgy weeks were prolonged into months as the Germans, though now fighting desperately on three fronts, refused to give in.

But it was a relief that British troops were at last striking directly towards Germany. Though the Allies had destroyed Mussolini's regime and were now fighting Germans hard in Italy, this had seemed a puny sideshow compared with the mighty advance of Stalin's Red Army. From 1942, leftwingers had been demanding a 'Second Front Now', to relieve Russia. D-Day ended British guilt over the way Russians had survived unheard-of sufferings and counter-attacked while British soldiers had yawned in camps at home.

That was only one reason why D-Day 'meant' a great deal at the time. Posters for years had exhorted the British to work, dig and save for victory. Invasion of Europe was the necessary preliminary to victory. J. L. Hodson, a distinguished liberal journalist, strove to capture the mood of the times in diaries.

June 5th, 1944 Pieces of English life can be normal still. At Lords', on Whit Monday, a vast host sat in the sun watching cricket. Yesterday I golfed in sun and a high wind. Just after we had finished, the heavens were filled with a great roaring, and we saw, very high, in the dome of heaven, formations of Liberators flying towards France . . . It was the same roaring we used to hear over the Weald of Kent in 1940, but in those days the aircraft were German. So the wheel has come full circle . . . It is said that Russia is being bled white. But we are being bled white also. And so is Germany . . . *June 6th, 1944* The Second Front has begun – one of the most important days in this war and in world history.

Though written for publication under restraints of wartime censorship, Hodson's diaries honestly convey feelings of doubt and even remorse current at the time. They take us into states of mind when British people were conscious, day by day, of making history, but could not be sure what the shape of that history was.

As recently as 1986 the Belgian Marxist Ernest Mandel was confident enough to bring out a book – excellent in its way – called *The Meaning of the Second World War*. Just as old-style British 'Whig' historians felt they could place 1688 and 1707 and 1815 accurately in a trajectory of 'progress', so Mandel believed that humankind had one story in which 1939–45 had one meaning. In fact, since the prestige of Soviet 'socialism' was at a peak in 1943–5, and Roosevelt's New Deal was presented by Americans as a triumph for the common man, there was a degree of convergence when people assigned 'meaning' to the Allied effort at the time which now seems very queer. It was a 'people's war'. It was a war to liberate humankind not only from right-wing tyrannies but from the poverty and unemployment associated with their rise. It was, in some vague way, a 'revolutionary' war.

Look at the speeches and articles of Quintin Hogg MP, now Lord Hailsham. He led the Tory Reform Group of young politicians who, unlike many in their party, were hotly in favour of implementing the Beveridge report of 1942, with its plan for social security for all from cradle to grave and its still more attractive 'assumption' that there would be a National Health Service. Hogg told the Commons in February 1943 that he heartily approved of the 'redistribution of wealth' implied by Beveridge. Later in that year he announced to *Evening Standard* readers that the 'comradeship' of war must persist into peace, agreed with Michael Foot that a post-war government must have 'overriding authority over property' and asserted 'We are living in revolutionary times. There are some who regard the war as an episode from which they can return the moment hostilities are over into a comfortable atmosphere of "normalcy". But they must be very few.'

At the time, then, D-Day fitted into the story, told by government propaganda as well as left-wing publicists, of 'people's war'. In 1940 Britain, 'alone', had stood against Nazism. Bombed, regimented and rationed, the people had concentrated all their best efforts on producing the munitions and food required to defeat Hitler. Now the Allies had at last amassed the forces necessary for a second front which made victory, sooner or later, certain. The reward of victory for the people who won it must be a fairer, more generous society, freed from the blights of mass unemployment and gross social inequality.

If that was one 'meaning', the main one, assigned to D-Day at the time, what 'meanings' can we attach to it now?

Those who argued that the Second World War, like the First, was an 'imperialist' conflict always had an unanswerable case. The further events recede into the past, the more clearly their underlying *material* basis juts through the rhetoric which they generated. The Protestant Reformation, for instance, looks more and more like a series of episodes related to the rise to economic dominance of northern Europe. When the twentieth century began, Germany's increasingly overweening position in the European economy was resented by its

neighbours and was not reflected in its relatively puny overseas empire.
Forced back in 1914–18, Germany, under Hitler, tried again and was
more savagely defeated. Since then, revived German superiority has
been accommodated within the European Union.

Meanwhile, the USA, rightly thinking that for the moment the
Germans were more dangerous than the Japanese, intervened massively
in Europe (while doing enough to secure Pacific victory) and established a world hegemony – de facto 'empire' – challenged only by the
Soviet bloc, itself a kind of empire, though differently based. So it was
premature for the patriotic Hodson to rejoice when he learnt that equal
numbers of British Empire and US troops had landed on D-Day. The
invasion was a decisive step towards US victory in the war of empires.

However, as the twentieth century ends the resurgence of China is
clearly reshaping 'world history'. In a hundred years' time, historians,
even in the West, may be no more impressed by D-Day than by the
Japanese 'Ichi-go' campaign of April 1944. Determined to make China
useless as a base for the Americans, the Japanese totally routed Jiang
Jieshi's Guomindang armies in Henan, weakening the US-backed
'Nationalist' leader vis-à-vis Mao Zedong and his Red Army, and so
assisting eventual Communist victory. Meanwhile, famine in Bengal,
resulting from incompetence on the part of the ruling British, killed 3.4
million people and destroyed the administrative credibility of the Raj as
well as Britain's 'moral' claims to rule India on behalf of its natives.

I would like to suggest three ways in which D-Day 'means' something
to us in Britain now.

First, the men and women who fought Hitler almost all believed in
the justice of their cause and no amount of revisionism could convince
me that they were wrong. Nazism was an entirely evil creed. The fact
that the British themselves mostly subscribed to views which we now
see were racist paradoxically makes their struggle more, not less, valid.
The Nazis took European racist thinking beyond the point where it was
morally acceptable, and fighting them made many British people more
alert to their own prejudices and predisposed them to criticize racist
pseudo-science.

Second, D-Day represented the final culmination of the 'forging' of
British national identity. Linda Colley's brilliant study *Britons* has
recently explored the early stages of this process, from the Union of
England and Scotland in 1707 to the accession of Victoria. Britishness
reached its apogee in the 1940s. The 'British' Broadcasting Corpor-
ation, having accorded special authority to middle-class southern
English speech, now opened the airwaves up to 'regional' voices. Scots,

Welsh, and very large numbers of Irish, from the south as well as the north, moved all over Britain as the demands of the fighting services and 'war industry' dictated, giving people as never before the sense of belonging to one community which was so faithfully propagated by Ealing Films. Though the big push in June 1944 came from southern England, where forces had been concentrating for months, material support and will-power from the whole north-west European archipelago flowed behind it.

One of the problems facing Major and his colleagues when they absent-mindedly considered commemorating D-Day is that the 'break-up of Britain' as Tom Nairn called it two decades ago, has now reached a point where media people in Scotland, not necessarily radical, have been genuinely puzzled by the apparent absence of any 'Scottish angle' to D-Day. Whatever 'it' is to be commemorated, 'it' now seems like a southern English affair. Hampshire now looks from Scotland like foreign soil.

However, thirdly, the coincidence that the Chunnel opens at just this time reminds us that D-Day was a key moment in 'Britain's' relation with 'Europe'. In 1914–18 the UK had been dragged much further into European war than had been willed or foreseen. In 1943–4, under the wing of the USA, British forces went in to sort out Europe. Now that Britain was bankrupt, the US was successfully loosening our hold on India and the colonies, prior to its own takeover of world power.

June 1944 can be seen as the moment when Britannia, having ruled the waves of every ocean, attached her destiny to a choice (which proved to be no real choice at all) between a 'special relationship' with her 'transatlantic cousins' and identification with Europe. Singular imperial grandeur was no longer an option. Since the US wanted, and still wants, Britain to be 'in Europe' that is where the English, Scots, Welsh and Irish are now, whether they like it or not.

1994

The Wars of Ian Hamilton Finlay

Scandals in the visual arts, like literary feuds, are two a penny. The major wars of Ian Hamilton Finlay are of a different order from tabloid fusses over the acquisition of piles of bricks etc. by publicly funded galleries, media shock-horror over 'inappropriate' portraits or memorials, or bitch-ins filling the columns of literary journals, although an innocent eavesdropper might have supposed them to be 'that sort of thing'. I will try to discuss them so that the general issues involved emerge clearly over and above media angles, misrepresentations in good and bad faith, and squabbles over these misrepresentations. As Patrick Eyres wrote in 1986:

> There is a view, perpetuated by the art establishment, that the Little Spartan War is a digression from the work of Ian Hamilton Finlay. Even the Minister for the Arts has stated that he is 'genuinely concerned that Mr Finlay is continuing to dissipate his energies.' This view wilfully ignores the classical thrust of Finlay's poetry during the last decade, and his recognition of the spiritual potency embodied in classicism.
> (' "Hedgehog" Stonypath and the Little Spartan War', *Cencrastus* 22, 1986)

Understanding Finlay's classicism involves detaching the values aspired to within the tradition he acknowledges from the actual behaviour of the people who have recognized these values. Pitt the Elder belonged to the circle of Whigs who found in Lord Cobham's classical garden at Stowe the embodiment, in a peculiar relationship between nature and art, of libertarian political ideals. Pitt's gung-ho, commercially motivated imperialism as a war leader does not discredit Stowe's Temple of Ancient Virtue. Finlay, working as poet with a succession of collaborators skilled in visual arts and crafts, assumes, like other neoclassicists, the existence of meaningful language and values objectively, as it were, in the public domain. Personal quirks expressed in his tactics are irrelevant to our judgement of his overall aims and the values which support these aims.

Just as the defeat by the French of a very young Virginian colonel named George Washington in the Ohio country in 1754 can be seen as marking the start of the Seven Years War, forever associated with Pitt, which ended nine years later, so the first action in the 'Little Sparta War' (1984–8, revived 1993) came in 1978 when Finlay withdrew work, just before the planned opening, from an exhibition in the Scottish Arts Council's Charlotte Square Gallery, in protest against actions by SAC officials. The material withdrawn related to the garden which Finlay and his wife Sue had been creating since 1966 at Stonypath.

While the SAC broke off communication with Finlay, Strathclyde Regional Council withdrew the rates exemption previously granted to the gallery in the Finlays' garden, one reason given being that it enjoyed no SAC grant . . . In 1980, Finlay transformed this gallery into a 'Garden Temple', but Strathclyde refused him the rates exemption given to religious buildings. A body named the Saint-Just Vigilantes, after a previous invention of Finlay's, rallied to defend Stonypath, now known as Little Sparta in homage to the most austere and militant of ancient Greek city states. The first battle of Little Sparta occurred in the presence of the media on 4 February 1983, when a sheriff officer acting for Strathclyde attempted to seize, for warrant sale, work in the Temple. He was repulsed. A medal was struck and a monument erected on the battlefield. But on 15 March, in the Budget Day raid, a number of works were removed, several of which belonged to purchasers who were unable to reclaim them from the bank vault where they were placed. Little Sparta was closed for a year.

For years, Finlay has been tormented by the Strathclyde bureaucracy. In 1984 the SAC asked Strathclyde to hold fire while the Garden Temple was reassessed, but the region remained unmoved by subsequent pronouncements to the effect that the term 'temple' was valid, though the SAC could not say what it meant. Meanwhile the vigilantes liberated two neoclassical stone reliefs by Finlay from SAC head-quarters and installed them in the Temple as war spoils. In 1988, the region finally returned the art works taken from Little Sparta, along with several thousand pounds arrested from a bank account. Five years later, however, Strathclyde sent Finlay a new summons for a large amount in rates as well as an inhibition to stop him selling artworks at Little Sparta. The matter remains in suspense as moves proceed to put Little Sparta under the control of a trust.

Two fundamental issues overlap in this intricate, sometimes hilarious, sometimes puzzling story. One concerns the role of state funding in the arts. The SAC acts on a remit from successive governments to support artistic activities which would not otherwise be viable commercially. Unlike former rich patrons, such as Virgil's Maecenas or the Popes of Rome, the state does not require that resulting work represents its own taste or meets its own propagandist or educational requirements. So far, so good: the public (whether it likes the results or not) gives, through its taxes, disinterested support to artists who are allowed to be creative on their own terms. But the state, inherently bureaucratic, cannot desist from applying an economic, 'input/output' approach to funding. To fit in with this, Little Sparta would have to be defined as a 'gallery' and administered by a board producing accounts for scrutiny by SAC finance people. Its 'performance', or 'product', year by year, would be assessed on the basis of income, expenditure and attendance figures. A garden open to the public at the discretion of its creators, who claim that its central feature is a religious site, is impossible to subsidize on normal terms.

United Kingdom laws permit free expression of religious belief in buildings dedicated to spiritual purposes, and tax concessions are available to the proprietors of such buildings, in which any artworks are presumed to have a valid sacred purpose. The fact that an artist commissioned to produce windows or statuary for a church may be a non-believer and may be paid a large sum of money is immaterial to the legal status of their work. Finlay invokes a classical tradition very strongly represented, albeit in refracted form, in European literature and art, but not amenable to present-day law and bureaucracy. Many Africans would understand at once that a family which constructs a shrine for its own use, incorporating images relating to tutelary ancestors and other spirits, is practising religion. But 'religion' in this primary sense, involving ties to family, city, country and conceptions of virtue, is an indigestible proposition for the bureaucratic state. It cannot understand that artworks not placed in churches – which have a definite legal status like football clubs and trade unions – may nevertheless possess a religious function. They are conceived to be saleable objects, their value wholly determined by market forces. Yet our liberal-pluralist society cleaves to the baneful idea that 'art' is something different from the rest of life, set apart by 'beauty for its own sake'. That, rather perversely, is why bureaucrats, lawyers and most other people buy some sort of art for their homes, even if it is only wally dugs or reproduction Van Goghs.

So Finlay's assertion of his own rights over the display of work by himself and various collaborators, which he and they deem to have a religious function, painfully exposes contradictions in a culture which officially desires and promotes art but wants art to behave in the market like other 'products' and wants it to have no effective meaning but 'beauty for its own sake'. That art may be created not primarily for sale but to make urgent statements of principle and to incite action is most inconvenient. Clever people like Lord Gowrie, chairman of the Arts Council of England and a declared 'admirer' of Finlay, may be able to fall back on sophistries derived from notions of absolute formal beauty. However, the element of political challenge in Finlay's work – which has nothing to do with 'party politics' but attacks the culture in which party politics take place – is clear, explicit and unmissable. It should logically empower him to negotiate with patrons, including states, who want, in spite of it, to use his skills, for conditions under which it can be freely expressed. They should have to buy the kind of thing they see, which is what they claim they want.

Unfortunately, the international reputation of Little Sparta, which had led to commissions for garden installations executed and admired in England and on the Continent, was not enough to gain Finlay victory in his second major war, against French cultural bureaucracy.

Involved here were issues surrounding the role of the liberal-pluralist state in promoting commemoration of 'national' history. Imagine the stushie if an independent Scottish government, in 2010, felt compelled to commemorate the 450th anniverary of the Reformation, and a Hungarian artist were asked to celebrate John Knox. Finlay's French war began with controversy over the representation in art of images associated with militarism, which were apparently related to the original commission and the proposal with which Finlay responded to it only through a campaign of misrepresentation and slander in the French media. However, as the dust of combat settles it seems clear that the artist's neoclassicism and its political implications were at stake in every aspect of the affair.

In 1986, the French Ministry of Culture began to discuss with Finlay a possible commission for a garden commemorating the bicentenary of the Declaration of the Rights of Man. He was the obvious choice. Beside Little Sparta he had created notable outdoor installations at, for instance, the Max Planck-Institut in Stuttgart and the Kröller-Müller Museum in the Netherlands. His work for years had foregrounded his interest in the ideas and personalities of the French Revolution, notably in Saint-Just (1767–94), the 'incorruptible' Jacobin leader. The new garden was to be at Versailles, on the spot where the National Assembly had convened in the summer of 1789 and sworn an oath to continue meeting until liberty, equality and fraternity were permanently enshrined in law. A formal invitation to Finlay followed in 1987, and in that year there were three exhibitions of his work in and around Paris.

'Certain gardens are described as retreats when they are really attacks': Finlay's 'Sentence' published in 1986 seems prophetic of the coming French war. What he proposed was a delightful 'retreat'. But its 'pastoral' character, determined by neoclassical values, inflected the meaning of 'Rights of Man' so as to subvert the possibility of consensus, even of fudging, over the significance of the Revolution of Robespierre and Saint-Just for the France – and Europe – of 1989. Edwin Morgan has written of 'epic pastoral' as a presence in Finlay's work.[1] The 'Rights of Man', proclaimed on that spot in that time, was fighting talk. Finlay's text, from 1987, in a print accompanying a design by Gary Hincks of a guillotine entwined by flowers, expresses a certain issue very clearly: 'Both the garden style called "sentimental" and the French Revolution grew from Rousseau. The garden trellis, and the guillotine, are alike entwined with the honeysuckle of the new sensibility.'[2]

Nevertheless, Finlay excluded any hint of provocation from his proposal.[3] A lawn would occupy the area where the deputies had once sat, so that visitors could choose to picnic on left, right or centre of the Assembly. The public could furthermore pick, in season, cherries from trees alluding to the pastoral aspect of the Revolution, pears from trees arranged so as to allegorize equality. The Tree of Liberty would stand just inside the garden gate. On the far side of the lawn a line of poplars *(peupliers)* would not only symbolize the people *(peuple)* and their Fraternity, but also recall the grave given to Rousseau on an island in another garden, by the Marquis de Girardin, at Ermenonville, which is graced by trees of this species. Thus the 'Rights of Man', and the thinker most associated with them, were to be celebrated in such a way that neither the artist nor the visitor would be obviously identified with any particular faction in the Revolution.

However, this scheme was presented in a political climate determined by a forthcoming general election in which left–right issues were salient, and were playing on the deep uneasiness within French culture over two dates in history, 1940 as well as 1789. On the one hand, the status of the regicides, Marat, Robespierre and Saint-Just, had never been resolved: less than a third of French schoolteachers, polled that summer, believed that Louis XVI should have been executed. The Thermidorean Reaction which had executed the Jacobins in their turn had headed the Revolution away from the radical, democratic and neoclassical values which Finlay's proposal, however quietly, affirmed. On the other hand, as R. J. B. Bosworth has shown in *Explaining Ausch-witz and Hiroshima*, recent anathematization of Jacobin violence by the historian Furet can be related to the inability of his colleagues to come to terms with their nation's defeat by Nazi Germany in 1940, and the subsequent participation or connivance in Nazi measures of many French public figures, who were thus implicated in Hitler's Final Solution.[4] Finlay's French war broke out only months after the much publicized trial of Klaus Barbie, a German ex-policeman.

The 'execution' by Finlay and his collaborator Alexander Chemetov of the garden proposal would almost certainly have provoked some kind of 'war' anyway, in a context where some French artists were sure to be piqued over the award of such a commission – and so much current exhibition space to boot – to an alien artist. However, issues were confused and inflamed by the actions of a disgruntled ex-collaborator who disclosed selected excerpts from correspondence with Finlay to the French press. Jonathan Hirschfeld, the Canadian-born sculptor in question was, unfortunately, Jewish. Finlay sued for slander. Hirschfeld was eventually adjudged guilty of disseminating fragments of Finlay's correspondence which risked being misinterpreted. But meanwhile this, and disinformation spread by others, confirmed in many people's heads the baseless idea that Finlay was both anti-Semitic and pro-Nazi.

A radio forum on 25 March 1988, of which no one had forewarned Finlay and where no one represented his own position, cast this slur so emphatically that within hours the Ministry of Culture withdrew its commission. On the air, a misreading (or rather a deliberate non-reading) of part of a recent installation by Finlay, *Osso*, which included the Waffen SS double-lightning symbol as one part of a work on three stones, was used to support the charge that 'the work of Finlay is nourished intellectually by an ambiguous rapport with Nazism'.[5] Allusions to the Second World War in the Little Sparta garden were used in the ensuing smear campaign by people who had never been there so could not have understood the ironies clearly involved. In this sorry, prolonged fracas the Scottish Arts Council, in the person of its chairman, Sir Alan Peacock, honourably took up the cause of its undefeated Spartan foe. He wrote to the new French Minister of Culture, Jack Lang, calling for the commission to be reinstated. 'There is no need for me to add the Scottish Arts Council's voice to the refutation of the baseless allegations of anti-semitism and Nazism laid against Mr Finlay since your Ministry has already stated that it does not accept them.' Like similar letters from many other quarters, Peacock's received no reply.

As he himself has reiterated, the methods used by Finlay's opponents recalled witch-hunts by the Nazis themselves. An atmosphere was created in which the Ministry of Culture, unable to concede that the attacks on Finlay were justified (since these were not only mendacious in themselves but impugned its own judgement in offering him the commission), was equally unable to proceed with his garden proposal. The aim was to celebrate a famous event in French history. Finlay's opponents ensured that the creation of the garden would have gone on causing controversy inimical to nationalistic whoopee. Underlying unease over the significance of the Revolution itself would have been stirred up again and again. RIP Jean-Jacques Rousseau? Not likely.

Meanwhile, in France as in other countries, films depicting Germans in Second World War action continued to be seen, and books and magazines presenting Nazis and their weaponry without explicit condemnation were uncontroversially on sale. Nazi insignia were legal market commodities. Only in the sacred realm of art did some people insist they were taboo.

Visual artists, since Picasso's *Guernica,* have offered remarkably little in the way of serious representation of the gigantic wars of the last century. United States abstractionism and pop art evaded Vietnam as successfully as Stalinist 'realism' obscured the Eastern Front. Yet no candid person can fail to admit that the shapes of aircraft, battleships, even guns, such as are imitated at Little Sparta, convey artistic 'aura'. Finlay's correspondence with Speer about the garden which the war criminal created in jail was adduced as evidence of pro-Nazi proclivities by people who never dreamt of arraigning publishers who made money out of Speer's self-extenuating memoirs. Finlay's French war exposed the extent to which honest engagement in art with old Revolution and recent war are alike unacceptable to the bureaucratic patrons of liberal-pluralist democracies. That states have been founded on violence and have pursued their 'histories' by bloody warfare are facts unsuitable for public inspection except when sanitized in a National Curriculum.

Scots are not the likeliest people to understand these 'wars of Finlay', for three reasons.

First, it is unhelpful to set them in the flyting tradition, as revived by MacDiarmid and others from the days of Dunbar and Montgomerie.

Flyting involves competitive displays of feigned contempt. In a game of two players, who should be well matched, both use the same weapons. The SAC and Strathclyde Regional Council could hardly have replied to Finlay's campaign with a counter-shower of postcards and their own reciprocating street theatre.

Second, the prominent physical presence of a species of commercialized neoclassicism in parts of Scotland, especially in Edinburgh, will mislead the unwary into conceiving it to be a decorative style which provided icing, as it were, for the rich Enlightenment cake. Robert Adam, that archetypal Scotsman on the make, used opportunistic study of ancient ruins *in situ* to add the appearance of serious scholarship to the package of services he offered to Brits who wished, when remodelling old houses or building new ones, to display to admired effect wealth great and often very ill-gotten. ('Just raped Bengal, sir? I have the very fireplace for you.') Finlay's comment on Adam's best-known Scottish 'masterpiece' was made in 'The Third Reich Revisited', a sequence of architectural drawings with mock-scholarly commentaries dating from 1982, which he himself describes as 'the Little Sparta War in an earlier form'.[6]

The last item in the sequence, 'Redemption (Renovation) Scheme, Charlotte Square, Edinburgh', displays the square

> converted into a pine forest. The adjacent Edinburgh New Town functions as a rigidly formal, horizontal 'plinth' for this planned 'natural' wilderness, reminiscent of the paintings of Caspar David Friedrich and symbolic of 'desecularisation' . . . Prior to Desecularisation the Square was synonymous with the Scottish Arts Council. Before work on the Scheme had commenced, the SAC HQ (the infamous 'Number 19') was attacked by the so-called 'Saint-Just Vigilantes' and 'Ayatollah Aesthetes'. The art-files, artist case-histories and reports of the Censoring Committees, were burned, and the façade was hung with extremist slogans (some of them misspelt).[7]

Adam's decorative classicism is quite fairly assimilated with Finlay's target, 'secularization'. In what is described in the Penguin Guide to Edinburgh as the 'grand finale of the First New Town', Adam's design for Charlotte Square mixed Venetian windows with his 'own version' of Corinthian columns, and Egyptian sphinxes on the rooftops may have masonic overtones. However much we may regret changes, Victorian and later, affecting Adam's unified design for the square, this never intended more than a stylistically eclectic celebration of the marriage of affluence (nay, opulence) with taste. Robert Reid, redesigning St

George's Church for completion well after Adam's death, went for something 'simpler and loftier' with, to quote the Guide again, 'a plain monumentality'.[8] This starker, less 'secular' neoclassicism did not save the church from transmogrification, in quite recent times, into 'West Register House', a repository for 'case histories . . . reports' and the like and not so much a symbol of secularization as a straightforward example of it.

The third reason why Scots will find it hard to understand Finlay's wars is that MacDiarmid has lumbered us with a potent local version of that favourite bourgeois myth: misunderstood genius. A simple example of this myth disposes of Keats, a more sinister one of Blake. Keats writes wondrous verse. Gets bad reviews. Dies broken hearted. Is found to have been a genius. Victorians assimilated this sad story with their ideology of progress. Pioneering genius suffers, but before long everyone is benefiting from genius. This of course raises the disappointing thought that Keats was only a middlebrow one step ahead of popular taste. So your really tasteful and intelligent bourgeois needs myths like Blake's. Here, neglected genius is presented as inherently incomprehensible except . . . to learned, patient and inspired adepts who know, contrary to appearances, that in order to 'understand' even the most directly affecting Blake lyric, you have to get very, very deeply into Plotinus, Swedenborg and other authors not normally available in Menzies.

To the great embarrassment of Scottish intellectuals, all the major figures in our cultural tradition made their points instantaneously to large publics, not even excluding keelie elements. Lindsay's community theatre, Burns's satires and songs, Scott's novels, Stevenson's poems and stories, like the paintings of Ramsay and Wilkie, connected immediately with contemporary taste and imagination. Please forgive me for presenting a strip-cartoon reduction of MacDiarmid, who decided that matters, for him, must be otherwise. Correctly assessing that bourgeois taste in Scotland was deplorable, he embattled himself against it in ways which confirmed that a major writer like himself could only be 'unpopular' and offered himself as misunderstood genius. This has provided ample scope for Ph.D. students, while ensuring that the general reader still rebounds, in awe if not disgust, from MacDiarmid's self-advertised difficulty.

MacDiarmid's fight with Finlay was border skirmishing, not real war. 'Concrete poetry', especially the 'one word poems' with which Finlay experimented in the 1960s, stands, as any child indeed can at once perceive, at the furthest extreme from MacDiarmid's literally interminable later work. Interviewed by Duncan Glen in 1970,

MacDiarmid conceded Glen's point that 'the creative mind needs a sort of relaxation':

MacD: Oh yes. Play. It's part of play.
Glen: Now this would bring into mind instantly something that you would perhaps reject – Ian Hamilton Finlay.
MacD: Yes?
Glen: The play element is very, very strong in that sort of 'concrete' work, isn't it?
MacD: There's nothing else but the play element.
Glen: Going round the Bond Street galleries, Finlay would fit in there very well.
MacD: I don't doubt it.
Glen: This is not poetry, of course.
MacD: It is not art either.

(*Akros* 5:13, 1970)

Now, the 'play' element in art is fundamental, and certainly something to be taken 'very seriously'. MacDiarmid, never well up on visual arts, assimilates Finlay's work with Bond Street fashion and the corruption of the art market only when prompted by Glen. In the wider context of the interview, where MacDiarmid has just had another go at his favourite butt, 'folk poetry', it would seem that his basic objection to Finlay's work is that it is childishly simple, 'playground' stuff. Up to a point, he is not too far wrong.

The wars of Finlay arose not because a great artist ahead of his time was misunderstood, but because his opponents knew perfectly well what he was saying and could not cope with the contradictions in our culture which he so deftly exposed. The presence of conspiracy against him during the French war distracts attention from the cardinal reason why his art was incompatible with official celebration of the revolutionary bicentenary: the silence of the French government, faced with repeated challenges to restore a commission suddenly and unjustly withdrawn, suggests not conspiracy, but embarrassment. Cultural bureaucrats and politicians could say literally nothing which would satisfy themselves, let alone others. If the 'art' of Robert Adam represents successful adjustment of taste to wealth and power, Finlay's restores, in ways conducive often to merriment but never to complacency or ease, the awkward questions posed, not resolved, by serious neoclassicists in Adam's own day. To quote from Finlay's *Table Talk* of 1985, 'Classicism aims at Beauty; neoclassicism at Virtue'. Neoclassicists raised awkward issues to do with the balance between nature and culture, wildness and order, the relationships between beauty and terror, creativity and violence, and the attempt to achieve both private and civic virtue harmonized with liberty, equality and fraternity. The wit, grace and aura of Finlay's works make neoclassical points instantaneously. And, to paraphrase Miss Jean Brodie, creation of Ms Spark's equally drastic vision, for those who do not like that kind of point, that is the kind of point they do not like.

In Scotland, where most sound chaps and chapesses conventionally approve of Adam and his decorative, 'beautiful' classicism, we have neglected Gavin Hamilton, the greatest of our eighteenth-century artists. His neoclassical treatments of subjects from Homer and Roman history, executed in Rome for private patrons but seen all over Europe in engraved versions, inspired J-L. David, painter of the *Oath of the Horatii*, *Brutus* and *Death of Marat* and the artist most identified with revolutionary Jacobinism. Duncan Macmillan, a consistent and acutely informed supporter of Finlay in his wars, has recently made the first significant contribution for decades to the very small body of scholarly work on Hamilton. Of *The Death of Lucretia*, he writes that Hamilton 'demonstrated memorably the ability of art to deal on its own terms with issues central to the well-being of society and to make visible the nobility of the ideals of those who sought to change it for the better'.[9]

This seems as apt a point as any with which to end this brief history of the wars of Scotland's present-day champion of classical, pastoral, civic-republican and heroic values. Hamilton and David operated in a culture where 'sacredness' was still understood, and they could represent virtue without irony. Finlay has to use words, often ironically, to spell out the significance of his chosen images. But taking both together, his statements are clear. And that is why they provoke such embarrassment, which then blunders into enmity.

1994

References

[1] I. H. Finlay, *Evening Will Come They Will Sew the Blue Sail: Ian Hamilton Finlay and the Wild Hawthorn Press 1958–1991* (text by Edwin Morgan) (Edinburgh: Graeme Murray).

[2] Peter Day, *Ian Hamilton Finlay: The Bicentennial Proposal: The French War: The War of the Letter* (Toronto: Art Metropole, 1989), p. 93.

[3] Yves Abrioux, *Ian Hamilton Finlay: A Visual Primer* (revised edn) (London: Reaktion Books, 1992), pp. 132–3.

[4] R. J. B. Bosworth, *Explaining Auschwitz and Hiroshima: History Writing and the Second World War 1945–1990* (London: Routledge, 1993).

[5] Day, *Ian Hamilton Finlay*, pp. 31–3.

[6] Abrioux, *Ian Hamilton Finlay*, p. 141.

[7] Ibid., p. 144.

[8] John, Gifford et al., *The Buildings of Scotland: Edinburgh* (Harmondsworth: Penguin Books, 1988), pp. 291, 293–7.

[9] Gill Perry and Michael Rossington (eds), *Femininity and Masculinity in Eighteenth Century Art and Culture* (Manchester: Manchester University Press, 1994), p. 95.

2

WHAT DID YOU DO
IN THE WAR?

Campaign Honours: The American Revolution

Review of Charles Royster, *A Revolutionary People at War: The Continental Army and American Character, 1775–1783* (Chapel Hill: University of North Carolina Press, 1979).

This book, as its author shows he recognizes, advances into landscapes as dangerous as that unconquerable American terrain which defeated Lord North's armies. Its title alone is enough to muster sharpshooters against it. It presumes that a whole 'people' was engaged in revolution, whereas much recent scholarship has emphasized the extent of loyalist feeling. It further presumes that we can talk of an 'American' character in that period, when thirteen disparate polities had combined in an uneasy confederation. Then, as we move on to the book itself, it emerges that Professor Royster believes that the 'American' people lived, not by bread alone, but in terms of high ideals which moved their psyches profoundly. Surviving the questions he begs, he deserves proud campaign honours. Using letters, diaries, sermons, poems, all manner of documents, he seeks to generalize about attitudes within Washington's army, and views of the fighting, and the army, among civilians. He writes up his wide research rather too well. It is fine that he deploys eighteenth-century concepts with respect, rather than glibly translating the mental throes of his people into Freudian or Marxian terms. It is excellent that he can produce a measured prose of his own which, assured in cool epigrammatic irony, recalls good writers of his chosen period. But his book makes demanding reading, and I wished he had included more of those passages of direct, vivid narrative which, as a most original device, he juxtaposes with his abstract argumentation, presenting a person's experience, or a small event, without generalizing comment.

It was a real revolution, with an ideology as potent and universally subversive as that of Lenin. Its ideals were cosmic in scope. People could not live up to them. Charles Thomson, secretary of Congress, burnt his papers before he died, having refused to publish a history of the revolution. 'I could not tell the truth without giving great offence. Let the world admire our patriots and heroes. Their supposed talents and virtues (where they were so) by commanding imitation will serve the cause of patriotism and of our country.'

The revolutionaries had begun euphorically, with hopes of a swift victory of God's chosen people over a tyrant who sought to reduce them to slavery. Those who now proclaimed themselves to be 'Americans' saw themselves as guardians of liberty for the whole world. In their feats and their virtue, they hoped to surpass the heroes of Republican Rome. 'We have it in our power to begin the world again', Tom Paine assured them. John Adams, writing from Paris, echoed the founder of Massachusetts, that visionary puritan John Winthrop – American was 'the City, set upon a Hill'. Americans were consciously making *revolution,* not 'rebellion', and our modern use of the former term derives from them.

With another term, likewise, they set a new fashion. The tearful ecstasies of the followers of Whitefield and other evangelical preachers during that wave of revivals which smote both shores of the Atlantic from the 1730s and formed what Americans call the 'Great Awakening', had been branded by gentlemen and rational intellectuals with the obnoxious word 'enthusiasm'. Now Americans commonly used it in a positive way. It was right to be 'enthusiastic' in the 'sacred cause of freedom'. Royster rightly sees the 'Awakening' as an important element in the causation of 'revolution'. But I think he must be overestimating the hold of evangelicalism somewhat. It is odd to have a view of 'American character' which does not seem to apply to Benjamin Franklin or Thomas Jefferson. Royster's arguments would be strengthened by recognition that the pull of rationalist deism was, in relation to 'enthusiasm', both countervailing and conspiratorial. The undoubted religious afflatus which certainly moved many revolutionaries needs to be set in a spectrum of ideas and feelings including also the 'neo-classical' vision which appealed to Americans who were as suspicious as Edward Gibbon of 'fanatics' and their deluded intolerance. Somehow, it was possible to range the Elder Brutus alongside the biblical prophets, to combine the biblical millennium with the myth of the Golden Age.

An 'American Liberty Song' of 1775 proclaimed:

> With the beasts of the wood
> We will ramble for food
> And live in wild deserts and caves,
> And live poor as *Job*
> On the skirts of the globe,
> Before we'll submit to be slaves.

Royster's book is at its fascinating best as he reveals the implications lurking in this naive-seeming ditty. 'Liberty', for Americans, meant freedom from government interference, freedom from war, freedom from heavy taxation, freedom above all from such standing armies as the dread George III seemed bent on quartering upon the Chosen continent. Any revolutionary snatching time to read that current best-seller, Gibbon's *Decline and Fall,* would have found even an English writer who disapproved of American rebels drawing received American wisdom from the Latin classics: 'The army is the only order of men sufficiently united to concur in the same sentiments, and powerful enough to impose them on the rest of their fellow-citizens: but the temper of soldiers, habituated at once to violence and to slavery, renders them very unfit guardians of a legal, or even a civil, constitution.'

When God's Chosen People rose in what Royster calls their *rage militaire* in 1775, according to their millenarian vision charismatic leaders should have led volunteer citizen-soldiers to swift victory over George III's mercenary army. Because, contrary to fond hopes, the improvised or non-existent drill of American amateurs did not at once confound the manoeuvres of the tyrant's redcoated slave-automatons, liberty-lovers were given ample time to see how revolt itself might deprive them of liberty.

Though volunteer militiamen were needed throughout the war, they could not win it. They were apt to go home when they felt like it, and prone to plunder the homes of their fellow Americans. A standing army was essential. Washington wanted a properly disciplined one. But, as every patriot knew, such an army was a fount of corruption, where discipline shaded into slavery and patronage bred sycophants. The necessary evil was accepted. Minimum service, one year at first, was raised to three before long, and thousands of morally suspect heroes actually enlisted for the duration. 'Once a long term army became necessary', Royster drily notes, 'the public decided that it was the duty only of some men – mainly unmarried sons of farmers, farm labourers, servants, apprentices, slaves, and mechanics – to fill its ranks.' Such low persons were lured to sacrifice their liberty by the offer of bounties. Citizens who purchased substitutes to serve in their stead were buying freedom, in effect, from the demands of their own government. Though they could and did claim that their sacrifice of cash was patriotic, recruitment proved to be an arena of ingenious graft of many kinds.

And as that 'Liberty Song' implied, the vast acreage of America made government problematic. Even without adopting the last resort and fleeing west, men could live in quiet, untouched by war, enjoying already the freedom which others were fighting for. If the British appeared in overwhelming force, liberty-lovers could gain further quiet by professing loyalty – but a demand that they should fight for the king would of course alienate them at once. Royster believes that the majority of ex-colonials were in fact in sympathy with the revolution despite the apparent quiescence of so many. The problem for Congress, and Washington, was that sympathy with ideals of liberty and paradisal peace predisposed citizens *not* to enlist or submit to discipline.

A German, Baron von Steuben, from 1778, was able to bring increasingly good order into Washington's rag-tag ranks because he understood that these soldiers were different from Europeans. Dregs of society though they might be, they insisted on their right to reason why. Men also insisted on wearing long hair and sporting individualistic headgear. The desertion rate was huge. Those who stayed, despite inadequate pay and the shortage of provisions which arose as civilians found they could make more money selling food to civilians, or to the enemy, did so, Royster argues, because they were patriots. 'The distinguishing feature of the recruits was their willingness.' They *wanted* to fight for liberty.

Their officers, it appears, were more complicated. It seemed clear enough, whatever Tom Paine might imply, that officers ought to be 'gentlemen'. Alas, the land of new Scipios and new Joshuas proved to be short of authentic gentlemen, though fecund in aspirants to that station in life. Sons of prosperous farmers and artisans who got commissions inevitably behaved with exorbitant self-consciousness. They emphasized their difference from common soldiers all too like themselves. They paraded their 'honour' and fought duels with each other. They were disastrously sensitive about promotion and seniority. Courting heroic death in the intervals of flaunting their mayfly consequence, Washington's officers began to feel a caste apart. Since civilian revolutionaries, after a time, thought as little as possible about this distressing war, army men had some right to opine that they alone represented the revolution, and they alone would be worthy, afterwards, of esteem and power in the new polity.

But, in the end, the spectres of Caesar and Cromwell were laid. Washington did not make himself dictator. The regular army disbanded peacefully. And civilians decided that it had not won the war. Victory had been the work of the American people. This view imposed itself as 'history'.

Ideals of national character had, Royster argues, been shaped and tested through war. The fact that many had failed the test – that alarming numbers had run from the enemy, had profiteered, had bought bootleg British provisions from smugglers, had professed loyalty to both sides – could not be altogether evaded, and the shape of the American constitution would reflect in due course the view of Washington, Hamilton and other officers that citizens who could not man or supply an army adequately were hardly fit for paradisal liberty. But Washington himself – the most overrated commander of all time – had been, if incompetent, upright and dedicated and in contemplating their hero men could believe that the ideals of 1775 had had real basis. And the existence, in Benedict Arnold, of a perfect scapegoat, helped to maintain the citizen's self-esteem. A Roman hero after his epic march to Quebec, this man, grafting, obsessed with promotion, epitomized the worst qualities found among the sinister officer class and finally proved a cold-blooded traitor. 'By pillorying Arnold, Americans seemed to be trying to prove that such corruption did not exist or that it could be extirpated.'

It remained – and remains – the case that to be an 'American' was not just an accident of nativity, but a matter of living up to an ideal of character. Royster relates this to the 'Great Awakening'. 'The test of patriotism bore some likeness to the test of evangelical conversion: one did not ask, "Was I born an American?" or even, "Do I choose to be an American?" but rather, "Am I worthy to be an American?" ' The strain, as in religious revivals, was too much for some. Two of Royster's narrative interpolations concern prominent people who committed suicide. Some accounts of the revolutionary period make it seem that one of the fundamental episodes in world history came about, in effect, gradually, as loyal English subjects broke hesitantly with a crown they had venerated. It is a great merit of Royster's book that he suggests how disturbing, how *revolutionary*, the times were. Men really thought that they could donate to their descendants something like the kingdom of heaven on earth.

Royster does not explain, what is perhaps inexplicable, how a common sense of American identity could have emerged so suddenly amongst people scattered through thirteen polities geographically as different from each other, at the extremes, as Scotland was from Spain. Though he suggests that service in the army helped people to 'think Continentally', his book implies strongly that serving soldiers were untypical people, and shows, anyway, that sectional discord persisted. 'Friction between soldiers from New England and those from the middle and southern states sometimes made it hard for the army to direct its hostilities towards the enemy. Washington, who had hoped to create a national army, wound up in 1780 and 1781 using Pennsylvanian troops to quell mutiny in the Connecticut line and New England troops to quell mutiny in the New Jersey Line.'

Was there really *one* 'American character'? Leaving the definite article out of his subtitle, Royster recognizes, but also evades, an issue. To give us the many insights with which his book provides us, he has had to generalize riskily. His Americans advance as one body. Will their 'Americanness' disintegrate, will they break into sections and disperse, as scholars take aim at his hypotheses?

1980

Civil War Soldiers

Review of Reid Mitchell, *Civil War Soldiers: Their Expectations and Their Experiences* (New York: Viking, 1988).

No major conflict of the nineteenth century was larger or lasted longer than the US Civil War. It marked the beginning of modern life. Cause, shape and, arguably, result, were provided by industrialization. Over the huge theatre of war, the North had emphatic superiority in rail transport, and while both sides used hot-air balloonists to direct artillery fire, it was the North which first employed the electric telegraph to send messages back to ground, and first took aerial photographs. One could go on – this was the first war in which both sides carried rifled muskets, producing fearful casualty rates, especially when fired from defensive trenches, and the first in which cavalry never played a decisive part: a prophetic observer might just have imagined the Armageddon of 1914–18.

Another aspect was also exceptional. In an age of generally rising literacy, North Americans above all were equipped to record, as soldiers, their views and experiences. And since the war was staged, and would be remembered, as an epic struggle for the future of a continent, soldiers' letters and diaries were very likely to be preserved. Reid Mitchell, to write *Civil War Soldiers*, has raked through over 300 sets of papers, armed, he tells us, with a set of questions suggested by the 'post-Vietnam' and 'post-Civil Rights' conjuncture in which he became a scholar:

Why did you fight? What did you think of your enemy, your American enemy? How did you feel about slavery and race and all the unfinished business that means in some way the war you fought is still not over? What was it like to be in battle? . . . How did you accept that you yourself were a killer? What did you take home from the war? What legacy have you left us?

He has explored, he believes, 'the moral dilemma at the heart' of the USA's past. Between 1861 and 1865, the soldiers he has studied 'created a new American history, a potent source of myth and identity'.

Himself a Southerner, he argues that Southern identity was a creation rather than a cause of the war. At the start, the Confederation was short of distinctive symbols. Its ideology was 'American', its constitution copied that of the US, its supporters 'had to use American symbols because they regarded themselves as the true Americans'. By 1865, they possessed their own potent mythology, binding Southern whites together. The sagacity and courage of Generals Lee and Jackson, the superior valour of the grey-uniformed soldier, the aristocratically mannered lady running a plantation tended by loyal slaves – these would compel the imagination as much as tales of the Jacobites, and more momentously. The myth of Southern chivalry insisted as concomitant on that of black inferiority.

Lincoln's Emancipation Proclamation, Mitchell believes, united the white south as cautious Northern politicians had feared it would. The average Confederate soldier could not accept the Union's black troops as legitimate foes, and massacred them when occasion arose. 'In the lines around Petersburg, where black troops were used, a Pennsylvania regiment found it advisable, when replacing a black regiment on picket, to call over to the Confederates "that the 2nd Pa was back again".' As one man in that regiment explained to his mother, an informal truce was kept up while white troops were on picket, but as soon as blacks appeared Confederates started a constant fire: 'they hate a niger worse than they hate a coperhead Snake.' Mitchell is careful to preserve the uncertain orthography and punctuation of his soldiers: a good practice, since a historian assessing evidence needs to be able to judge how capable its author really was of expressing his experience. Individual black soldiers have not, it seems, left much trace.

Yet, by the end of the war, blacks made up a tenth of the Union army. Most were ex-slaves, who had fled to the Union lines or had won their freedom, in the loyal slave states of Kentucky, Maryland and Missouri, by volunteering to fight. The Union government's handling of them was racist. Initially, they were paid less than whites, were treated as labourers rather than fighters, and provided almost no officers. As they proved their valour, respect increased. But Northern mythology would remember 'the boys in blue giving blacks their freedom, not black soldiers helping to free their race'. How was it that blacks could be soldiers, yet somehow still not worthy of citizenship?

Mitchell points to the paradox that, in volunteering to fight, blacks sought a role which whites feared would degrade them. 'If blacks could be soldiers, did it mean that soldiers were no better than blacks?' 'I will Never fight by the side of A Nigger & that is the feeling of the army where ever I have been', wrote one Union soldier, echoing many. Later, black participation was more accepted – at least it saved white men's lives. But if blacks were good, even better soldiers, this confirmed their inferior nature. Blacks were said to make better soldiers because they were more subservient, they were said to make better soldiers because they were more savage. Discipline and savagery, as we have seen, were desirable traits in a soldier. They were not necessarily desirable in citizens.

Granted that black soldiers were beasts who 'fought like tigers', they were ideal foes for barbaric Confederate troops – white Union men could praise themselves as incapable of behaving like either. 'Conversely, the image of black soldiers as slaves in uniform obeying a new set of masters gave men unhappy with their own submission to authority an example of more total subservience.' American ideology inherited and boosted the legacy of the 'free-born' Englishman and the Britons who 'never, never will be slaves'. Northerners denounced the South as aristocratic. A Northern brigadier wrote from Alabama in 1863: 'We are not fighting for the negroes only – no indeed we are fighting for the rights of the poor white trash of the South, men who tho' good enough originally have been so kicked and abused that they themselves now believe themselves inferior beings – indeed they are.' The inconvenient fact that the democratic process in the South had produced Secession was, for many Northerners, inconceivable. Contrariwise, Southerners held that the North had fallen into 'an odd combination of anarchy and despotism'. According to one Confederate officer, Northern elections towards the end of the war were farcical because 'Each party strove to prove its candidate to be a better friend to the soldier than his opponent. They feared not only the votes, but the bayonets of their own hirelings.' He claimed that Lincoln – commander-in-chief of the Union army – had 'changed a free republic to an obsequious despotism'.

As Mitchell presents matters, this last view had some basis. In both North and South, soldiers were understandably intolerant of civilian dissent. The Confederate government took more care to allow free speech than the Union, but even so reacted viciously to strong Unionist insurgency. On both sides, soldiers were ready to argue that people who did not support the war efforts had forfeited their rights as free citizens. They 'habituated themselves to the notion of repression' and (to quote perhaps the most striking sentence in Mitchell's book) 'Power joined liberty as a fundamental American value'. The drive to enforce communal unity after 1865 would lead to violent suppression of

Republicans and Populists, white as well as black, in the South and state-approved violence against the labour movement in the North. A recent issue of *Index on Censorship* (July/August 1989) prints a scene from Arthur Miller's 1950 translation of Ibsen's *An Enemy of the People*. Introducing it, Miller describes Ibsen's theme as 'the crushing of the dissenting spirit by the majority'. It is curious that this theme bears more strongly on the present-day US with its written democratic constitution than on Britain where the 'majority' has no effective say. But in both societies the purported need to defend liberty against 'subversion' from within has been lavishly used to legitimate the power of elites. Mitchell's analysis suggests that the Civil War was a key point in the trajectory from those Salem witch-hunts which Miller has dramatized to the era of Joe MacCarthy and Oliver North.

But, as he points out, attitudes to power in 1861–5 were powerfully conditioned by Protestant evangelicalism. Power must be a tool of the righteous. While men on both sides could agree that American sin was the prime cause of the war – 'God's chastisement of his disobedient American children' – interpretations of His will of course differed. A Northern Presbyterian (Irish-born, ironically) believed that God would 'carry on the war until that he [made] all flesh free'. But a North Carolina chaplain was sure that the war would end soon because so many Southern soldiers were undergoing 'conversion': 'I don't believe that God will deliver us over into the hands of our enemies while we take Him to be our refuge and strength.' Another Southerner averred that his people were 'destined to freedom, as the christian is to inherit eternal bliss in a future state'.

In the event God, or Grant's use of the railway system, brought Northern invaders into the South. Mitchell's fourth chapter, 'The landscape of war: the Union soldier views the South', is perhaps the most interesting in his book. Though the Union fought to keep the South as an integral part of the nation, its soldiers often wrote of it as if it were a foreign country. They did not, by the usual standards of war, behave too badly on Southern soil. But burning plantations, that long remembered offence, could be seen, Mitchell suggests, as a 'concrete manifestation of the desire to remake the South in the North's image'.

Strong as folk culture was in the South – whether in the Uplands with heavier Ulster and German influence, or Lowlands which retained English ways – this was not a case where Northern representatives of mature industrial society confronted slovenly archaic ways. Folk culture persisted in the North as well – a Northern soldier was often comparing his folk with theirs. Reactions were mixed up with responses to landscape. The South was conceived in advance as lush and exotic. When the landscape failed to provide what one romantic Union captain had dreamed of – 'orange groves . . . bright winged birds and southern skies' – it merely related to poverty, sloth and slavery. 'The few houses we've seen', wrote a Connecticut sergeant south of New Orleans, 'are a kind of hut filled with nigger or poor dirty-looking white folks', and the Mississippi mud, he added, was 'the nastiest, slipperiest stuff you eyer saw'. In the Louisiana swamps the trees were 'all huge and misshapened monsters' covered with grey moss. Snakes and 'devilish looking' alligators abounded. Plantations seemed ill kept up, disorderly. Towns were smaller, and lacked the regular grid patterns of the pioneering North West and plains. Captain Pierson from Michigan was contemptuous of Clifton, Tennessee – a major city by local standards but a 'miserable place' compared to 'Yankee Towns of the same importance'. Another Union man observed, 'The rule in North Carolina seems to be that it takes two houses to make a town & that three and a barn constitute a city.' The fact that large plantations provided many of the resources offered by Northern towns escaped Yankees for whom the town was a central institution. Without proper towns, it seemed to them, the South could have no law, politics, education or business of a civilized kind; it must be primitive and undemocratic. Even in larger places, gracious houses for whites mingled offensively with shacks for blacks.

The American ideology of progress, which has dominated the world in the twentieth century and still seems to thrill eastern Europeans, was already present in the reaction of an Ohio soldier who referred to a Southern town as 'beautifully situated on a branch of the Murfrees-boro and Chatanooga railroad'. The railroad, Mitchell notes, was 'beautiful to those who believed in Progress'. But most Northern soldiers were rural men, and the backwardness of its agriculture, for them, confirmed their right to conquer the South. In Virginia, land exhausted by tobacco had reverted to forest, and, according to one Union soldier, 'Old tobacco fields with the last ridges of the plow still visible grown up with pine fifty feet high were good representations of the wastefulness and wickedness of slavery'. In the spirit of progress, Northerners conflated economic inefficiency (often more apparent than real) with immorality. Slavery was opposed not so much as being unjust to blacks, but because it wasted natural resources. And laziness – either cause or result of slavery – was the Southerner's cardinal fault. The same charges of indolence and inefficiency had earlier been used to justify white expropriation of land from Amerindians. No doubt there are still people who earnestly believe that the destruction of Brazilian rain forests is a Godly way of making use of God's neglected gifts to Man.

Near the end of his magnificent recent addition to the Oxford History of the United States, *Battle Cry of Freedom* (1988) covering the Civil War, James M. McPherson remarks that while 'Union victory . . . destroyed the southern vision of America and ensured that the northern vision would become the American vision', before 1861 North, not South had been 'out of the mainstream'. The war years confirmed US, and world, history on a new course: McPherson quotes George Tickner, a retired Harvard professor, as writing in 1869, 'It does not seem to me as if I were living in the country in which I was born.' Reid Mitchell's study, composed with wry wit, makes an invaluable companion to McPherson's masterpiece because it documents US consciousness at a moment of revolution, standing comparison with Charles Royster's splendid ten-year-old study of 1776–83, *A Revolutionary People at War*. When Sherman's army paraded through Washington after victory, one soldier wrote: 'As I listened to the steady footfall again I experienced the odd feeling of excitement, and the fancy of the dreaded "Mill" grinding to atoms Kings, & Kingdoms, Emperors & Empires, Tramp, tramp, slow but sure. I thought that tramp of freemen is grinding to dust tyrants and tyranny.' He could not know that it was marching towards Edison's electrical lighting, Coca Cola, the Model T Ford and beyond the Ford to Alfred P. Sloan and the freedom of consumers to choose between different models of goods complete with built-in obsolescence; towards the trenches of Flanders; towards the defoliation of Vietnam.

1989

Britain's Good War

It was easy for the British to convince themselves in 1945 that they had had a 'good war'. In the armed forces, more than a quarter of a million young men and women had died, and as many had been wounded. Over thirty thousand merchant seamen had lost their lives in the desperate fight to bring essential cargoes to the island. Double that number of civilians had been killed by German bombs. But compared to the calamitous loss of young British lives in the 1914–18 war such sacrifice seemed relatively trivial.

Houses, hospitals, schools and churches had been destroyed, and even those cities which had escaped heavy bombing were shabbier than before the war. Food had been more and more severely rationed, so that at a peak, in August 1942, an adult officially got no more than roughly half a kilogram of butcher's meat per week, and only 55g of butter. But people in general approved of rationing, as the fair way to distribute food and other essentials, and the nation's diet was overall healthier. Full employment meant that many of the homes previously poorest were better provisioned. Children got free milk.

The phrase 'People's War' became current early on, defining the sense that rich and poor, civilians and fighters, were 'all in it together', that privilege was or should be in abeyance and that even conscripted effort had a voluntary character. It also implied for many, and not only for those who had previously identified themselves as socialists, the idea that the 'Old World' of capitalist boom, slump and war was being bombed and planned out of existence, so that victory would be followed by social justice. The report on social security by a committee of civil servants headed by Sir William Beveridge, which the government published late in 1942 just as the tide of war had turned decisively in the Allies' favour, sold 650,000 copies. It was Beveridge's assumptions, more than the rationalization of existing provisions for social security which his report proposed, which won the enthusiastic approval of the vast majority of Britons. He assumed that there would be 'family allowances' for all children and a National Health Service free to all, both of which indeed came about soon after victory, and that there would be 'full employment', which by previous and later standards was virtually achieved in the first two post-war decades.

The British could see themselves as deserving of such reward for their truly exceptional efforts. They alone had kept the beacon of European democracy burning in the dark period between the fall of France and US entry into the war. They had mobilized more thoroughly than any other major combatant. By D-Day, June 1944, the USA had drawn 40 per cent of its people into the armed services or civilian 'war work'. For Britain, the figure was 55 per cent. Conscription of women went so far that by 1943 it was virtually impossible for a woman under forty to avoid 'war work' unless she had heavy family responsibilities or was looking after a 'war worker' billetted on her. British agriculture, in a trough between the wars, expanded to fill every corner which could be cultivated, while non-farmers set about 'Digging for Victory' in gardens and allotments. A man might quite normally work extended hours, 'war industry', drill as Home Guard or serve as Fire Watcher afterwards, then spend much of his weekend cultivating potatoes. Retired people and housewives worked in their homes making aeroplane parts. Though many expressed guilt that their sacrifices and efforts in no way matched those of the allied Soviet peoples, most might still feel that they had 'done their bit' and 'pulled their weight'.

Inevitably, Britain's war experience fostered complacency. Churchill's magnificent rhetoric as he rallied the nation's will to fight in the frightening summer of 1940 would have looked ridiculously fustian had Britain treated for peace or lost the war. As it was, every word uttered by him on 18 June after France had fallen seemed to shine as true prophecy:

> Hitler knows that he will have to break us in this island or lose the war. If we can stand up to him, all Europe may be free and the life of the world may move forward into broad, sunlit uplands. But if we fail, then the whole world, including the United States, including all that we have known and cared for, will sink into the abyss of a new Dark Age made more sinister, and perhaps more protracted, by the lights of perverted science. Let us therefore brace ourselves to our duties, and so bear ourselves that, if the British Empire and its Commonwealth last for a thousand years, men will still say, 'This was their finest hour.'

Mention of the United States advertises that with this speech, as with all his other public announcements, Churchill was concerned as much with American as with British public opinion. The 'bulldog' defender of the British Empire which he loved so fully was, ironically, the man whose continued defiance ensured that it went bankrupt and finally conceded world hegemony to the great republic on which it depended for survival. The process of 'decolonization' would be all but complete within a quarter of a century. Churchill's state funeral in 1965 would be the first given to a commoner since Wellington's more than a century before. The 300,000 people who filed past his coffin were involved in the last rites of Empire. But the British remained entranced by the image of themselves as defenders of world democracy in their finest hour.

Twenty-five years after victory, in 1970, Henry Pelling published a useful short study of Britain and the Second World War. He concluded:

> The average Briton might be impressed, at least for two or three years, by what he took to be the exceptional military prowess of the Soviet Union, and wonder what the reason for it was; but the war did not really weaken his [*sic*] adherence to his own distinctive national institutions and customs. Parliament, the political parties, local government, the press, the law, the trade unions all emerged from the war with slightly different surface features, but basically unaltered. There had not been much of that 'inspection effect' which is supposed to be one of the by-products of war; or, if there had been, it had found most institutions not unsatisfactory, and so served to reinforce the view which so many people in Britain still retained: that somehow or other things in their own country were arranged much better than elsewhere in the world . . .

The left as well as the right in British politics still largely shared in the 'view' noted by Pelling. While Conservatives forgot that their party's MPs had mostly resented Churchill's seizure of the helm from Neville Chamberlain in 1940, as they gloried in the defeat of the 'Hun' under the leadership of the man who had then become their first post-war prime minister, the Labour Party had an equal emotional investment in the myth of the 'People's War'. The 'people', in a general election held between VE Day and VJ Day, had voted Churchill out and voted in a Labour government which had rewarded them for their wartime efforts by creating a 'Welfare State'.

This might be held to have perfected British political life, fulfilling the promise made by propagandists to America in 1940 that Britain, contrary to appearances, was a truly democratic country. To an extent which now seems surprising, post-war Conservative leaders accepted the Welfare State as just and inevitable, sustaining it during their thirteen years of rule after 1951. War service had bonded men from different regions and classes together. Bombing and privation had likewise given civilians rich and poor a sense of shared experience. When Buckingham Palace was bombed in September 1940 just a few days after the Luftwaffe had set the London Docks alight, the Queen remarked, 'I'm glad we've been bombed. It makes me feel I can look the East End in the face.' She wrote to her mother-in-law a month later: 'I feel quite exhausted after seeing & hearing so much sadness, sorrow, heroism and magnificent spirit. The destruction is so awful, & the people so wonderful – they deserve a better world.'

Pelling did not mention the monarchy among the institutions 'inspected' and approved in 1939–45, but the roles played by the Queen and her husband, sustaining morale as they toured bombed cities and imitating in their palaces the 'austerity' measures enforced on their subjects by rationing and shortages, certainly strengthened greatly an institution brought into jeopardy by the scandal surrounding the abdication of the pro-Nazi Edward VIII in 1936. The warmth of feeling which George VI evoked among the people helped ensure that the televised coronation of his daughter in 1953 was an event shared and remembered by virtually everyone, amid talk of a 'New Elizabethan Era' of new Shakespeares and Raleighs. (A revival of British drama did indeed occur, but the entrepreneurial energies of the earliest phase of overseas colonialism were hardly evident in a British economy soon lagging further and further behind its German rival.)

The young intellectual members of the ruling elite who had turned towards Marxism in the 1930s had mostly joined enthusiastically in the war effort. Even the out-of-step Orwell became a BBC propagandist, as did the poet MacNeice. Erstwhile Surrealists found that the weird sights of Blitz went far beyond imaginings from their subconscious, and one of them, Humphrey Jennings, created in propaganda documentaries the most potent and durable film images of 'the People's War'. The social justice for which the left of the 1930s had called seemed to be more or less achieved by the defeat of Fascism and Nazism and the arrival of a Welfare State. Its intellectuals, if they chose, were now part of the 'Establishment', that fraternity of former students of Oxford and Cambridge universities which dominated British public life.

The BBC, friendly face of the establishment, continued to purvey, on TV as well as radio, the balance of populist and culturally elitist output which it had achieved during the war, when its reputation as the truthful voice of freedom had become enormous all over the world. It also presented 'balance' in the broadcasting of political views. The genuine respect for freedom of expression which much of the press shared with the BBC and its new rivals in commercial television helped ensure that dissent, for decades after the war, was easily muffled, diffused and co-opted. The 'Angry Young Men' of the 1950s – playwrights and novelists – swiftly became part of the literary establishment, and their works were set as school textbooks. Student revolt in Britain in 1968 was extensive, but moderate and playful compared to events on the Continent. Serious anger was directed outwards, at the USA's war in Vietnam. The need for drastic change in British institutions was recognized only very slowly. Leaders of the Campaign for Nuclear Disarmament, which began to march in the late 1950s and rallied the left in and out of the Labour Party, could be heard talking as if it was Britain's immense 'moral' standing in the world which might ensure that the country's unilateral abandonment of nuclear weapons would exercise decisive 'moral' influence even on the superpowers. The image of the dome of St Paul's Cathedral riding over the smoke and flame of the Blitz had come to symbolize Britain's lone stand for Christian values against Nazism. Now CND proposed exemplary, Christlike renunciation.

Parliament had not been seen at its best during the war. An increasingly unrepresentative House of Commons elected in 1935, which had supported Neville Chamberlain's appeasement of Hitler, debated but could hardly much influence decisions taken by the War Cabinet. Its chamber was destroyed by a bomb in May 1941. But before this it had provided a theatre for Churchill's oratory. As 'the Mother of Parliaments', purportedly the prototype of representative assemblies throughout the world, it evoked loyalty to its strange, anachronistic procedures even in men and women of the left who sat in it; none more fanatical than that of Michael Foot, fierce critic of the 'Guilty Men' of the Conservative Party in a famous pamphlet reacting to the retreat through Dunkirk in 1940, prominent CND campaigner, and eventually the leader who guided Labour to disaster against Margaret Thatcher in the 1983 general election. Foot's Parliament-worship was echoed by right-wing Conservative opponents of greater integration with the European Community a decade later. Though by then a serious debate on constitutional reform had begun in Britain, that it arrived only four decades after the war suggested how thoroughly Britons had bought their own propaganda line then, that even with the wholly unrepresentative House of Lords thrown in, their country had the finest democratic constitution in the world. Nothing had done more to delay

Britain's entry into the EEC, or to pervert relations with its partners thereafter.

In 1960, though Britain's cities had recovered only slowly from the effects of bombing, and though rationing, which continued for some goods into the 1950s, had only recently yielded to consumerist affluence (Harold Macmillan had just won the Tories a third term with the slogan 'You've Never Had It So Good'), a student like myself visiting the Continent could still be forcibly struck by how 'primitive' conditions seemed even in France. Continental lavatories evoked shudders. Italy was a cheap country for hitch-hikers. Thirty-five years later, contrasts are all reversed. Spotless and efficient sanitation greeting the hordes of Britons who now seek Mediterranean sunshine contrasts with the sordid toilets of British pubs. Except for wine, Italy, now industrially ahead of Britain, seems distinctly pricey. And the British tourist is less likely to encounter veterans of the Resistance grateful for British support against Mussolini and the Nazis. Intelligent Britons can see with their own eyes that many things work better on the Continent, and the bank balance of gratitude created during the war has been squandered by yobbish football supporters. (Scottish supporters, including myself, have made a point of behaving impeccably, to distance ourselves from the dreaded English.) Very, very slowly Britons are achieving a realistic sense of themselves, as inhabitants of a country which has become a second-rate economic power, with much to learn from more successful neighbours.

Complacency was sustained for so long partly because of the shortage of honest representations of wartime experience in the media. Post-war films generally presented it with unqualifed pride. In the 1970s, a very popular TV series, *Dad's Army*, was based on one of the platoons of Home Guard assembled in 1940 to defend Britain if the invader came. Its chirpy signature tune – 'Oo do you think you're kidding, Mr Hitler?' – overrode the farcical inefficiency displayed by its part-time soldiers to suggest that these doitered old men would indeed have 'fought on the beaches and in the hills' as Churchill's oratory had threatened – and they would have won.

The British during the war had praised themselves for being less efficient – because less ruthless – than their German enemies. J. B. Priestley, in those broadcasts in 1940 which had given him influence comparable to Churchill's, had jeered at the Nazis as 'robot men', just as Churchill himself, in his 'finest hour' speech, had associated them with 'perverted science'. Deep into the post-war period, 'carrying on' and 'muddling through', as the British were held to have done during

the Blitz, continued to seem morally superior to 'Continental' rationality. Outdated customs in industry and business were thus legitimated.

Nicholas Cull in a recent brilliant study, *Selling War*, has shown in
detail how American journalists in London conspired with British
propagandists in 1940 to create an image of embattled 'England' which
would wean their compatriots away from neutrality. 'The British and
Americans shared a common pool of ideas that summer, and the interpretations of each influenced the other in a spiral of cooperation . . .'
Observing the results, I drew up in my book *The Myth of the Blitz*
(1991) two columns of opposites:

England	Germany
Freedom	Tyranny
Improvisation	Calculation
Volunteer spirit	Drilling
Friendliness	Brutality
Tolerance	Persecution
Timeless landscape	Mechanisation
Patience	Aggression
Calm	Frenzy
'A thousand years of peace'	'The Thousand Year Reich' dedicated to war

This worked well at the time and must have helped to counteract
some of the negative tendencies in British life, notably widespread anti-
semitism, which surfaced in 1940 in a temporarily successful clamour
for the internment of refugee Jews as 'enemy aliens'. Yet the British had
acquired, not always without brutality, a very large empire, circum-
scribing where they did not obliterate it the 'freedom' of non-white
subjects. Their racialist contempt had erected 'colour bars' in Africa,
Asia and the Caribbean. It was the RAF, not the Luftwaffe, which had
planned pre-war the types of planes most suited to the long-distance
aerial bombardment of cities; this mode of attack was by no means
'improvised' in 1940 as a way of striking back at Germany. Though
much was done – as in other combatant countries – by voluntary effort,
Britain conscripted soldiers from the outset of this war and later
conscripted women into industrial production.

But the British internalized an Anglo-American view of themselves
at war, incorporating with the 'finest hour' notions of volunteer
improvisation and 'muddling through', which in effect stood in the way
of realistic representation, or hard questioning, of their wartime
activities for about three decades. Just before the concluding paragraph

which I quoted earlier, Henry Pelling notes 'the lack of original contributions in the arts' in 1939–45. There are explanations for this. A serious novelist ending on an upbeat a book set in the war was horribly liable to be contradicted by events; downbeat closure would be unpatriotic. The much-maligned soldier poets of the day suffered from comparison with Wilfred Owen and others who had fixed the experience of the 1914–18 trenches indelibly in memory. 'Rosenberg, I only repeat what you were saying', wrote the brilliant Keith Douglas, killed in 1944, in one of his poems from the north African desert. Sorley Maclean's verse from the same arena stands comparison with any of the century, but it was written in Scottish Gaelic and was almost unknown till the 1970s. In fact, the war years produced notable music, some of it propagandist, from Vaughan Williams, Walton and Britten, but this did not have to be specific about current realities. The painters conscripted as official war artists did, and produced images acceptable at the time which in at least two notable cases achieved permanent currency. The great sculptor Henry Moore turned draughtsman to portray the frightened people who took 'deep' shelter in London's underground railways system in 1940 as representative humans in calm repose, thus reinforcing the message sent to America that these shelterers were not cowardly but somehow heroic. Stanley Spencer depicted Clydeside shipyard workers as heroes also, figures in an epic cooperative endeavour.

It is not at all strange or discreditable that the less attractive features of life in Britain and in the armed forces were not given prominence during the war. What is odder, both symptomatic and causative in relation to national complacency, is the shortage of really impressive works of art handling such subjects in the decades since. The appalling experiences of Bomber Command (at least half of the men who flew died or were maimed) are suggested in one good novel by Len Deighton, but no one has produced memorable, serious fiction about the bloody, dismal fighting of Montgomery's soldiers in Normandy and beyond after D-Day. Poets who served in battledress have rarely returned to the subject. Film-makers have created nothing to compare with certain drastic movies and TV serials about 1914–18.

Since the heavy bombing which the British called 'Blitz' dominated 'life' for most people on the island in 1940–1, it might be supposed that there would be much vivid writing about it. Certainly, there was even at the time fine, honest factual writing, little of which remains in print. But if one notes that Robert Westall's *The Machine Gunners* (1977), a novel about juvenile delinquents in the Tyneside Blitz written for the children's market, is as powerful and memorable as any dealing with the bombing, one exposes the failure of major 'serious' novelists to confront that experience.

Elizabeth Bowen, whose *Heat of the Day* (1949) was a post-war best-seller, did so brilliantly, in a fiction involving her heroine's love for a pro-Nazi traitor. Two considerations about Bowen arise. First, she was Irish, though committed against Nazism, as was the poet who wrote best about the Blitz at the time, Louis MacNeice. Both had a certain detachment from the English folk around them in London. Second, Bowen continued something like a tradition, started by Grahame Greene in his Blitz novel *Ministry of Fear* (1943) and also evident in certain impressive wartime films, of exaggerating, in effect, the presence of active German and pro-German subversion in Britain.

Bowen and Greene, who supported the aim of 'People's War' and accepted, up to a point, that it had been realized, could only, it seems, work with the sentimental and almost bland version of the Blitz which was necessarily current by introducing the piquant zest of treachery. It is significant that the outstanding British fiction about the Second World War was produced by a snobbish Catholic reactionary, Evelyn Waugh. His *Sword of Honour* trilogy (1952–61) takes from outbreak of war to victory a Catholic hero, Guy Crouchbank, who volunteers on the verge of middle age in order to 'crusade' against Nazism and is appalled by the British alliance with Stalin, who seems to him to represent identical godless evil. Waugh despises the rhetoric of 'People's War' and satirizes it mercilessly. Unfair and even inhumane as some of his emphases may seem, his dissident position permits him to write with extraordinary candour about demoralization and bad behaviour in the British retreat from Crete in 1941. His books may be seen as the most powerful exception proving the rule that the mythology of victorious 'People's War' inhibited for decades realization of what war had in fact entailed and prevailed in a collective suppression of memory.

1995

Further Reading

Paul Addison, *The Road to 1945* (London: Jonathan Cape, 1975); Angus Calder, *The Myth of the Blitz* (London: Jonathan Cape, 1991); Nicholas Cull, *Selling War: The British Propaganda Campaign Against American 'Neutrality' in World War II* (New York: Oxford University Press, 1994); Tom Harrisson, *Living through the Blitz* (London: Collins, 1976); Alan Munson, *English Fiction of the Second World War* (London: Faber, 1989).

GIs: The American Occupation of Britain 1942–1945

Review of Juliet Gardiner, *Over Here: The GIs in Wartime Britain* (London: Collins, 1992); Judy Barrett Litoff and David C. Smith (eds), *Since You Went Away: World War II Letters from American Women on the Home Front* (London: Oxford University Press, 1992).

Second World War V-Mail was the immediate ancestor of microfilm. To save valuable transport space, in a situation where the US authorities knew that letters from home were vital to the morale of enlisted men, wives and mothers were asked to write on specially designed 8½ by 11 inch stationery. The results were photographed. Mail which would have weighed 2,575 pounds was in this way reduced to 45 pounds. The film was flown overseas, developed, and letters were handed to sendees in photographs half the original size.

In September 1943, *Yank*, a servicemen's magazine, carried as an illustration a V-Mail to Corporal Samuel Kramer. He had written in: 'Dear Yank: I desire to lay claim to having received the shortest V-Mail ever received.' It read: 'Mr Kramer: Go To Hell! With Love, Anne Gudis.' Naturally, this example of the dreaded 'Dear John' missive caused a furore. 'Approximately one hundred GIs, sailors, men in the Royal Marines, women in the United States, and others wrote to her. Some sought dates and others wanted a pen pal. Worse for Anne were those who chastened her for damaging morale, for possibly putting Samuel in danger, or for otherwise not living up to the "unwritten law" of how women should behave in wartime.'

Oh what a wordy war! What Sam had done to light Anne's always short fuse on this occasion is not made precisely clear in *Since You Went Away*. But it emerges from the extracts from this 'courtship by mail', which Litoff and Smith have edited with verve and skill, that Kramer probably hinted at, or admitted, infidelities, during his service in England. In spite of their long-distance tiffs, this pair married in 1945 and were still together in 1990. Whereas Audrey Davis who wrote to her brand-new husband in the navy as 'Precious One', 'Angel' and so on was divorced after only fourteen years. A vast amount of wartime mail, including, perhaps, some of hers, must have been devoted, under the 'unwritten law', to covering up what the girls the men had left behind were really doing and feeling.

Since You Went Away is a fine book, the result of devoted search in military and university archives and in private hands: the editors now have a personal collection of 25,000 letters written by about 400 American women. They have tried to present the diversity of classes and ethnic groups across America, and amongst their most moving examples are letters written to her 'Shigezo San', a Japanese farmer in California interned in 1942, by his wife Soroko, who was soon 'relocated' to Arizona with their three children. She is so very 'American': 'This coming Sunday is Father's Day and our thoughts will be with you especially.' Attempts to find letters from African-American women have been, in contrast, almost totally unsuccessful.

I do not think Litoff and Smith will think me captious if I point out that the effect of this book, carelessly read, could be to convince people that US life in 1942–5 was monopolized almost completely by 'family values' such as Dan Quayle evokes. For all the evident candour of many of the correspondents, the dominant theme has to be 'wish you were back safe'. And the instruments carrying this are, so to speak, the massed violins of white heterosexual monogamy. A more sensitive ear than mine will be needed to pick out of this book the strains of homosexuality, male or female, or discords of class and race.

'Gay' life is also absent – I find this surprising – from *Over Here*, an absorbing study by a former editor of *History Today*. Juliet Gardiner has researched exhaustively, using not only unpublished manuscripts but her own interviews with both GIs and Britons. The general reader will be entirely captivated with the result: as a historian who will almost certainly want, one day, to quote some of her very quotable quotes, I must pedantically regret that her way of summarizing her debts, without pinpoint, numbered references, will frustrate my own efforts towards secure accuracy.

Another quibble, maybe unfair: the copious illustrations (even the delightful Giles cartoons) all come in the cheerful or heroic varieties which could be issued at the time without disturbing always volatile relations between Britons and an 'occupying force' rising to over a million and a half in less than two and a half years between January 1942 and D-Day. Are there really no photographic records *at all* of aggravation and armed battles between white and black GIs, of the activities of the massed prostitutes known as 'Piccadilly Commandoes', of the detritus which the Yanks left in and around their camps when they went home? Did not the police, or the US authorities, take any such pictures?

Perhaps, though, the contrast between bland pictures and frequently disturbing text will make important points clear to any sensible reader. Officially what was going on was inspired cooperation between two mighty democratic powers united against a uniquely evil enemy. What actually emerged was a dubious interface between the proud subjects of an ascendant imperial power and native people unconscious for the most part of their own Empire's decline. One reason why the British tended to side with surprising vehemence with segregated black GIs against white troops who had Jim Crow attitudes was that African-Americans found the island's depleted wartime standards of living much more acceptable, after what they had known, than did their steak-reared ofay compatriots: blacks were grateful, and polite.

Gardiner's war is the obverse of Litoff and Smith's. In the situations which she so vividly evokes, the sexual fidelity of any GI seems almost like a weird aberration to be carefully explained, when women from twelve to fifty were so eager to trade virtue for PX luxuries and dancing with men in smart uniforms to high-class swing bands. In London, one GI observed, 'It usually took a Pole about ten seconds to tell a girl he wanted her. It took us a little longer.' Fidelity to something different – male peer group bonding – emerges from her account of the lives, commonly brief, of the very young men who flew Boeings for USAAF in daylight raids out of East Anglia. 'During the 1,008 days that the "mighty Eighth" was in action, it lost nearly 5,000 planes and sustained over 45,000 dead, wounded and missing . . .' An image which will linger with me is of the CO at Framlingham, on the day when 95th Bomb Group lost ten planes and 103 men, pacing up and down with tears in his eyes, repeating, 'What's happened to my boys? What's happened to my boys?'

So much for the typical British joke: 'Heard the one about the Yanks who went to a war film? One fainted and the other got a medal for carrying him out.' All competently produced Home Front books will, like these, produce a wonderful array of anecdotal and incidental information. ('Fried spam for Easter dinner *in the US.* Gosh!') But both these do more than titillate. They vividly evoke a period when the US, with all its internal divisions, was overall the confident standard-bearer of democratic values, exporting its wonderful new culture of moving pictures and swinging music along with troops ready to die bravely for the cause, as it seemed, of Jefferson and Lincoln. I do not know whether my own notion that even the films and the music are not so good now, fifty years on, types me as a silly old nostalgic. But I thrilled to the words written on VJ Day by a Massachusetts woman to her husband serving in China: 'I love my country and I'm not ashamed to admit it any more. Perhaps I am only thinking along the lines the nation's propagandists want me to think. But I know I am proud of the men of my generation.'

1992

Review of David Reynolds, *Rich Relations: The American Occupation of Britain 1942–1945* (London: Harper Collins, 1995).

Memory does not always deliver fact. Every historian using a tape recorder to tap the memories of veterans and witnesses knows this, or should know it. Near the end of his wonderful study of GIs in Britain during the last three and a half years of war, David Reynolds recounts two apposite stories.

'It took Leon Standifer forty years to remember that he had killed a German in hand-to-hand combat.' On patrol on the Siegfried Line in January 1945, he was surprised by an enemy and slit his throat. Afterwards, he convinced himself that this was nightmare, not memory. Only in 1986, at a divisional reunion, did his former platoon commander convince him that he had done it. When Shirley McGlade from Birmingham tracked down her father, a former GI, in California in 1987, he could not remember her mother, Lily, at all, though in 1945 theirs had been a close and loving relationship over six months during which he had become part of her family. He had been recuperating from an encounter with a landmine in France, and Reynolds sees both these cases of amnesia as 'a psychological legacy of combat trauma'. Others suppressed memory deliberately. One veteran of D-Day told Reynolds, 'I could see it was hurting my health to re-create these vivid terrible things.'

'Memory', suggests Reynolds, 'is about therapy as well as remembrance. Its function is as much to forget the past as to record it.' Historians must work with memory, and Reynolds uses written memoirs and oral testimony throughout his book. But the historian's function is to get behind memory.

The British have remembered the GIs as 'over-paid, over-sexed and over here'. We recall that they gave gum to little boys and nylons to their big sisters. As the *Daily Express* put it in 1979, the GIs 'came with saunter and swagger, with brashness and boisterousness . . . one joke heralded a new brand of knickers: "One Yank and they're off." ' Their condoms littered parks and alleyways after they had drunk the pubs dry.

Previous lively and useful books about the GIs have tended to confirm this stereotype. Only Graham Smith, in his powerful but limited study of black GIs and the British response to them – *When Jim Crow Met John Bull* (1987) – made much use of the archives on both sides of the Atlantic which lay virtually untouched before Reynolds, in 1981, began to dig into them. He sought out and used approaching thirty.

Thanks to these monumental labours, he can see clearly that 'the three million GIs passing through Britain each had an experience as distinctive as his own personality'. There were indeed brash, hard-drinking GIs who sneered at British penury and snobbery. There were also scholarly, peaceable Anglophile GIs. Men from New York would respond to urban Britain very differently from white 'trash' Southern farmboys. The experience of USAAF men stationed for months or years in East Anglia in huge bases outpopulating nearby towns was radically different from that of black GIs in small service units engaged in 'routine manual labour without much obvious relation to the war', or that of men who passed briskly through on their way to the European battlefield.

Geographical sense is one of Reynolds's many strengths. Though its population was one-third of that of the USA, the whole of the UK would have fitted into the state of Wyoming. Men from a big, new country, largely from ethnic groups imperfectly melted in the pot of US identity, confronted the people of a small old one long bonded in many ways but divided by class.

Their arrival and subsequent movements were dictated by diplomatic fencing between the British high-ups who wanted to keep control of the war they had started and American counterparts deeply suspicious of Britain's greedy imperialism. Not until well after D-Day, at the point where Eisenhower took over direct command of the Allied armies in Europe from Montgomery, was it allowed to become plain that only American might could beat Hitler. High-level politickings and mistakes account for why GIs were where they were when they were and Reynolds writes about them very acutely.

He has also established a clear and detailed view of the factors which made the GIs seem 'over-paid'. The truth was that America had been so severely depressed in the 1930s that many were better fed and clothed than they had dreamed possible. The British overall had fared less badly just before the war, but bombs, rationing and shortages had reduced their standard of living steeply. When GIs disembarked in Britain, the dimout in Manhattan where they had boarded 'bore no comparison to the Stygian darkness of Glasgow or Liverpool'.

Reynolds memorably, and rightly, describes the British Army as an 'underemployed underclass'. Tommies too were uprooted, subjected to the boring routines of army life, and tired of waiting to go into action. No wonder they were incensed that GIs got paid three times as much as they did. But political pressures on Roosevelt and the Pentagon to make sure that GIs were comfortable were acute and persistent. Isolationist sentiment still affected many voters, and the US economy was booming. While citizens might grumble that their boys were suffering in someone else's war, GIs might well feel that men and women in the factories were exploiting their own absence and privations as they earned high wages. 'Over-paid' is a relative term.

So, of course, is 'over-sexed'. Reynolds's very careful examination of illegitimacy rates before, during and after the war permits him to query whether 'immorality' in fact increased during the US 'occupation'. If it did not, this was despite the fact that British society had been so thoroughly disrupted that the boy from Kansas entering Birmingham (for instance) would encounter young women from Scotland, Ireland and the north, far from home and desperate for fun after long hours of boring factory work. For many 'landgirls' their new rural environment was perhaps more alien than it was to farmboy GIs. Notoriously, girls in their early and mid teens threw themselves at the occupying soldiery. Was this surprising when Dad was in the army, Mum was at work till late, and schooling had been shredded by evacuation and bombing?

'Over-here' – but not everywhere. It was the Poles who stole the girls in Scotland, which saw few GIs except in transit. The 'occupation' was very uneven, concentrated in three areas: in Northern Ireland; in East Anglia; and in a triangle based on the south-west coast from Hampshire to Cornwall, with its apex stretching towards the ports of disembarkation in the north-west. A recent sortie of my own into the Mass-Observation Archive (of which Reynolds himself makes very good use) suggests that the 'occupation' impinged surprisingly little on the lives of many of those who sent their diaries to M-O. If you lived in Sussex or Cumbria, for instance, you had little reason to think much about them. Where you could not miss them was in central London, the only place in Britain, Reynolds suggests, where a man with a pass out of camp could have a really good time on his 'Liberty Run'. Here the 'Piccadilly Commandos', blackout prostitutes, plied their trade, and here enlisted men bored by training, or suffering combat exhaustion, could exercise their spending power by 'swaggering' into expensive restaurants or going on colossal, highly conspicuous benders.

Rich Relations touches on so many fascinating topics that a reviewer can hardly convey its scope and its excellence. For instance, his sections on the rather different story of the Canadians leave one tantalized, wanting more. Reynolds marries the 'new' military history which studies armies in social and psychological terms, to political, diplomatic, economic and social history, and he articulates his astounding range of material with the fluency of a first-rate novelist.

Perhaps epic, though is a better comparison. Montgomery, whose optimism and rapport with his men outweighed his vanity and other limitations, emerges as a hero, but less fully one than Eisenhower, whose commitment to sustaining good US–British relations helps explain why this was perhaps the most successful military alliance in history, But the paramount hero of Reynolds's book is GI Joe himself, eventually tested and not found wanting in the battles in France to which Reynolds at last turns. I will not tell you how the story ends. I fancy the last page will move others, like myself, to tears.

1995

Mass-Observation's War

With the end of the Second World War, the British people were released from collective nightmare. The worst possible imaginings had been confirmed when the Nazi death camps were broached. The best result had followed, when Hitler had died like a hunted rat in the ruins of his chancellery. Many British women had dreamt about Hitler. Chaplin, jeering at him in *The Great Dictator*, had missed the point by making him ridiculous. He was potent and he was frightful. And Britain's war had been frightful, from those silly days in the autumn of 1939 when city children had been decanted into the hostile countryside and cars moving through the blackout without real lights had mown down pedestrians in droves, to the point, as late as the end of March 1945, when the shower of German flying bombs and V2 rockets finally ceased.

Cut to 8 May 1941. The air-raid sirens have just gone over Birmingham. Sid and Vera, fortyish, married with one child, are having a quarrel or, as she will put it in her diary, 'a heart to heart talk about the effect the war has been having on him'. Sid works in 'war industry' – in engineering, supplying munitions. Vera says she has been hoping that his new job 'would make it that we were happier together through the fact of him having more money and more freedom with his own work'. Sid says sharply, 'Well haven't I been more generous and spent money where necessary, haven't I tried to make a difference?' Vera concedes this but says, 'it's been overcrowded by your reactions to the war.' Sid retorts, 'I can't help how the war affects me, can I, the fools that are running it, we shall lose it if they go on in the same way they are doing.' Vera: 'Are you the only one to have feelings?' And so they bicker on. Though they are not to know this, Birmingham is not the main target tonight. The Nazis are going for Hull.

Vera and Sid are still together in August 1945, when news comes of the A-Bomb on Hiroshima. 'The minute it was announced, Sid said, "That's it, that's my dream." At the beginning of the war he had a nightmare . . . which he could never explain to me but which caused him to wake up in a wet sweat and he looked ghastly. The Atomic Bomb, that was the dream, and he said, "Now you can understand why I was afraid of this war. I was always waiting for this to come on us, I could never understand the bombing being no worse than it was – I was always waiting." ' The distant horror of Japan breaks Wizard Fear's spell on Sid, achieved how? By the screening pre-war of the H. G. Wells fantasy *Things to Come*? Through the gloomy prophecies of politicians and civil servants that Britons would die from bombing in millions? Or from a grown man's apprehension of extreme evil loose in the world, inducing reactions like a child's to the tales of Grimm?

'Vera' and 'Sid' are not their real names. Vera's diary was sent in instalments to Mass-Observation. This was social survey founded in 1937 by Tom Harrisson, who could loosely be described as an 'anthropologist', and a poet, Charles Madge. They had recruited hundreds of voluntary 'observers' on the understanding that M-O could quote their writings as it liked, without revealing their identities. Vera and Sid are probably dead, but researchers using the M-O Archive at the University of Sussex still have to respect her confidentiality, and that of the roughly five hundred other people who for greater or lesser periods kept M-O diaries during the war. Like those of most of the rest, the later life story of Vera is unknown.

There are many kinds of material, stored in many places, where the historian can feel in strangely intimate touch with the war years. Fragile newspapers at the Colindale annexe of the British Library give you the bombast of leader writers on provincial weeklies and the daily flow of information about petty crime against wartime regulations. The Imperial War Museum holds posters, other memorabilia – and, indeed, diaries. But the latter were retained by their owners to the stage where hindsight was possible. Disillusionment with Churchill in 1942 might have been expunged. References to Uncle Fred's dealings in the black market might have been reconsidered and dropped. Once Vera and the other Mass-Observers had posted their monthly batch of entries, they could not touch them again.

Since the diaries are stored by month, not writer, it is physically difficult to follow a particular contributor through from start to finish. One tends to encounter them in the middle of things. Who is this troublesome relative? Where in the whole wide war is this diarist's son serving? Who is Fred and who is Margie? Opening a box is like dropping into a succession of draft short stories by Chekhov, except that characters create themselves in one's mind as much by handwriting as by what they say. Some type pretty well. Some write almost illegibly in pen. The generous middle-aged Irishwoman living in Monmouthshire who was one of the hard-core faithfuls uses pencil and is very hard to read.

In compensation for effort of reading, there is the utter immediacy of the text. Since the past of these diarists is obscure and their future unknown, there is the effect of agelessness. They do not grow old as we that know more grow old, to adapt Binyon. Some, like the lovers on Keats's Grecian urn, are 'forever panting and forever young'. Take 'Muriel Green', for instance, as the M-O archivist Dorothy Sheridan rechristened her when she published portions of her diaries in an anthology, *Wartime Women*. At the start of the war she had been eighteen and with her elder sister Jenny, also a Mass-Observer, had been helping their mother run a garage and sweet shop in a small Norfolk village and noting wrily the bad relations which developed between local people and evacuees from London. In 1945 both sisters were employed at a hostel for war factory workers in Somerset, where Muriel helped in the hostel shop. Her boyfriend lived far away in Devon. Here she goes . . .

February 13. Went to the Sports Club dance . . . My usual dancing partner whom we will call O took me and B's (her sister's) usual partner these days who we will call M took her. M was originally my partner, but then O came along and we double-crossed one another and B has pinched M and O has gradually taken charge of me. I have spent a lot of time talking and flirting with O lately. Of course we have been friendly since last July when he came to the hostel and we were thrown together in the amateur theatricals. It has been nothing but acquaintance growing into platonic friendship up until about the New Year. Lately it has verged on more than platonic friendship, but I don't want it to become more, because of my boy-friend D and also because O is a married man of over 40. I have known for several months that O has been very much attracted by me and he has shown in many ways that he is gradually falling in love with me. I am not sure what to do about it as now I am getting fonder of him every time I go out with him. Life is very complicated!

February 15. My day off and O took me to town to the pictures, tea, and back to the hostel for dinner to go on to a factory dance. It's no good pretending any longer, O is very much in love with me and I am (temporarily) in love with him. And that's that! The old old story of hostel life and married men. Most of the girls here get tarred with the same brush in the end . . . not necessarily going further than just running round and flirting with them, but the hostel gossips always think the worst!

Oh, Miss Green, what became of you and your D and your O? Dorothy Sheridan tried in vain to contact you. Did you emigrate, as so many did after the war, to the expanding African colonies? Have I seen you yellowed and wizened marshalling your black boy through a shopping expedition in Harare? Or did you do well in Britain, retire to Argyll? Did I pass you in tweeds on the promenade of say, Tarbert? But at least I know what you did on VE Day, and how you reacted to news of Japan's capitulation, before you vanished into the silence which preserves you, so to speak, in eternal youth.

What became of Leopold and Molly Bloom? One could imagine a Joycean polyphony constructed out of the M-O diaries which would have an effect not far from 'stream of consciousness' fiction. Different diarists react so differently to the same war news. Some write about little except the war news. On the other hand, a young housewife in Wales paid attention, pen in hand, to nothing but the weather and her small child . . .

Without foresight or hindsight the diaries present to us the British people at war as dominated by itch and twitch, urge and apprehension, pining and craving. Their 1945 is not the year which historians have written about, in which the British were delighted by triumphs on every battle front and confidently rewarded themselves by voting out Churchill, deemed to be a great war leader no good for peace, in favour of a Labour Government which would give them a Welfare State.

Shortages of so many things – eggs and cigarettes, razor blades and coal, nice clothes and tasty food – were particularly unendurable at the start of 1945. Miss Cope, a local government clerk in Bury St Edmunds, complained:

> With life as short as it is, I chafe at the interminable housework required to keep body alive. In the year of our Lord 1945 one should at least be able to pour milk from a bottle and heat it in two minutes, switch on a fire and draw hot water for bottles. Instead I make a coal fire and light an oil stove and stir and stir powdered milk in a jug of water, adding a bit of butter in lieu of cream. The rain comes down the chimney, the smoke goes up and comes down again in gusts. I add coal and coal and coal as the fire burns rapidly notwithstanding. Then I get powdered egg and mix it with golden syrup and Bournvita . . . The milk now looks hot enough to pour in with the rest.

To cap all privations the war news had been ominous. On 16 December General von Runstedt had launched a counter-offensive against the advancing Allies, in the Ardennes. The 'Bulge' which he created was not finally squeezed back till mid-January. Thereafter, news was almost solely of victorious advance, or of heavy Allied bombing raids on Germany. But the Russians were advancing faster – 'Keep it up, Joe,' a teenage clothing manufacturer's assistant adjured Stalin in his diary for 26 January – 'Hope you get to Berlin first.' The particularly ferocious winter weather dominated civilians' lives. Thoughtful Miss Elmwood worked in an office in Glasgow. '25th January was "the coldest day yet" – I have heard that phrase over and over again. Today people are trying to decide whether the 26th is worse, better or the same. At 11.30 a.m. (time of typing) the fog is coming down . . . wonder in my mind whether it is the "coldest day in my whole life" (an almost unanimous opinion) or whether the rations have lowered our resistance.' A Lincolnshire parson, Manley, worried about what the weather was doing to church collections. 'So few people realize that the cost of running a parish is the same whether they are at Church or not, and if they miss a Sunday through bad weather or any other cause, they never think of putting in double the next time.'

But, in his part of the world, people were spared the 'doodlebugs' – pilotless planes – and the V2 rockets which continued to cause devastation and death in the south-east. Carter, a south London diarist in his eighties, was obsessed with them:

February 1. A quiet night, but a rocket came down just as I got out of my bath this morning. One never can tell where these things are going to fall, neither can one learn where they have fallen in London when they come close.

February 2. A rocket came down while I was at breakfast this morning and made a great noise which rumbled like thunder for some time and spoilt my appetite . . .

February 3. 11.15 a.m. A rocket which shook the windows came down some-where to the north. 11.27 a.m. Another rocket, nearer this time, to the north.

He consoled himself with the thought that a 'front seat in Hell' would be comfortable compared to living in Berlin. He did not know that the one which came down 'not very far away' and shook him in his bunk on 27 March would be the last, but his entry continues as if he were the voice of Father Time marking *finis*: 'I dug up a fairly large piece of the rocket casing on the plot today. This is like steel but as light as aluminium, but it is crumpled up like a piece of paper now.'

The latest news was exhilarating. Montgomery's troops had at last crossed the Rhine. Mrs Squire, a 'county' lady in Oxfordshire, had been thrilled by a description on the radio of 'air born troops being dropped in great numbers . . . Winston is at the Front, a lovely account of how he went on a short *cruise* down the Rhine. How he would enjoy it all, but I hope on the whole he did not take too active a part, but just sat smoking his cigar and making the "V sign".' On 27 March the BBC newsreader began his bulletin in a 'terribly funereal voice' and Mrs Squire was dismayed – 'I thought, goodness, Winston has been killed.'

But it was Lloyd George who had died, the victorious prime minister in the 1914–18 war, and Mrs Squire, not shocked, could write, 'The news is simply marvellous. The whole German line seems to be breaking.' Others were not quite so ecstatic. Mrs Birch, in her late twenties, was a Cambridge graduate working on aircraft development. Her war had gone wrong. Early in 1941 she had married her doctor fiancé and become a happy housewife. But her Jack had been called up and was now in India, and she was morosely marooned alone in Hampshire. On 28 March, as she recorded, 'M. came into the office reading his paper and saying, "it looks pretty good doesn't it?" I asked him if he still thought that it would be December before the war was over in Europe. He said, "Yes. Don't you?" I replied that I would stick to my original date of September.'

People were inured to disappointment – advance in the West since D-Day had been so slow, the conquest of Italy was taking so long, the war with Japan showed no sign of ending (though that was rarely in the minds of those who did not have dear ones serving in the Far East). In 1943, the might of the Red Army, pushing the Germans back on the Russian front, had fuelled the naive pro-Soviet feeling which brought scores of thousands of young people into the Communist Party and inspired sermons from WEA lecturers on the obvious superiority of the Planned Socialist Economy. But Miss Cope, though generally left-wing, was developing doubts. At the end of March she read an article on Russia by the Labour MP John Parker which confirmed her fears about Stalin. 'Big pay and big rations for the ruling classes and a sort of legalised black market to allow the ruling classes to receive all they desire. Just as in England.' The death of President Roosevelt in mid-April was a grave check on optimism about the post-war world. Miss Lake, a retired nurse living in Sussex, lamented, 'The best are taken while evil men live on to work still more evil. Undoubtedly the war work killed him. In 1940 I wrote to Mrs Churchill that Mr Churchill must take care of his health.' Mrs Grant, a shorter-winded diarist, a middle-aged housewife in Gateshead, wrote: 'Roosevelt's death – We are all profoundly shocked. We do feel we've lost a personal friend . . . All peoples have lost a champion.'

Meanwhile, obsession with shortages, especially of food, continued. Parson Manley rejoiced on 16 April: 'I have at last found a use for funerals. I had to go back to my old parish to take a funeral and came back with a lb of rice, 1lb of tea, 18 eggs, 1lb of butter and a sack of potatoes being sent to me by rail.' Less self-centredly he reported meeting, at the village church, two young men on leave. As so often in early 1945, apprehension not hope is to the fore.

> I had prepared both of them for confirmation, one is now a squadron leader in the RAF, and the other is a Major in the army. Before the war they were both farm hands. What will they do now the war is over? When I asked them, they said they hadn't an idea, but they were not going back to the farm . . . Will they end up being disgruntled men all their lives?

The Americans had overrun Buchenwald. Then the British found Belsen, and on 19 April Richard Dimbleby broadcast an unforgettable report of its horrors to BBC listeners. Mrs Grant of Gateshead, though very left-wing, was also fiercely anti-semitic. Her disgust, however, provoked an equal and opposite anti-German racism: 'The men and women SS ought to be systematically shot.' Miss Lake's anger exploded in another direction. Many of the camp victims, she noted, were Germans.

> And Chamberlain said in that broadcast before he handed over Czecho-slovakia to that devil Hitler, 'I realise vividly how Herr Hitler wishes to champion other Germans . . .' Chamberlain's ashes are buried in Westminster Abbey. Much as I love the Abbey I would willingly have heard it had been bombed to destruction to obliterate that stain on it.

Though it has been said that people in rural areas who could not see the horrific newsreels screened in towns remained sceptical about 'atrocity stories', Parson Manley in Lincolnshire reported the opposite. 'One hears nothing else talked about. The German prisoners coming from work in the fields have got guards again, which is a wise protection as things are.'

As victory in Europe approached, the diaries remind one of a factor bearing on civilian morale throughout the war. Desperately bored though many young women had been in the jobs assigned to them in 'war industry', working long hours at repetitive tasks, little as many young men had liked life in or indeed out of the army, the young were young and could make excitement on the dance floor and love in the fields and alleys. Conscription to forces or industry took them far from home and peacetime inhibitions. Miss Cope, back in January, had commented with wry tolerance about how the young went to it.

> It sounds like my fellow lodger Regina's Ronnie downstairs. Fortunately, he's quieter than most of them. I'd never have dreamed, at their age, of entertaining 3 or 4 fellows, perhaps the worse for drink, as these girls (Joyce and Regina) do. I wonder how the Police find proof that anywhere is a brothel? If people watched the men coming and going here I should think they might easily imagine Joyce and I carried one on.

If people who were young in the war years are nostalgic about them, this is the universal phenomenon of nostalgia for lost youth. For the elderly, frightened of blackout, of bombs, of rowdy young servicemen, and of children loosed from parental restraint into deliquency, and for middle-aged people worried about offspring in the forces or in the disrupted schools and despairing over the destruction of normal home life, the war was never fun. Mrs Flowers, a teacher in Sussex, aged about forty, with a child at home, reported numbly on 2 May: 'Hitler died yesterday. And I don't think we are very excited. We are too much satiated with news.' Mrs Connolly, fiftyish, asked several people how they would spend V-Day. A local government official in his twenties said he would probably go on a pub crawl 'and get plastered if the beer holds out'. A forty-year-old man said, 'If the weather is good I will put in a day in the garden.'

The months ahead after victory held for older diarists, as they perfectly well knew, further struggle against shortages. By 23 May, Miss Elmwood would be reporting

> much talk of further cuts in food. Recently they have been selling nice ice cream in Glasgow and offices send out for large supplies of wafers. There have been more cakes and better cakes, and biscuits have been comparatively plentiful. Apparently there are to be declines all round. Even sausages are to be fewer.

Mrs Birch, attending a packed-out concert at the Albert Hall on 10 June, would observe, 'What a dowdy crowd of people it looked. An occasional scarlet coat showed up, but otherwise everyone looked drab.' The general election which followed Labour's break from

Churchill's coalition would cause deep dismay, as the great man rounded on his loyal Labour colleagues and accused them of totalitarian ambitions, violating the wartime ethos of national unity which he himself had done more than anyone to build. Labour's victory would delight many, of course, but would fill others with gloomy apprehension. Old Mr Carter, a Tory, retreated into nostalgia: 'August 4. I enjoyed listening to Sir Harry Lauder on the wireless. I remember hearing him in London in 1894, more than 50 years ago, but all I can remember now is the crooked walking stick he brought on the stage.'

For the young, however, this could be a time of pristine joy. They had survived a war in which hundreds of thousands of their generation had been killed or maimed. They were free to take such pleasures as might still be found – like milling in the centre of London on VE Day, climbing lamp-posts and splashing in fountains, singing, cheering the King and Churchill, and getting guiltlessly drunk. (Mrs Flowers could hardly be so abandoned; on that day the doctor told her that her boy had mumps.) Muriel Green should have the last words. On 7 May, when everyone expected the announcement of victory, her hostel was celebrating its third anniversary with a cricket match, men versus women. (The men had to play left-handed and bowl underarm.) Double Summer Time, a controversial innovation, meant that the match could still be in progress when chimes of Big Ben counted in the radio news at 9 p.m. A general cheer went up when it was announced that VE Day would be tomorrow. The match was resumed and tied at nineteen runs each side. Then more serious fun ensued – dancing to records.

> About 11.15 p.m. an American sailor who was being entertained by some of the Irish girls forced his way up to the platform where the mike was. He, as well as the girls, was obviously the worse for drink. He said he would do an impersonation of Bing Crosby (rousing cheers) and sang 'Irish Lullaby'. The girls who were sitting below the stage asked him to sing 'If You Ever Go To Ireland', which he then followed up with another Irish song at their request. The last was unknown to the English people present who were by this time not so enthusiastic in their applause. In the corner where we were sitting undertones were saying 'The Irish hadn't won the bloody war' and 'It's time we had an English song'. A drunk boy beside us said, 'What English song can we sing?' and E said, There'll Always Be An England'. In the next interlude the drunk boy led off . . . and in no time everyone in the room was singing it.

Muriel, still at the hostel, found the news on 10 August of Japan's offer to surrender 'simply a knockout'. On 15 August, proclaimed 'VJ Day', she exulted

At last, at long last! The day we have waited for nearly six long years has come round. A new era has dawned in which it is up to the survivors and the young people to let it not happen again. A new people's parliament has opened and the world is ready for better things.

Oh 'Muriel', if you are still alive somewhere – you would only be in your early seventies – how do you respond to the world which the young and the survivors made? Apart from the fun, does your generation's war seem worth it, now, after all?

1995

New Zealand Women at War

Review of Lauris Edmond (ed.), *Women in Wartime: New Zealand Women Tell Their Story* (Wellington: Government Printing Office, 1986).

'The early war was very much a British war, a BBC war; David Niven and "A nightingale singing in Berkeley Square".' Thus, a woman who was a Wellington schoolgirl in 1939. Though this witness goes on to emphasize that the arrival of US troops in New Zealand (from June 1942) provided a very different perspective, making 'the war real for us in a way that the black and white films of the day, and the patriotic messages had not', a leitmotif of Lauris Edmond's anthology of anonymous short memoirs is the total identification with Britain felt by many (was it most?) New Zealanders.

Another then schoolgirl, from Papatoetoe, recalls 'the feeling aroused by a soloist singing "Land of Hope and Glory" at a patriotic concert'. A third (Hawera) remembers filing into the assembly hall to the strains of music over the loudspeaker system, 'always a patriotic marching song, "Sussex by the Sea", "There'll Always Be An England".' Later, she helped run the local Boy Scout Club den. 'I had a group of boys between nine and eleven – they spent a lot of time talking about the air raids over London, their attitude one of excitement and glamour.' This was a milieu in which some fifth-form schoolboys asked the teacher for a lesson on Rupert Brooke's *The Soldier*, an overlocking machinist had her work cut out supplying a 'never ending line' of orders for Union Jacks, and a young soldier heading for Egypt with New Zealand's 'First Echelon' wrote in his girl-friend's autograph book 'England expects that every man this day will do his duty'.

As New Zealanders remember it, food rationing was introduced because 'Britain needed all the food we could send'. A merchant seaman's wife, then living in Wellington recalls (and I find this almost incredible) that 'fruit always seemed in short supply. I became so used to going without fruit that even years after the war . . . I seldom bought it until I had re-educated myself to its luxury taste.' Ample statistics prove that New Zealanders sacrificed themselves for the Empire to the very limit of their capacity – the highest proportion of war casualties of any Commonwealth country, the highest productivity of agricultural labour per head of any combatant nation. Yet Edmond's witnesses combine to produce the image of a quiet provincial society, faithfully, wistfully mimicking the heroic metropolis as far as it could. An umbilical cord joined two corners of planet Earth. When a secretary took over the additional duties of office mail clerk after the young men joined the forces, she found that

> Mail work increased. A large portion of our correspondence was with the UK, and because enemy action might stop the mails from getting through, we always had to do three mailing copies of each letter. These I sent off at six-weekly intervals. The British firms did the same thing when they wrote to us.

Barely a note of Kiwi nationalism sounds in this book. One learns from the useful chronology at the end, not from the main body of text, that 'God Defend New Zealand' was made the national hymn in May 1940.

BBC News ensured that New Zealanders knew promptly what they had to do to keep in step with the Motherland. The New Zealand 'Home Guard' was created three months after its British model and dutifully conformed to the 'Dad's Army' image. 'My husband was . . . given a gun that was used in the Maori Wars, and he had one bullet!' 'We used to watch in great amusement whenever they marched down the main road on their way to take up their position near the Pencarrow Lighthouse.' In mid-1940, so dangerous for Britain, Lord Haw Haw broadcast the 'true story' from Germany to New Zealanders as well. After Pearl Harbour there was real cause to fear Japanese invasion. 'The Northland coast was considered a threatened zone, and all the Home Guard was called up. Overnight, the women, many quite inexperienced, had to manage the farm . . . Frequently, the talk was what to do if the Japanese came.' A woman in Hawera's Home Guard Intelligence Corps recalls being summoned to stand by one night, for hours; later, she learnt that a Japanese submarine had been sighted off the coast. A serviceman's wife living in Plimmerton relates: 'We were issued with instructions to keep a little case packed with necessities, and at a given signal were to head for the hills. I had visions (and still do at times) of myself, a baby on one arm, clutching a three-year old with my free hand, forcing my very pregnant form through the bush and up into the hills. I don't know who was going to carry the case of necessities.'

Just as in Britain, the demonic Squander Bug featured in anti-waste propaganda. Just as in Britain, black and grey markets developed. A South Island woman who kept bees became 'very popular', adding 'I remember being approached by one of the bank managers to see if I would sell him a four-gallon tin of honey.' Sadly, Italy's entry into the war provoked the same reaction in Eastbourne, near Wellington, as it did in British towns large and small. 'One young man, not long out from Italy, had a barber's shop in the village, and one night a group of local men smashed it to pieces.' But (clearly to the chagrin of some) New Zealand could not replicate the psychological and social tensions caused by evacuation and bombing in Britain. A young mother read of 'the courage of Londoners in the Blitz' and developed a 'sneaking fear' that in like circumstances she might 'go to pieces and be useless'. One morning a huge explosion woke her. Believing that an air raid was in progress, she calmly roused and dressed the children and packed a basket with food for twenty-four hours before proceeding, as arranged, to a neighbour's basement shelter. It later transpired that a bomber had crashed taking off from a nearby base. But she was proud of herself. 'I had not panicked. I had done the right things. I had passed my test of fire.'

At home, then, there was war in the mind only, while oceans away New Zealand servicemen, and servicewomen, experienced real horrors and triumphs. The great tests for young mothers were, in fact, loneliness, 'coping' and, still more, holding family life together afterwards, when a strange man had returned after years abroad to meet strange children of whom he was jealous and who were jealous of him, over Mummy. 'Both men and women had changed', muses one witness. 'We women were not now so submissive.' But their warriors, 'and New Zealand as a whole', wanted a return 'to the kitchen and to maternity'. Another displays her acceptance of the prescribed role. 'Having made all the decisions in the bringing up of the children while the men were away, it was not easy for us to adjust to father's firm hand – which actually was badly needed, and finally gratefully accepted.' A third, a teacher who confesses to being something of a 'feminist', sets Father in a different light, with a surprising yet entirely plausible allegation which may have some application to British post-war experience also. Standards of honesty among children, she says, dropped after the men returned. 'After experiencing four or five years in situations where property was not private (belonging either to the government or to the enemy) and souveniring common, the men brought their attitudes home with them. They returned as heroes to their children, and the loss of honesty was quickly communicated.'

Edmond, as she explains in her Foreword, resisted the idea of selectively emphasizing feminist viewpoints. She wanted to represent women as they were at the time, 'on the other side of the modern upsurge in women's social realignment', when 'women not only endured with few complaints such injustices as getting lower pay for doing a man's job while he was away, and then losing it when he returned', but 'actually felt honoured by their inclusion in the national drama'. She admires their unconscious 'generosity of spirit'. She was a young woman herself during the Second World War. In 1984, she suggested to the Government Printing Office a project of collecting memoirs by women of both world wars. Advertisements trawled in this rich catch. Edmond took what was freely offered and did not solicit material on specific aspects (though thirteen interviews are included, and here there are some traces of 'leading' questions). So the project was not exhaustive, nor even particularly systematic. However, as Edmond claims, the range of response is wide enough to provide a sense of the whole society – at least, for 1939–45. The few First World War memories scattered throughout the book provide only a sketchy basis for comparison. They evoke a markedly rawer society, dominated by distance, with little motor transport and no radio, and point up how much livelier conditions became over the succeeding quarter-century.

Even on rereading, I have not detected the key to the book's arrangement in three sections, but Edmond is a distinguished poet, and she has contrived a sequence of utterances which keeps one turning the pages avidly. The result is substantial, captivating and moving.

She suggests that her chosen narratives form 'a collection of short stories in which all the tales are true'. Some do indeed have haunting literary quality. As historical evidence – this goes for all such material – they have the virtue of vivid suggestiveness, and the limitation that memory selects, distorts and is sometimes plain wrong. One former alumnus of Wellington East Girls' College implies that soon after war started in 1939 the headmistress delighted pupils by saying that, because of shortage of woollen goods, they could wear white socks instead of long black stockings. But a contemporary at the same school recalls carrying on 'the time honoured practice of disguising the holes in our stockings by using our fountain pens to colour the flesh underneath them with blue-black ink'. The two accounts may be somehow compatible – I have no way of checking this. However, I am quite certain that the Luftwaffe's 'Baedaker' raid on Bath, England, apparently remembered by a New Zealander who was then a social worker in Bristol, occurred in 1942, not 1943, and was a reprisal for British bombing of Lubeck, not of Dresden.

But Edmond, who herself points in her Foreword to other contradictions and errors, was wise to eschew pedantic corrections and annotations. Memories are historical 'facts' in their own right. What this book gives us is the significance of wartime experience as registered by women in late-middle and old age. Edmond urges, justly enough that 'we no longer believe – if historians ever did – that the truth of human activity is to be found in a single "accurate" chronicle.' A 'truth' which seems to emerge through these pages is that the experiences of New Zealand women at war were extremely diverse, yet contained common factors explicable by geography, by history, and most of all by gender.

Almost all, because they are women, had their expectations in life disrupted more sharply than men (who are socialized to be warriors) by the exceptionally complete mobilization of a country with a population of only 1,600,000. Change was registered more swiftly and starkly than in large and lavishly differentiated British society. (A statistical jump from one to ten, put it this way, is much more dramatic than three jumps from one thousand to ten thousand.) A witness who can remember 1914–18, when women took over men's farm work and handled baggage and mail off the steamers as porters, was nevertheless impressed by her sex's efforts in the Second World War. 'The women sprang into action to support their men. Who could forget the girls on the overcrowded trams, coping with overhead lines, keeping the friendly drunks in order, and battling through the mass to collect the fares before the next stop!' She herself acquired the office job of a young man gone to the wars – at half his pay. But as a middle-aged divorcee she was grateful for the new direction her life took. 'The war gave me opportunities that I could not have obtained as a married woman.'

Younger women chalked up many 'firsts'. One group could claim to be 'the only girls in the world driving 10-wheeler trucks for the US Navy'. The Women's Herd Testers Reserve completely replaced men, and even achieved equal pay. The very first woman government herd tester to be appointed in the Antipodes, recalling her jolting tours round the countryside in a horse-drawn buggy, still writes with warm delight about the kindnesses she received from farming people. Less spectacularly, but for the individuals concerned no less momentously, banks which would never before have employed women now engaged them, and the Auckland daily newspapers 'were forced to take on females. Opening journalism to women was a big thing that the war did

for us.' In the Land Army city girls learnt how to ride horses, killed and
sheared sheep. One recruit observes that 'The health of some girls was
affected and some had to live under poor conditions, but that was not
my experience. Being a land girl completely changed my life.'

That remark, of course, points to diversity. Depending on age,
temperament, background, luck, the experience of bringing up children
single-handed, or that of being 'manpowered' into unexpected work,
might be felt as positive or negative. The same went for other aspects of
the war. When US troops arrived in force, they dominated some areas
completely (though an Invercargill woman 'never saw an American
serviceman during the war' and doubts 'if any came south of Christchurch', and a Maori mother of eighteen encountered Yanks only on a
rare holiday in Auckland). A sailor's wife recalls with disgust the
physical and moral squalor they brought to Wellington, where

> they urinated in shop doorways, anywhere; they fornicated in shop door-
> ways, alleys, and lanes. When daylight came, Willis Street and Manners
> Street, probably because they were dingy and dark, looked like the streets of
> a slum. There were condoms thrown everywhere, soiled knickers, puddles of
> urine and stranded faeces, fag ends and paper rubbish, and pieces of food.
> Wellington's rat population doubled.

Chacun à son goût. The clever girls of Victoria College in the same
city delighted in the Yankee invasion – 'Chesterfields and Camels we
had by the carton' – and gave an 'exultant "view halloo" when "the
curse" – except it was mostly seen as a blessing – made its monthly
appearance.' But a young woman whose father was Liaison Officer
between New Zealand and American forces in Whangarei nobly
resisted American charm. 'I longed to find someone to love, and there
was not one New Zealand soldier among the thousands that I met that
fitted the bill.' She turned down an offer of marriage from an American
doctor and eventually wedded a demobbed New Zealand lieutenant.

For one serviceman's wife in Dunedin the war entailed constant
fearful suspense – 'We lived for the sound of the postie's whistle.' Yet a
Christchurch woman who actually lost her husband and trained as a
beauty therapist to support their two children found this a 'marvellous
job'. She adds 'Despite everything, we were in great heart during those
war years.' After news came that her fiancé was killed, a Gisborne
woman stood in the hall of her parents' home and screamed, 'and a
part of me is screaming still and always will be'. Serving in the WAAC
in Italy, she barely fought off three Arab auxiliaries who tried to rape

her, and saw appalling death and devastation. Then she lost a second, British, fiancé. She considers herself a 'war casualty'. Yet she enjoyed her spots of leave in Venice, in England, as 'sheer magic'. Another witness writes of the war years as 'exhilarating' – though she had a painful time as a war bride in the USA, where she encountered fierce anti-'Limey' prejudice, before she brought her American sailor husband back to New Zealand. A Belmont child had found life 'incredibly dull' before war broke out. But now 'it began to be exciting'. Grown-ups who hardly exchanged a word before 'were always talking together these days whenever they saw each other . . . They even waved their arms about in great circles or patted each other affectionately, even though they weren't special friends.'

British testimony of similar kinds displays the same contradictions. But an intelligible pattern emerges, common to both countries. The war did not decisively 'liberate' women, or even make many of them 'liberation' minded. After strains and deprivations, the general reflex when peace returned was to try to re-establish pre-war habits, including that of masculine domination. But this did not mean that women's encounter with 'history' had had no positive effect. Many had discovered new capacities or had experienced, however bitterly, an independence. Much 'war effort' suited traditional roles – by the end of 1941, Edmond's chronology tells us, New Zealand women had knitted 98,000 mittens, 95,000 scarves, 94,000 balaclavas, and so on. But the first ten women police had begun training. In 1944 the Presbyterian Church voted to support admittance of women as elders. In 1946, the first two women would be appointed to the legislative council. From our vantage point we may assume, and I think rightly, that long-term trends in Western society were bound to promote, however patchily and inadequately, chances of greater independence and status for women. But during the war, women were conscious of something remarkable happening in their own lives. The trend was dramatized unforgettably.

The last, deeply thoughtful, contribution to this book (is it by Lauris Edmond herself?) makes the crucial but usually forgotten point that 'War was the process by which the abnormal became the normal.' Men brought up to shun murder were now praised for killing. Women nurtured in housewifely skills were 'manpowered' into heavy jobs, responsible jobs, exciting jobs. Our witness continues: 'I think it is true to say there was hardly a moment when I didn't feel mentally involved with the process of being at war, and still constantly aware of trying to reconcile the ordinary with the extraordinary.' Her husband remained at home, her doings were those of an 'ordinary' housewife. But 'total war', that novel phenomenon of our century, permeated lives, like hers, in New Zealand many thousands of miles from Europe's bombed cities, many hundreds from the Allied–Japanese front. Dominating consciousness then, it still overweens in the stories which people tell themselves and others about their own lives, helping to focus, as blurred peacetime continuities cannot, a sense of what it has meant to be lover, mother, member of society, woman. Edmond's storytellers are not betraying the liberationists of younger generations. They offer a usable version of past experience on their own terms, the terms of the people who laboured and laughed and suffered. They rarely solicit pity, and deserve much better than condescension. They were 'England's still, colonial', but feeling and thinking their way into a Pacific, as well as a pacific, future. It must be in great part a credit to their values, as passed on to or shared with society, that the Government Printing Office of their nation should publish a book so subversive of masculine heroic concepts. It could not happen, alas, in Thatcher's Britain.

1988

The People's Peace

'This was their finest hour' . . . 'Everyone was in it together.' Popular memory, as directed by the media, seems to enshrine the Second World War as a time of wonderful social solidarity uniting the people of Britain as never before or since. It was a 'good war', fought for a just cause and it was 'the People's War' in which ordinary folk shrugged aside the qualms of cowardly toffs and the mistakes of obtuse bureaucrats and 'went to it' themselves, defying Hitler and at last defeating him.

This myth does have much basis in fact. People did help their neighbours through the Blitz. The vast conscript army did bring men from all classes and regions together in shared privations and terrors. Workers in 'war industry' performed great feats: over 100,000 aircraft by June 1944, 700 major war vessels, and so on. During the war, public opinion overwhelmingly approved of rationing, as the fair way to share scarce necessities, and of the government-commissioned Beveridge Report on Social Security, published in 1942, which promised a financial safety net to everyone in Britain 'from the cradle to the grave'.

A pacifist brooded in his diary just after VE Day

> While the war was on there seemed somehow to be an urgency – an importance – about everything one did, and a feeling of comradeship and working together. Even I, a conscientious objector, have felt that. There was a real aim in just carrying on daily life and getting some enjoyment and satisfaction out of it and in helping others to do the same.

Now he felt 'depressed' that the old peacetime selfishness was returning.

But historians realize that two conflicting stories may both be equally true. Widely shared feelings of warm solidarity coexisted with furious resentments and tensions. While some rural householders, shocked by the undernourished and verminous state of evacuees from the cities dumped on them, cried out for social reform., many others did everything they could to avoid taking such creatures in. In every blitzed area, after heavy raids, there were stories told against local notabilities who sped out of town in big cars when, or before, the sirens went. Some men from state schools got army commissions, but not enough to break down the intimate connection between high rank and fee-paying education. Dr Jeremy Crang of Edinburgh University observes in his study of the wartime army that even in the 1960s public schoolboys still formed an absolute majority of all new officers. Despite wartime restrictions on provisions and goods, 'the fundamental rights of officers to a separate mess, to be valeted by batmen, to a more comfortable accommodation when it could be secured, and to a better general standard of day-to-day living than the men, remained unchallenged'. There was much talk of the war bringing 'social revolution', but that was not how young Anthony Bailey saw things when he returned late in 1944 to suburban Hampshire, aged nearly twelve, after four years as an evacuee boarding with a family in Dayton, Ohio.

His memoir of his adolescent years, *England First and Last* (1985), is a wonderfully evocative little masterpiece. After the USA, 'Everything was smaller. It wasn't the suddenly reduced "standard of living" so much as it was that everything was closer, denser, more tangible. Like Gulliver in Lilliput I found it hard not to bump into things.' No more hamburgers – toad in the hole. No more angel food cake – spotted dick. Dried eggs from a tin, mixed with water, formed a 'lumpy yellow splodge that gradually hardened into a sort of pancake'.

The fierce winter of 1944–5 – said to be the coldest for fifty years – was followed by another bad one in 1945–6 and catastrophe in 1946–7 when snow followed by floods paralysed large areas. People huddled round scarce lumps of coal in their living-room grates and went shivering to bed with stone or rubber hot-water bottles. Chilblains were epidemic, hot baths sheer luxury. Meanwhile, food got scarcer. Even powdered eggs disappeared for a while in 1946. In August 1947 the prime minister, Attlee, announced a crisis austerity plan for the British economy, food rations were cut again and the basic petrol ration was abolished, to stamp out 'pleasure motoring'.

The moral atmosphere generated by such hardships is accurately, though farcically, represented in the film *A Private Function*, scripted by Alan Bennett (1984), in which leading citizens of a small town scheme to fatten and eat a black-market pig. The grasping snobbery of the chiropodist's wife portrayed by Maggie Smith is instantly recognizable

by those of us who remember the 1940s and early 1950s. As the British
struggled fretfully with their disappointing peace, young Bailey
certainly not aware of an egalitarian 'social revolution'. He note
when the NHS arrived in 1948, many doctors 'seemed to vent
grievance at "nationalized medicine"' by maintaining 'scarc
furnished, barely lit, and generally ill-heated waiting rooms. If nothin
was wrong with you when you joined the other patients sitting there,
shivering and sneezing, the chance was good that there would be by the
time you left.' In his free grade school in Ohio, there had been 'no one
who represented the extremes of wealth and poverty'. For Bailey
'coming back to Britain' was 'coming back to class' – the reverse of the
experience even now, of the UKanian going to America who suddenly
finds that social markers like accent and clothing are unheeded and
experiences a sensation of classlessness, almost like flying free of gravity.
('Where are you from, bud?' a man in working overalls asked me once in
a bar in Connecticut. 'Britain', I replied in my RP accent. 'Oh, yeah,' he
said, 'New Britain. That's what, fifteen miles up the road?')

The Butler Education Act of 1944, establishing 'secondary education
for all', had not mitigated class distinction – on the contrary. 'In the late
1940s', Bailey noticed, 'there seemed to be an even greater distinction
between those students who went to grammar schools and those who
went to the ill-named "secondary moderns" than there was between
expensively educated public school students and those at grammar
schools.' In Scotland, a similar effect was produced by the division
between five-year 'senior secondary' schools and 'junior secondaries'
which provided inferior three-year courses for what one inter-war head
of the Scottish Education Department had called 'the majority of
distinctly limited intelligence'. In 1951, 87 per cent of the occupied
population of Scotland had left school at fifteen or younger. As T. C.
Smout has put it, 'The system had defined the overwhelming majority
of the population as stupid, and reaped the miserable consequences.'

The 1940s did little to break down class divisions and much to
reinforce them. Full employment and some 'levelling up' of income
related to increased trade union power brought novel prosperity and
security to the working class. But its members, mostly, stayed where
they were, or where their dads had been. With the great exception of
domestic service – where numbers dropped from 1.3 million in 1931 to
under 350,000 in 1951 – patterns of employment reverted to pre-war
normality. The proportion of women at work post war – just over one
third – was barely higher than in the 1930s, though many who would
formerly have been housemaids were now clerks. There were nearly as

many miners in 1948 as in 1938, almost as many textile workers, rather more construction workers, slightly fewer clothing workers: but employment in the dynamic, innovating industries which had produced planes, guns, tanks and ammunition to beat the Nazis – metal, engineering, chemicals – swiftly returned to levels only slightly above pre-war. Working-class life resumed its old patterns, enhanced by the fact that more people could now afford to spend a bit more money on favourite leisure pursuits – pub, cinema and dance hall. Attendance at football matches and other sporting events soared. So did betting.

And so did voting Labour. The party – which now, in 1995, crows over a recent leap to 300,000 – had over 600,900 members in 1947, over a million in 1952. In the general elections of 1950 and 1951, it was backed by nearly two-thirds of working-class voters. 'Labour', as an American historian, James E. Cronin, has remarked, 'was an avowedly class party . . .' So, 'its coming to power brought an escalation of class antipathies.' The Conservatives, in those elections, took an almost identical share of the middle-class vote. The Liberal Party was squeezed almost to extinction. In Scotland, the trend to class polarization overrode the brief 'home rule' afflatus marked by the SNP's first parliamentary election victory at Motherwell in 1945 and two million signatures in support of John MacCormick's 'National Covenant' of 1949 which called for self-government within a federal system. Notoriously, in the 1955 general election, the Conservative and Unionist Party actually gained an absolute majority of the Scottish vote.

Class, in fact, dominated the 'people's peace'. A limited Labour–Tory consensus, dubbed 'Butskellite' after R. A. Butler and his Labour front-bench opponent Hugh Gaitskell, supported the Welfare State as an arena of armed truce. It is significant that young Anthony Bailey used the NHS although his father was a bank employee and he had been evacuated to the USA under a scheme for the salvation of the children of 'professional' people. Free health care, family allowances, free selective secondary schooling and free university education greatly eased middle-class budgeting. The working classes, so long as full employment endured, were pacified with bread – which came off ration in the summer of 1948 – and, still more after TV asserted its universal spell, with circuses. In industry, opposed classes fought along battle-lines established in Queen Victoria's day.

In his jeremiad *The Audit of War* (1986), the right-wing historian Correlli Barnett raged over the way the war, because it was won, had confirmed the complacent British in their faith in outmoded industrial practices, while American mass-production and German efficiency portended the eclipse of the island's economic greatness. Two particularly sad stories relate to Britain's genuine and remarkable pre-eminence in science.

One of the brightest British ideas was radar, the secret device which helped beat the Luftwaffe in the 1940 Battle of Britain. When the story was made public just after the war, a *Times* headline exulted GERMANS BAFFLED BY BRITISH DEVICES – TRIUMPH FOR SCIENCE. But British industry had simply not been able to cope with what the scientists had given it. Underproduction of components had brought crisis in 1942–3. 'This newest technology,' Barnett remarks, 'had suffered from a galloping attack of the classic British industrial disease – fragmentation of resources and effort, overlaps in product design, batch production virtually by hand, utter want of standard-isation of parts and components.' Britain had 'failed to match either Germany's achievement in radio and radar of precision manufacture to the highest scientific standards (owing partly to superlative and abundant German technical education) or the American creation of a huge new mass-production capacity . . .'

The story of penicillin is better remembered. In retrospect, the greatest event of the 1940s was the arrival of new wonder drugs trans-forming humankind's relationship with time and nature. If a great epidemic had hit the West in the 1930s, doctors would have been as impotent as their predecessors faced with the Black Death in the fourteenth century. Scurvy could be beaten by vitamin C, syphilis treated with Paul Ehrlich's salvarsan, developed in 1908. Otherwise, there were treatments but no cures. The introduction in the war years of first the sulphanilamides, then penicillin, suddenly made many killer diseases curable.

Penicillin, discovered accidentally by Fleming in 1929, had been isolated for large-scale production by Florey, at Oxford, in 1940. It dealt not only with syphilis (a huge brake on the efficiency of armies), but with wound infections and gas gangrene, with boils and diphtheria, tetanus and impetigo. By D-Day, 1944, supplies were available for all the Allied forces. But large-scale manufacture had been possible only in the USA . . .

Barnett, emphasizing the gulf between British scientific brilliance, British military triumph and pathetic weaknesses in the British economy, argues that 'Britain's post war decline began in wartime British dreams, illusions and realities'. But this seems to be contra-dicted by his own conviction that deleterious attitudes long preceded the war. At the top of the British social pyramid were entrenched men educated at public schools and Oxbridge in the classics or history, uncomprehending of science and technology, contemptuous of 'brash' Americans and 'humourless' Germans. They were committed to counter-competitive ideals of 'fair play' and wedded to the dream of a non-industrial 'England', evoked by the music of Elgar and Vaughan Williams, where bells tolled the Anglican faithful to evensong and the crack of willow on leather was heard on village greens – or to the safe Scotland of Buchan and Barrie, stocked with faithful gillies, shrewd caddies, wise shopkeepers and skilled workers who might be a bit abrasive but supported Rangers and were truly the salt of the earth.

The origins of the 'British disease' must in fact be traced back to the moment of triumph in 1815 when Revolutionary France lay prostrate before Britain, which enjoyed universal hegemony. Britain's invincible navy enforced a virtual monopoly of overseas colonies. The 'Workshop of the World' likewise monopolized advanced technology. Britannia ruled, and her children had reason to feel complacent. As the Empire waxed territorially mightier and mightier yet their descendants failed to adjust to the rise of powerful competitors. The belief that Britain was really the greatest power on earth was evoked by Churchill in his 1940 speeches and helped to raise and sustain morale. Wise men had recognized in the last century that improved technical education and industrial reorganization were needed if Britain was to remain a world power. But the belief that Britain produced the best ships, bicycles, typewriters, radios, whatever, muddling on in its traditional ways, could not be shifted.

Could a really dynamic Labour government, with that landslide majority of 1945, have seized the opportunity to restructure British attitudes? Hardly. The first priority was to produce goods for export to a war-stricken world where competition at first was not fierce. The year 1945 was a deeply conservative juncture. People wanted above all to 'get back to normal', but without the blight of mass unemployment which had disfigured the inter-war period. Contrary to what is easily supposed, the mood of Britain during the 1945 election campaign was not vibrant and heady but subdued and rather morose. People were uneasy about changing government before Japan was defeated. There was general, deep consternation when Churchill in a radio speech, very stupidly, attacked Labour leaders who had served him loyally through five years of coalition, accusing them of wanting to set up a 'Gestapo' police state. If Labour spokesmen, in contrast, were persuasive, it was because they sounded constructive, sensible and safe.

The greatest issue of the election was not nationalization or even 'welfare'. It was housing. Two out of every seven houses had been affected by enemy action. In some places – Clydebank, Bermondsey – the proportion was over 90 per cent. Nearly a quarter of a million homes had been wholly destroyed. In the pre-war year 1938–9, 332,360 new houses had been built, but between 1941 and 1945 only 30,723 were erected. The post-war movement of working-class city dwellers from battered slum areas to boring suburbs or nasty tower blocks, so often the subject of nostalgic regret, reflected initially the dire need for new accommodation. 'Planners' in this area have often been blamed unfairly.

But the sanctification of the 'planner' was one result of Britain's war experience which certainly had long-term, and often injurious, effects. The Welfare State put in place by Attlee's government was undoubtedly rather more generous to the poor than Churchill's version would have been. But key changes – the Butler Education Act, the introduction of family allowances – had occurred under Churchill during the war. Though the language of Beveridge – a Liberal – in the introduction to his famous 1942 report had been 'revolutionary', the rationalization of social security had been a favourite project of bureaucratically minded persons of all parties and none. And some form of National Health Service was likewise an inevitability long before the war ended.

In one sense, Labour's electoral triumph in 1945 was indeed a 'victory for socialism'. As Profesor Joad, the philosopher of the war-time radio *Brains Trust* would say, 'It depends what you mean by "socialism".' Though Ernest Bevin, his enemy Nye Bevan, and other powerful ministers in Attlee's team were thoroughly working class in origin, and Herbert Morrison represented well the petty-bourgeois strain prominent in Labour's contribution to local government, men with Oxbridge degrees – Dalton, Wilson and Gaitskell, Crossman and Jenkins – were dominant in Labour's ideological stramashes. Often such men were 'Fabians', members of a society founded by high-minded middle-class intellectuals and professionals in the late Victorian era, and closely allied, by background and temperament, to the Whitehall bureaucracy. Their 'socialism' involved securing for, not by, the 'workers by hand and by brain' (to quote Clause 4) the full fruits of their labours. It was bureaucratic and paternalist, though also com-passionate and deeply idealistic. What triumphed in 1945, and had its twee *Götterdämmerung* in the inane 'Festival of Britain' which celebrated the island's character and achievements in 1951, was a Lib–Lab–wet Con centrist consensus which had matured between the wars and had come to dominate the organization of the Home Front and plans for peace. Its perfect expression was the magazine *Picture Post*, owned by a rich Liberal, largely written by socialists, and virtuously optimistic about planning.

Planners were impressed by Roosevelt's New Deal and some of them remained starry-eyed remarkably long about the 'achievements' of Stalin's Russia which had withstood and rolled back the full might of Germany. Their pitch was made easy for them by the great worldwide boom which surged from the 1940s through to the 1970s during what Eric Hobsbawm in his recent *Age of Extremes* calls, without irony, the 'Golden Years'. Though the British economy grew more slowly than that of any other industrial country, it still broke its own previous records. The loss of formal Empire in the East and Africa did not prevent profitable imperialist exploitation of less advanced countries. The persistence of class divisions in Britain did not discredit Harold Macmillan's Conservative election slogan of 1959, 'YOU'VE NEVER HAD IT SO GOOD'. British workers knew that life was indeed better. However politicians and planners bungled, there were more good things, and plenty of good new things.

In 1931, less than a third of British homes had had electricity. By 1938, the proportion had doubled. In 1948, despite the ravages of war, 86 per cent had electricity. In 1939, three out of ten households had had vacuum cleaners, but less than 5 per cent had had clothes washers and only 2.6 per cent had had fridges – this at a moment when half the homes in Depression-stricken America had had such appliances. By 1959, home life was transformed for the masses as such goods, which had been rarities, became taken-for-granted necessities, along with the increasingly ubiquitous TV set, pre-war only the plaything of a few well-heeled Londoners, but now driving down attendances at cinemas and sports arenas.

The novels, plays and films produced by the so-called 'Angry Young Men' of the 1950s demonstrate the frustrations attendant on living in a country where class still poisoned social relationships and choked aspiration and talent, yet the workers en masse showed no signs whatever of wanting to transform society. Albert Finney's performance as the deep-drinking, womanizing skilled worker in Karel Reisz's film based on Alan Sillitoe's *Saturday Night and Sunday Morning* epitomizes what, for the left, had gone wrong. From the same moment, we have the image of the Aldermaston marcher, ostentatiously classless in her or his jeans, sporting long hair and a scruffy sweater, plucking a guitar and singing folk-song or skiffle. And it is there, I suggest, in the late 1950s, not at the point of victory and Labour landslide in 1945, that British life begins to break its nineteenth-century moulds.

The first do-it-yourself music of youth was New Orleans jazz. Though its impact in Britain was first felt around the end of the war, it did not come with the black GIs as one might casually suppose. It was a response by local buffs to a white-led authenticist revival in the States. The black men who had created the New Orleans style had not been conservatoire-trained and a fair number of untrained young Britons now applied themselves to a music which was fresh and sassy but technically not too demanding. While 'trad' has boomed and bust several times since the 1940s, its 1950s offshoot, skiffle, has never shown signs of revival. But arguably it was more significant. That is where the Beatles started. People with minimal musical experience could cheer up their own generation with guitar, washboard and chirpy songs. Do-it-yourself skiffle converged with rock 'n' roll, surging in from the US by the mid-1950s, in the ideology and customs of a new youth culture which seemed, and up to a point was, 'classless'. Across the vertical dividing line between posh and prole cut the horizontal separating with-it youth from square oldies. That the youth market was open to exploitation by big business in a big way explains the mystique of the Swinging Sixties.

The values of the 1960s generation reversed those which had won the war. Peace not war, yes, but also me rather than us, doing your own thing rather than discipline. Thatcherite rejection of society in favour of the individual was paradoxically prefigured by left-wingers who sanctified Bob Dylan. They paraded their 'Up Yours' across a Britain which by 1970 wore a very different aspect from its post-war drabness. London and Glasgow had been slashed to pieces by roads created to cope with the insatiable demand for private cars. In other cities, also, development had destroyed many more landmarks and cosy corners than the Luftwaffe. The cloth-cap uniform of the working class was giving way to the hard hat as real ale (much of it truly disgusting) had yielded before keg and lager and mousetrap cheddar, sole cheese of the 1940s, had retreated before Brie and Gruyère. The norms of working-class Britain, variously preserved, like flies in amber, by *Coronation Street, Sunday Post* and *Beano*, were crumbling with the Cooperative Wholesale movement. Yet the power of trade unions, still led by men whose confidence had been braced by the full employment of the war years in which Ernie Bevin had had their bosses over a barrel, was still sufficient to bring the Heath government down in 1974.

The general election of 1983 presented a spectral apotheosis of the class politics of the 1940s. In the blue corner, Thatcher (whose 'refained' and strident accent hit me like a dentist's drill without anaesthetic, remembering as I did so many Tory ladies like her who had blighted my suburban childhood with their invincible prejudices). She had grown up in the 1930s, when mass unemployment had kept wages down and the poor, who were by definition feckless, had got in her view, exactly what they deserved. Even petty-bourgeois types like her adored father had been able to afford servants, and a bright girl like Margaret could wing her way via Oxford to marriage to an older man rich enough to support her political career. Those horrid Labour people had beaten her idol Churchill out of office in 1945 and imposed the pall of paternalist bureaucracy on the laissez-faire instincts which created wealth (at least for people like her Denis). In the red corner, Michael Foot, public school, Oxbridge, of distinguished Liberal parentage, and Tony Benn, ditto and aristocratic into the bargain, but both of them residuary legatees of the Lib–Lab consensus behind planning which had built a sort of New Jerusalem after 1945 and leaders of a movement still dominated by trade unions which had been deprived by a modest increase in educational opportunity, and consequent upward mobility by bright proles, of the services of such rough-diamond brilliance as Ernie Bevin had displayed.

The British people trusted neither Thatcher nor Foot. Division on the left kept Thatcher in office with a declining share of the vote. Survey after survey revealed that the British people remained attached to the values of the Welfare State and to the idea that public services should be publicly owned, though they remained unimpressed by nationalization and socialist planning. The aspirations – to fairness, full employment, prosperity – which had given the Lib–Lab planners their chance in 1945, remained entrenched. Looking back, the ludicrous British electoral system, which awarded Labour its colossal majority in 1945 with less than half the vote, and Thatcher hers with much less than half, is a key to understanding the islanders' twitch and distress as Britain slumped further and further down the league of industrial powers. The first-past-the-post system, coupled with the class-based polarization of British politics in the 1940s, ensured that the raw resentments inflamed by war and post-war conditions continued to pre-empt rational debate and to stifle democratic expression of opinion. That has been the most pernicious legacy of 1945.

1995

Terence Rattigan's Deep Blue Sea

Terence Rattigan's play *The Deep Blue Sea* opened in the Duchess Theatre in London's West End on 6 March 1952. It starred Peggy Ashcroft, convinced critics and public alike, and tallied over 500 performances. Its success confirmed Rattigan's status as the leading British dramatist of his day. Though it had many amusing moments, its theme was timelessly serious: love in its form of obsessive lust, conveyed through characters so trapped in English reticence that 'the physical side' is their strongest expression for it.

In a mediocre rented flat in the genteel but shabby Ladbroke Grove area of west London, the play opens with Hester Collyer lying on the floor near her unlit gas fire. Her lover Freddie Page is away playing golf at Sunningdale. He failed to return last night for her birthday dinner *à deux*. (She is in her middle thirties – Freddy is a few years younger.) Hester swallowed a dozen aspirins and turned on the gas, but omitted to put more money in the meter. The gas ran out and her attempt at suicide has failed. Landlady and neighbours come to her rescue. A neighbour phones her estranged husband, a lawyer whom she left ten months ago, since elevated to the bench of judges.

Mr Miller, a neighbour, gives her medical attention. He is a refugee doctor, presumably Jewish, from central Europe, temporarily detained in 1940, like so many of his kind, as an 'enemy alien' on the Isle of Man, and subsequently struck off the medical register. The original West End audience of the play would mostly have thought that this had been for conducting 'back street' illegal abortions, but we may be sure that Rattigan imagined some homosexual indiscretion. The good-natured Mrs Elton, who has known, and now divulges, Miller's secret, remarks to Hester 'what he did wasn't – well – the sort of thing people forgive very easily. Ordinary normal people, I mean.' Her own charitable view is that 'It takes all sorts to make a world.'

Hester, a clergyman's daughter, childless but not by choice, far from physically alluring, met Freddie, we learn, at Sunningdale while her husband was playing golf. He was an ex-Battle of Britain pilot, DFC, DSO, at a loss in the post-war world. She had not thought he was 'particularly good looking' and was slightly irritated by 'that RAF slang . . . such an anachronism now . . . as dated as gadzooks or odds my life . . .' But he expressed his admiration of her and she fell passionately in love with him. She fusses over his dress and 'mothers' him but it is clear that she is driven by overpowering physical lust, inexpressible in her sterile marriage. She took the initiative in leaving her husband, who refused a divorce. They went together to Canada where Freddie had a job as a test pilot. After too many drinks, he crashed a plane. They returned to the sordor (by Justice Collyer's standards) of Ladbroke Grove. Now he is drinking heavily and she is in despair, an amateur artist seeking to raise cash by selling her paintings.

Rattigan's stagecraft was always admired even by people who did not like his plays. Over three acts he manages to manoeuvre his eight characters in and out of Hester's flat, in various permutations, with easy 'naturalness'. Her husband the judge, anxious to get her back, appears three times. Miller and Mrs Elton drop in. The young couple upstairs, Philip and Ann Welch, Home Office civil servants, are drawn in out of their depth. Freddie returns unexpectedly early – golf rained off – with an appointment to lunch with a man called Lopez whom he met at Sunningdale. Hester does not mention her suicide attempt, and has asked her neighbours not to tell Freddie about it, but he finds the note she had written for him. (Her carelessness with this hints that she may, at least subconsciously, want him to find it.) What happens to Freddie thereafter we cannot be sure of, since his first reaction is to get drunk, and all his statements in the second and third acts are suspect. He either lunches or does not lunch with Lopez, who does or does not offer him a job as a test pilot in Brazil which he makes an occasion for leaving Hester. He certainly rings up an old Fighter Command friend, Jackie Jackson, to whom, in the flat, fortified by whisky, he reads Hester's note. He then goes off bingeing and encounters the Welches. Judge Collyer implores Hester to return to him. She refuses. Late at night Freddie sends Philip round to collect his toiletries. The funniest scene in the play has this pompous young man, rather drunk, confessing to Hester that he too has had an extramarital love affair, an 'infatuation', but decided that 'the physical side' was 'really awfully unimportant'. Freddie is to fly off soon (he himself says) to Brazil. Hester rearranges herself for suicide. Miller spots what she is up to and persuades her that she must go on living – 'To live without hope can mean to live without despair.' Freddie unexpectedly returns. It seems clear that a word or hug from her would bring him back to her. Instead, she coolly ushers him out and lights her gas fire. She has decided, we infer, to live, and to live alone – perhaps, since Miller has encouraged her to esteem her own artistic talent, she will go to art school and 'start from the beginning again'. In 1952 serious critics thought that this relatively positive ending betrayed the play's essential tragedy. But a second, successful, suicide attempt would surely have been as crude as the pistol shot which Chekhov (an important model for Rattigan) decided must *not* conclude *The Cherry Orchard.*

'We're death to each other, you and I,' Freddie tells Hester after Jackie has left. Intellectually not her equal, he cannot reciprocate her intense physical need for him. He is good-naturedly abashed by his own incapacity to match her passion. Like Phaedra, Theseus's queen, she is the victim of '*Venus toute entière à sa proie attachée.*' The basis of *The Deep Blue Sea* is 'timeless', classical. Like Racine's tragedies it maintains 'unities' of time and place – everything happens on one set within one day – while focusing on doomed, lethal passion. But its original audience would have had no trouble placing Freddie as a contemporary 'type' – the Battle of Britain hero. Nor, perhaps, do we. The Spitfire pilots of 1940 acquired mythic status at once. They flew planes with beautiful clean lines against a brutal foe, denied the Luftwaffe command of Britain's skies, convinced Hitler that invasion was impossible, and so administered the first check to the Nazi war machine which had rolled over Poland and France as if invincible. As Churchill put it at the time, 'Never in the field of human conflict was so much owed by so many to so few.' For some good reasons, the myth of 1940 is still strong in British culture, so Freddie has not 'dated'.

This cannot be said of the Bomber Command men featured in Rattigan's wartime West End hit, *Flare Path,* written while he himself was serving very efficiently in RAF Coastal Command, and in *The Way to the Stars,* a notable documentary film which he scripted towards the end of the war after his transfer to propaganda duties. The tragedy of the bomber crewman after the war was that nobody wanted to hear about what he had done, battering German cities and slaughtering children. The tragedy of some of the fighter men was that they remained matchless heroes, Galahads of the air, trapped in their own special slang like flies in amber. It is difficult for rock stars and actors to live with stardom achieved by their early twenties. How much harder for a man whose stardom had been achieved by killing young Germans while watching his mates dying, and who then, if he wished to continue flying in peacetime, found the clinical discipline of the test pilot to be about as far from dogfights over Sussex as a desk job would have been. One reason for doubting Freddie's story about accepting an offer from Lopez is that he confesses to having hated test flying. It was not a job you could drink on. In August and September 1940 you got drunk every night with comrades who had survived, getting over the deaths of those who had not come back that day.

The fighter pilot, contrary to myth, was not a lone knight questing out a chivalrous or dragonish foe for man-to-man contest. Successful fighter tactics depended on teamwork. Military historians agree with all thoughtful ex-servicemen that the most important reason why people go on fighting in such desperate conditions as Freddie would have known in 1940 – back to battle again and again, your airfield bombed, kids with less and less flying experience sent in to replace your dead mates – is male bonding. You fight for your mates. Freddie's deepest relationship post-war has to be with his old comrade Jackie Jackson. (Rattigan's original audience would at once have thought of Britain's most successful fighter 'ace', 'Johnnie' Johnson, credited with forty-one 'kills'.) Hester perceives clearly what has maimed Freddie emotionally. She tells her husband, 'his life stopped in nineteen-forty. He loved nineteen-forty.' Though we must assume that Freddie, collecting his decorations, went on flying Spitfires after that year, presumably until the end of the war, Hester's simplification implies that heroic combat in the Battle of Britain rendered him incapable of relating successfully to anyone but a live buddy who also knew the dead ones, or of settling down in any life less hecticly exciting, less fraught with adrenalin, fear, grief and drink.

Rattigan knew at first hand that of which he wrote. In 1940, aged twenty-nine (so he was not subject to compulsory call-up), dissatisfied with the reception of his latest work, a comedown after his tremendous success with *French Without Tears* before the war, he took the advice of a psychotherapist who told him to join the RAF. He did well in training. He was posted to Coastal Command, which performed routine duties over the Atlantic and North Sea, normally not very dangerous. But he chose one of the most perilous jobs, rear gunner. Late in 1941, he was flying to Sierra Leone in a Sunderland which was shot up by a Heinkel, and, after one of its four engines cut out, was forced to jettison all inessentials and land in Gambia. Rattigan had rescued the first act of a new play from his suitcase just before that went overboard. The Air Ministry approved of his writing, had previously given him leave to work on film scripts, and was pleased by the success of *Flare Path*, produced in the West End in August 1942 after Rattigan's return from

Sierra Leone with the rank of flight lieutenant. A run of 679 performances rewarded Rattigan's reciprocated enthusiasm for the RAF.
Winston Churchill saw it, and told the cast that he was 'very moved' by
this 'masterpiece of understatement'.

Flare Path takes place between 6 p.m. on Saturday and Sunday
afternoon in the residents' lounge of a hotel in Lincolnshire near an
RAF base. An English-born actor named Peter Kyle, now a US citizen,
is back in Britain to arrange a new film. He arrives at the hotel to
pursue his erstwhile actress lover Patricia, now married to a Bomber
Command flight lieutenant. The old flame blazes up again, but just as
Patricia is about to tell her husband Teddy that she is leaving him, he is
ordered to bomb Germany that night. He returns safely, but breaks
down in her arms, shattered by a night in which his tailplane was shot
away. She decides that she cannot leave him, and Kyle slinks away
defeated . . . Enriched by representative types – a working-class air
gunner, a Polish count flying with the squadron who is married to a
good-hearted English bar girl, and gets back after landing in the North
Sea, while being written off for dead, the play ends optimistically with
a party.

This was strong patriotic stuff, such as could well have been commissioned by the Ministry of Information as propaganda if Rattigan
had not obliged by producing it spontaneously. He was duly transferred, in March 1943, to the RAF Film Unit. *The Way to the Stars*,
directed by his long-term friend Anthony 'Puffin' Asquith was made
while Rattigan was living in such luxury as the times afforded in rooms
in London's Albany, where J. B. Priestley, rival playwright and fellow
propagandist, also kept up a flat on the proceeds of his West End
successes.

In the 1930s, as a young aspirant playwright, Rattigan had joined in
demonstrations in support of the Spanish Republic. Now his lifestyle
kept him apart from the mostly leftish intellectuals of his own and the
succeeding generation. He golfed at Sunningdale, gambled and drank
heavily, ran a Rolls Royce and was generous to his homosexual lovers,
though he never let one of them actually live in with him. The most
important of these lovers for Rattigan was a young actor called
Kenneth Morgan. They had met before the war, which had pushed
them apart, but in the late 1940s they were 'together' again when
Morgan suddenly announced that he was going to stay in downmarket
Camden Town with an actor of dubious character and uncertain
prospects. This did not work out and after just six weeks, on 28
February 1949, Morgan gassed himself. Rattigan was devastated. It is

beyond doubt that this event inspired him to write *The Deep Blue Sea,*
where Hester leaves a rich husband for a somewhat shady lover who
deserts her, and Justice Collyer's position – deprived of a favourite
possession, helpless, guilty – is like Rattigan's own.

It has long been suggested that the 'real' ur-play was about a
homosexual triangle, and that Rattigan was too cowardly to put it
forward. Years later, after homosexuality between consenting adults
had been legalized at last, Rattigan remarked in a letter to John
Osborne, 'Perhaps I should rewrite *The Deep Blue Sea* as it was really
meant to be . . .' (Geoffrey Wansell, *Terence Rattigan,* Fourth Estate,
1995, p. 218). But metropolitan theatre in Britain, as in Louis XIV's
France and Tsarist Russia, had always been produced under censorship.
Rattigan, dedicated to his craft from his youth, had prospered in it
despite the constraints which prevented him from dealing directly with
the emotional predicament of a promiscuous homosexual such as himself. Beside which, the compulsion to repress the truth was a painful
part of that predicament. Insofar as *The Deep Blue Sea* is concerned
with Hester's anguished discovery that she had repressed her own
sexuality in marriage to Collyer, and her feeling that the lust which
drew her to Freddie is a shameful weakness, Rattigan's play powerfully
refracts aspects of his homosexual existence in the tragi-comic milieux
of Anglo-Saxon prudery.

Important colleagues in the theatre – his sometimes waspish friend
and rival, Noel Coward, his promoter 'Binkie' Beaumont, various
famous actors – were homosexual, and close heterosexual collaborators such as 'Puffin' Asquith knew about Rattigan's tastes and
accepted them. One of his lovers in the 1940s was a rich Conservative
MP. Yet such truths were so successfuly repressed that naive young
actors working on Rattigan's plays sometimes had no inkling that he
was homosexual, a fact which he successfully concealed from his own
parents. *The Deep Blue Sea* is not a 'coded' play about homosexual
attraction. It is a play about English reticence and hypocrisy about sex
'in general'. There is more of Rattigan in Hester than in Collyer. If
there is anything of him in Freddie, it derives from first-hand understanding of Freddie's compulsive drinking and gambling. Otherwise
Freddie is a 'type' observed in close-up during Rattigan's RAF years.

The 'type' had been established, like other elements in the myth of
1940, well before the outbreak of the Second World War. It had
originated in the earliest days of the Royal Flying Corps on the Western
Front in 1914–18. Silly nicknames, euphemism, understatement, devil-
may-care flamboyance overriding deaths of close friends in action,

careless flings with young female 'popsies' and above all constant heavy drinking, became part of the style of the brash young service which had popped up alongside the antiquated army and august Royal Navy.

Film audiences in 1938 had seen the mores attributed two years later to the young men in Spitfires displayed in a remarkably effective movie, *Dawn Patrol,* directed by Edmund Goulding for Warner Brothers. Errol Flynn and David Niven – close drinking and wenching companions in 'real life' – gave superbly moving and convincing performances as hard-drinking RFC buddies flying above the trenches in First World War France, free with the slang which irritates Rattigan's Hester, redeemed by courage and stoical will to win. It was to Rattigan's short-term advantage in 1952 that he did not have to 'explain' Freddie to his audiences. They would have readily imagined where he might have flown after 1940 – in France following D-Day, for instance. They did not need Rattigan's Oscar-nominated script for the film *The Sound Barrier,* another of his successes of 1952, to tell them that testing planes to the point where they might fly supersonically was not at all like dogfighting with Adolf Galland – this was part of the brave new peacetime Britain competing in advanced technology with its overweening ally the USA.

Nor, heading to see the show in the West End, would they have needed reminding that Freddie and his like had fought off a murderous enemy. There were still gapsites all over London where bombs had destroyed buildings. This included Ladbroke Grove. Rattigan's stage directions are precise and elaborate. His first describes Hester as living on the first floor of 'a large and gloomy Victorian mansion, converted to flats after World War One', with 'an air of dinginess, even of squalor, heightened by the fact that it has, like its immediate badly-blitzed neighbourhood, so obviously "come down in the world" '.

Rattigan's first audience would have sensed how themes of waste and self-repression related to the ruins and drabness of post-war Britain. Mrs Elton has learnt that Hester is not really 'Mrs Page' through seeing her ration book. Hester's frustration and Freddie's alienation echoed, however remotely, in many lives. Sensitive members of the audience might have wondered if death by gas had special significance for the Jew Miller. He and Hester are outsiders in a discontented society which has lived through crisis and triumph and found itself unrewarded for its 'sacrifices' and unsatisfied with the vistas following victory. Much of the power of Rattigan's play in 1952 must have derived from what he did not state, and understated.

'A well made play about boring middle-class people' would have been a common verdict on Rattigan's play ten years later. He was the chief casualty of the 'revolution' in British theatre attributed to the first production of John Osborne's *Look Back in Anger* at the Royal Court Theatre in 1956. The critics who led the taste of a new generation of theatregoers approved of anti-Establishment animus, thought the provincial working class was more interesting than the London middle class, and spurned the dramatists – Coward, Priestley and Rattigan – who had given the West End its great successes in the 1930s and 1940s. Coward had his acting and his singing to fall back on, Priestley his talents as a polemical journalist. For Rattigan there was only dramatic writing. *Separate Tables* (1954) and *Ross* (1960) both had very long West End runs. He remained in demand as a writer of film scripts. But his last five stage plays fell far short of his earlier box-office triumphs and he died in 1977 a saddened man.

In long retrospect, *Look Back in Anger* seems considerably more 'dated' than *The Deep Blue Sea* – and Osborne, like any sensible young dramatist, had learnt from Rattigan's superfine 'naturalistic' technique. The more devastating challenge to Rattigan's aesthetic came from the impact of Beckett and Brecht on British theatre from the mid-1950s. Naturalism was old hat. The 'Absurd', or explicit politics and sex and violence featured in such new drama as serious critics took seriously. Rattigan had made the prime mistake of writing with affection of 'Aunt Edna' in the introduction to his *Collected Plays*, published in 1953. Dramatists could not afford to offend the 'nice, respectable middle-class, middle-aged, maiden-lady with time on her hands and the money to help her to pass it'. He whimsically suggested that the likes of Aunt Edna had been the backbone of audiences for drama since ancient Greece. She had been his muse, in effect, as a young writer, though, as he had tried to establish himself as a serious dramatist, he had begun to distance himself from her. She 'must never be made mock of, or bored, or befuddled' but, equally, she must not be 'wooed, or pandered to, or cosseted'. These remarks were later gleefully quoted against him. While Coward's exceptional wit ensured that his plays were never shooed off the stage, a fairly modest revival of interest in Rattigan emerged only two decades after his death.

Muriel Romanes directed an excellent production of *The Deep Blue Sea* at the Royal Lyceum Theatre in Edinburgh in January 1999. The one liberty which she took with the text was to make Hester much older than Freddy – nowadays, she can point out, the sexuality of middle-aged women is freely acknowledged. (And, in this heyday of the 'mature student', the notion of a woman in her late forties studying to be an artist is not in the least bizarre.) Otherwise, Romanes obeyed

Rattigan's naturalistic stage directions and was scrupulous over period detail. Her very talented cast found the play fascinating. Rattigan, it became clear during rehearsals, is content to create puzzles which he does not solve for us round the motivations and natures of Hester and her husband, Freddie and Miller. Older members of the audience, brought up to admire Osborne, Arden, Pinter and Stoppard, often seemed to think the play engaging but still in the last analysis too 'middle class', too 'well made'. There was anecdotal evidence that younger people were not afflicted with prejudice against Rattigan, and were more open to his play's humanity and power.

To stick with the proscenium-arch convention of the missing fourth wall, as Romanes did, is to honour Rattigan's own naturalistic conventions. But revisiting her production for a second time one was more and more struck by the thought that a different way of setting the play could restore a sense of the context which its original audiences took for granted. To leave space around Hester's flat in which bombsites could be seen, and on which wartime and post-war newsreel footage could be back-projected, and to introduce typical music of the period might, paradoxically, by 'dating' it more precisely, make it less 'dated'. Conversely, to present the play more intimately, with a minimal set, 'in the round' might expose the explosions of powerful feeling which underlie the different modes of reticence displayed by Rattigan's characters. It seems pretty certain, anyway, that further revivals will take place and that Rattigan's stagecraft will prove, as he hoped, durable.

1999

3

REPRESENTATIONS OF WAR

The Hero from Homer to Now

Early in the 1980s, the traveller Christina Dodwell was riding a horse thousands of feet up in the Papua New Guinea Highlands. Resting in a pass in the mountains, she noticed that something was going on in a nearby valley. She went to investigate.

A battle with bows and arrows was in progress between two groups she recognized as the Engas and the Mendies. Men bunched at opposite ends of the valley. In the middle, 'there seemed to be an invisible skirmish line' to which the warriors ran to call insults at each other and let loose a few arrows. Then they rushed back to base, well out of range. Dodwell saw no one get badly hurt, though one man was hit in his buttock as he ran. When it began to rain, the war was abandoned, to be resumed some other time. The men did not want to get their ceremonial costumes wet.

According to Dodwell – and to anthropologists familiar with the Melanesian region – tribal fighting has formal rules like a sport. Indeed, versions of cricket have in some places replaced or supplemented it. In the New Guinea Highlands, wars are arranged when pigs are stolen or people are murdered or manslaughter occurs. Arrows of a special war type, with magical properties, are employed. People are seldom killed. If a killing occurs, the victorious group celebrates, the losers mourn the dead. 'Payback' war is then due so that the killing can be avenged.[1]

Warfare of this kind has occurred elsewhere in the world. And the element of ceremony and ritual in warfare was prominent in Europe until the nineteenth century. The conception of total war has more or less smothered it. The 'knights of the air' in the 1940 Battle of Britain in fact had no time for knightly challenges or courtesies. The modern soldier is meant to be a man with mechanical weapons, who is part of an overall killing machine. He may have to be braver than soldiers have ever been before, but his heroism will hardly approximate to that of Arthurian knights or the figures of ancient epic.

Of course, war was never exclusively ceremonial. Total war was prefigured in situations where groups – call them tribes – fought to the death for scarce resources. The expansion of the ancient Meso-potamian empires clearly involved both economic imperatives and drives arising from the very nature of kingly power, its tendency to protect itself by aggrandizement. No one reading Homer's *Iliad* could possibly imagine that the only motivation of the Greek heroes is to retrieve, for quasi-chivalric reasons, the beautiful Helen, wife of Menelaos. They are acutely interested in spoil – in valuable goods and in women. Homer's epic begins with Achilles' anger over the Greek general, Agamemnon's taking from him a woman he has seized. These men often look like pirates, besieging a town richer than those they have left behind them.

However, when the fighting starts in Book 3 of the *Iliad*, something not altogether remote from warfare in the New Guinea Highlands at once appears. Greeks advance, Trojans advance across the plain:

> Now as these in their advance had come close together,
> Alexandros the godlike lept from the ranks of the Trojans,
> as challenger wearing across his shoulders the hide of a leopard,
> curved bow and sword, while in his hands shaking two javelins
> pointed with bronze, he challenged all the best of the Argives
> to fight man to man against him in bitter combat.

'Alexandros' is better known to us as Paris. When Paris sees Menelaos striding towards him, accepting his challenge, he shrinks back from combat with the man whose wife he carried off. His brother Hector rebukes him in a long speech. Paris agrees: let the best man win. The long war can be settled here and now. Hector announces this to the Greeks. Both sides thankfully sit down to watch the show. A solemn sacrifice of lambs is prepared. Heralds distribute lambs' hairs amongst the princes in both armies. Agamemnon solemnly declares that if Paris wins the Greeks will sail off, if Menelaos wins they will get back Helen 'and all her possessions' and also receive a fitting 'price' for their efforts. Lambs' throats are cut. Prayers are uttered. The champions arm themselves splendidly. They fight. Menelaos is winning. But Aphrodite, goddess of love, intervenes and whisks Paris out of the battlefield and back to his bedchamber. The goddess Athene, in disguise, invites the archer Pandaros to shoot at Menelaos. He hits him. The war resumes.[2]

The Homeric heroes are defined not only by their relationships with men on their own side, but by taunts thrown, grudges maintained, challenges uttered, against the others. Though the armies at times seem quite large, both can be silenced to hear the voice of one man. And every killing, in those recitals which sometimes sicken the modern reader, is of individual by individual. The detail is often revolting, but few deaths are anonymous. Leaving aside the climactic scene when the noble Hector in single combat receives Achilles' spear through his neck, and the victor drags his body behind his chariot, each of the victims of Achilles' furious return to battle, after the death of his friend Patroklos, is personally accounted for until he reaches the river Xanthos and reddens its water with the blood of nameless fugitives. Then, very horribly, he comes upon a Trojan prince, Lykaon, who has stripped off his armour to cut wood to make rails for a chariot. Lykaon begs for mercy at the hero's knees. Achilles spurns him:

> So, friend, you die also. Why all this clamour about it?
> Patroklos also is dead, who was better by far than you are.
> Do you not see what a man I am, how huge, how splendid
> and born of a great father, and the mother who bore me immortal.
> Yet even I have also my death and my strong destiny . . .

Lykaon dies, like others, in a very particular way: Homer is precise about anatomy:

> . . . Achilleus drawing his sharp sword struck him
> beside the neck at the collar bone and the double-edged sword
> plunged full length inside. He dropped to the ground face downward
> and lay at length, and the black blood flowed
>   and the ground was soaked with it.

Then Achilles slings him into the river. 'Die on all', he cries. Every Trojan he meets must die, die 'an evil death':

> . . . till all of you
> pay for the death of Patroklos and the slaughter of the Achaians whom
> you killed beside the running ships, when I was not with them.

Sure enough, within a few lines, the guts of Asteropaios, son of Pelegon, from far away Paionia, are spilling out on the ground and shortly the eels are nibbling the fat that lies by his kidneys, while Achilles slaughters seven more Paionians, all named . . .[3]

Could any auditor, any reader, anywhere, ever, have identified with Achilles at this point in the *Iliad*, a slayer without mercy, whose excuse

– grief for his dear friend Patroklos, slain by Hector – is mixed up with guilt, as the passage I have just quoted shows, because Patroklos and others died while he was sulking in his tent refusing to do battle? The great epic which stands at the fountainhead of all European literature – poetry, drama, prose narrative, even historiography – has retained its power because it has offered in various aspects and passages all things to all men, though fewer, perhaps, to women. A Victorian imperialist and a CND member of the 1950s could both equally quote it for their own purposes. Partly, this must be because it is clearly a syncretic work, full of puzzles and anomalies deriving from a hybrid origin.

No one knows exactly how and when the Homeric epics were assembled. There is a scholarly consensus that they were more or less fixed in the form we know them by around 700 BCE, which was the time when the Greeks were becoming literate. But their origins are oral. Whether or not one supremely gifted individual called Homer travelled about collecting tales and traditions, details in the *Iliad* refer anomalously to different past periods. In the early Mycenean period, say 1600 BCE, Greeks had used huge spears, suitable only for close combat. Smaller, paired spears, one for throwing, are seen in the archaeological record in the fourteenth and thirteenth centuries BCE, but the hurling of spears in battle is a later development. Achilles, when he at last goes out to fight, begins with 'a spear which would seem most at home in the thirteenth century or considerably earlier', and 'finishes with one which acts as though it belongs in the twelfth century at the earliest, and possibly several centuries later'. Ajax has a tower-like huge shield made of seven layers of oxhide to which an eighth layer of bronze has been added. Suddenly, in the thick of battle, it acquires a boss. In this case an unwieldy item suitable in close combat characteristic of early Mycenaean times, then redundant as bronze body armour came in, is given a boss such as appeared on a different, lighter type of shield centuries later.

I draw these points from a highly persuasive recent essay by E. S. Sherratt. She confronts two problems at once – the inconsistencies of the Homeric texts and the incapacity of archaeologists to find, at the presumed site of Troy or anywhere else, objects confirming the historicity of the *Iliad*. Her answer is that many stable structural elements in oral composition, as detected in the poem, carry 'early' references with them. Just as the archaeological record shows us several stages in the development of Greek societies, involving the rise and fall of kingdoms, then increasing maritime activity after the palaces collapsed, before the establishment of the historical city states – so the *Iliad* is, as it were, layered.

But I do not want to get into archaeological niceties where I have no qualifications at all to follow Mrs Sherratt. There is a parallel very close to us for the coincidence in the *Iliad* of momentous heroic deeds and implausible use of hardware. I refer to the Hollywood Western.

Mrs Sherratt suggests that the final formation of the *Iliad* coincided with rapid colonial activity by the Greeks who retained the Trojan stories. As part of a process of consolidation, she suggests, there 'may have been an increasing emphasis on existing epic traditions' as possessions not just of individual families or groups of elites, but of other communities. The stories ceased to be the material of creative bardic song and were fixed in a structure to be relayed by a *rhapsode*. The epics had a unifying ideological function.[4] In some respects the mythology of the Wild West is similar. It validates the theft from Native Americans of the rich resources of the West, and can be used in various ways to insinuate values suitable to be shared by a nation of migrants and immigrants. Westerns carried the ideology of Cold War, then confronted the ideological crisis brought about the Vietnam War. Like Homeric epic, Westerns can be richly ambivalent. But in the end they provide reassurance, because, through necessary violence, some sort of justice is done. When at the end of his great recent movie *The Unforgiven* – I do not believe it is the *last* last great western – Clint Eastwood is moved by the murder of his black buddy to revive his foresworn gunfighting skills and go into the saloon to shoot the baddies, we know that this gruesome mayhem is squaring an ideological account. Blacks are part of this myth now, too. (Or, as Lorna Hardwick suggests to me, one might say that they are 'included to make the myth and its associated values acceptable'.)

The Unforgiven, like many recent Westerns, has an attractive patina of accurate historical reconstruction. Quite likely nothing wholly anachronistic or impossible occurs in the whole movie. But the Western mythology which it feeds off is as counter-factual as Achilles' spears and Ajax's shield. It is virtually impossible to fire a Colt revolver accurately from horseback. The mayhem of the actual American West where men called Bill Hickock, Wyatt Earp and Butch Cassidy really lived tended to take the form of desperate, confused, brief shoot-outs and drunken shambles. But while one part of our minds knows that, another approves the unerring justice with which Clint Eastwood's gun picks the right people. Heroism, this is my first main point, is not something arising naturally from conditions of violence. It is something constructed upon them because we need heroes. Heroes are not real: they are superreal.

This is not to say that conditions of what might be called true heroism never occur. Men-at-arms have often been astonishingly brave: that is, reckless. Consider 'Pickett's charge' at the Battle of Gettysburg, 1863.

The Confederates had been bombarding the Union centre with the heaviest use of artillery which they made in the war. But they aimed too high. In charge of the all-Virginia division ordered by General Lee to attack was George Pickett, thirty-eight years old. I quote James M. McPherson's great account of the war: 'With his long hair worn in ringlets and his face adorned by a drooping mustache and goatee, Pickett looked like a cross between a Cavalier dandy and a riverboat gambler. He affected the romantic style of Sir Walter Scott's novels and was eager to win everlasting glory at Gettysburg.' His three brigades, joined by six more from Hill's division, moved out to attack on a mile-wide front. As the grey infantry moved magnificently across rolling farmland, the Union artillery, thought to be disabled, poured shot, shell and canister among them. Then Yankee marksmen crouched behind stone walls opened up at 200 yards' range. Other Union forces attacked the rebel flanks. Only two or three hundred Southerners breached the first Union line, where they were slaughtered. Pickett's division lost two-thirds of its men. The South lost the battle and, of course, the war.[5]

Why do men advance in war when reason should assert that death is almost certain? The new school of military historians, led by John Keegan and Richard Holmes, ask this question and find answers in discipline, male bonding and, not least, strong drink. 'We must take account', Keegan observes near the end of his pioneering book *The Face of Battle*, 'of the undoubted willingness of some men at all times to risk, even apparently to enjoy, extreme danger and arbitrary cruelty . . . There were volunteers as well as slaves in the ranks of the gladiators.'[6] But during the Second World War most Allied soldiers broke down in combat and in about six months became useless. The strain was too much. War, so often discussed as if it were the product of irresistible human instinct, in practice violates our instincts. Achilles the Hero is, in his prolonged *aristeia*, Achilles the crazed, ruthless serial killer. And his type, as he himself knows, does not last long. 'So friend', he tells Lykaon, 'you die also . . . Even I have also my death.' Or, as George Chapman expanded it in his famous translation of 1598–1611, the one John Keats read:

Death and as violent a fate must overtake even me.
By twilight, morn-light, day, high noon, whenever destiny
Sets on her man to hurl a lance or knit out of his string
An arrow that must reach my life . . .[7]

In a famous dramatic sequence by Chapman's contemporary,
Shakespeare, we find a consolidation of the anti-heroic, anti-war
tradition which can also be traced to Homer. Shakespeare projects a
very unattractive picture of the Greek heroes in his *Troilius and
Cressida*. His Hotspur, in *Henry IV Part 1*, is much more appealing. It
is hard to resist his boyish zest for battle and glory. After the devious
Prince Hal has killed him in single combat, he pays honour to his
corpse – 'Fare thee well, great heart' – then pauses to shed a tear over
Falstaff, apparently slain by Douglas nearby.

But Falstaff is shamming dead. After Hal's departure, he rises to
address us:

Counterfeit? I lie, I am no counterfeit. To die is to be a counterfeit, for he is
but the counterfeit of a man who hath not the life of a man. But to
counterfeit dying, when a man thereby liveth, is to be no counterfeit, but the
true and perfect image of life indeed. The better part of valour is discretion,
in the which better part I have saved my life.

That follows his great diatribe, three scenes back, against honour;

What is honour? A word? What is in that word honour? What is that
honour? Air. A trim reckoning! Who hath it? He that died a' Wednesday.[8]

Falstaff is, generically, a cheat and a coward. But his points are those of
a reasonable satirist. And a reasonable view of war, utterly scornful of
heroism, is amply voiced by the greatest figure of the eighteenth-
century Enlightenment. In Chapter 3 of *Candide*, Voltaire has a brisk
go at his erstwhile patron Frederick the Great, disguised as the king of
the Bulgarians, in whose brutally drilled army his naive hero is serving.
The Bulgarians confront the Abarians:

Nothing could be so beautiful, so smart, so brilliant, so well drilled as the
two armies. Trumpets, fifes, oboes, drums, cannons formed a harmony such
as was never heard even in hell.
    First the cannon felled about six thousand men on each side; then the
musketry removed from the best of worlds some nine or ten thousand

scoundrels who infected its surface. The bayonet also was the sufficient reason for the death of some thousands of men. The whole might well amount to about thirty thousand souls. Candide, trembling like a philosopher, hid himself as best he could during this heroic butchery.

Finally, while both kings were having *Te Deums* sung, each in his own camp, he decided to go reason elsewhere about effects and causes. He passed over heaps of dead and dying and first reached a neighbouring village; it was in ashes; it was an Abarian village which the Bulgarians had burned in accordance with the rules of international law. Here old men riddled with wounds watched their wives die, with their throats cut, holding their children to their bleeding breasts; there, girls, disembowelled after satisfying the natural needs of a few heroes, were gasping their last sighs; others, half-burned, screamed to be given the *coup de grâce*. Brains were spattered over the ground beside severed arms and legs.[9]

Voltaire's satire often depends on exaggeration. But in this case he did not exaggerate. I quote from a report by Mark Huband in the *Observer* of 31 October 1993. He writes from Burundi, where the army, dominated by the minority Tutsi people, has overthrown the democratically elected Hutu president, generated a fierce Hutu backlash and embarked on massacre in retaliation:

We passed the Makwa zoological centre. A man with a staff sat motionless in the entrance archway. A body twitched on the ground at the foot of the steps leading up to the house. Another lay face down in the mud. A third was splayed close to the road.

Shoes, bags of food and a few clothes lay smoking in a pit beside the house. The man lying outside the door turned over, his gaping eyeballs rolling as he peered over the ash-strewn garden. Blood poured from his right foot, which had been all but torn from his leg. From his neck downwards he was soaked in blood, which had left a trail smeared down the steps.

Only the murmurs of the dying men and their soft breathing, broke the silence which hung over the deserted village.[10]

Such is war. Such are the 'Disasters of War' as Goya etched them from 1810 to 1813, in one of the few attempts by a major visual artist to portray war as it truly is. In 1822 Byron launched a sustained assault, in the Falstaff tradition, on notions of military heroism in his account of the attack in 1790 on Ismail on the Danube, by the Russians, in Cantos VII and VIII of *Don Juan*:

> Oh thou eternal Homer! I have now
> To paint a siege, wherein more men were slain

With deadlier engines and a speedier flow
Than in the Greek gazette of that campaign.
And yet like all men else I must allow,
To vie with thee would be about as vain
As for a brook to cope with ocean's flood,
But still we moderns equal you in blood . . .[11]

However, a couple of years later Byron himself died a hero, because his life was seen as sacrificed to the cause of Greek freedom which he was helping to advance by force of arms.

The Enlightened view that war was horrible and should be avoided ran counter to the tendencies in the Enlightenment itself which led men to seek freedom from alien rule and class rule. The Voltairean spirit in Bryon clashed with his neoclassicism. And it was the classical scholars and neoclassical artists of the eighteenth century, rediscovering Homer, who developed what became an acceptable version of heroism for modern man. It involves on the one hand the idealization of energies seen as natural to humanity and most forcefully displayed in a savage, or near savage, state, on the other the elegiac freezing of the deathly results of these energies in images both pathetic and inspirational. From Enlightened thinkers concerned about the submergence and loss of generous passion and human solidarity – attributes of the 'primitive' tribe – in contemporary commercial society came ways of affirming, as it were rationally, the beauty and duty of self-sacrifice in war. From neoclassical sculptors and painters came techniques of design and composition which presented war as something indeed daunting and awesome, but set the deaths of dutiful patriots far above and wholly apart from butchered old men, burnt villages, raped girls. However, along with his life, the hero sacrificed his individuality: he was transformed into the heroic type. And eventually even the names of heroes became almost insignificant, as they appeared on memorials listing many, many dead, typified by one or two soldiers or groups of representative soldiers.

Neoclassicism elevated Homer from being merely one of the major ancient poets to a uniquely godlike stature matched only by Shakespeare and Dante. It did so as part of an agenda which directed pure, true feeling and noble emotion against social corruption and its concomitant sophistication and cynicism. As Hugh Honour puts it, 'The qualities which distinguished ancient poetry could be visually represented only by a style of equally primitive simplicity. For the literary and artistic cults of the primitive were two manifestations of a more profound urge to purify society and re-establish natural laws which were based on reason and recognised the dignity of man.'[12]

As Homer was revalued, the concept of heroism found in his work was refictionalized in terms of the myth of the noble savage. This process began well before the popularity of Jean Jacques Rousseau's views from the 1750s onwards. We can see it beginning with Alexander Pope.

Pope's vastly popular translation of the *Iliad* was published between 1715 and 1720. It met, like Pope's other work, the taste of an expanding, wealthy bourgeoisie. It was not for curious scholars but for all serious people anxious to form in themselves proper taste. Pope broke decisively away from the tradition, represented by Chapman and Shakespeare, which brought Homer's heroes down to earth, where they might even be burlesqued. This is his version of the death of Lykaon:

> Sudden, Achilles his broad sword display'd,
> And buried in his neck the reeking blade.
> Prone fell the youth; and panting on the land,
> The gushing purple dy'd the thirsty sand.[13]

Not for nothing do such couplets go by the generic name 'heroic'. The balance, the dignity, the formulaic use of language (properties, incidentally, which may be less foreign to Homer's original than the lighter, more vivid style of recent translation) give both murderer and victim stature. Blood gushes purple: that is a royal colour.

Rendering Homer thus, Pope had to contend with two facts which were bound to make high-minded, genteel eighteenth-century persons uncomfortable. First, the ancient poet believed in a plurality of gods. Not only were these gods false, the product of superstition; their behaviour was frequently petty and deplorable. Likewise, the heroes were often extremely bad mannered, to put it mildly. Pope's ratiocinations around these problems point forward to the neoclassical solution.

His preface points up Homer's closeness to nature – 'Our author's work is a wild paradise . . . What he writes is of the most animated Nature imaginable; every thing moves, every thing lives, and is put in Action.' His wonderful diversity of characters, speeches, incidents derives from nature, played upon by matchless invention. Pope admits that Homer has an excess of invention. But other objections to his art, admittedly less polished than Virgil's, 'proceed wholly from the Nature of the Times he liv'd in. Such are his *grosser representations* of the

Gods, and the vicious and *imperfect Manners* of his Heroes.' All is justified therefore by Homer's accuracy in depicting life as he saw it – he was 'the only true mirror of that ancient world'. Not so very far away, Hebrews were writing divinely inspired scripture. And the 'Grandeur and Excellence' of Homer's sentiments 'in general' is proved by their 'remarkable . . . Parity with those of the Scripture'. 'Simplicity', Pope avers, 'is the Mean between Ostentation and Rusticity. This pure and noble Simplicity is nowhere in such Perfection as in the *Scripture* and our Author.' From his work, Pope deduces the character of Homer himself – a sociable chap, but a patriot, and 'of a religious Spirit . . ., inculcating in every Page the worship of the Gods.' For a pagan, Pope tries to show, he got remarkably close to Christian truth, and he had 'a Notion of the Soul's subsisting after this Life'.[14]

Continuing qualms about the vices of Homer's gods and the bad manners of his heroes help to explain the rapturous reception of James Macpherson's Ossianic epic poetry in the 1760s. The heroes and heroines attributed to the dark-age Celtic bard Ossian were irreproachably chaste; as for the religious element, this was so pure as to be invisible – David Hume complained that 'all these Celtic heroes are more complete atheists than were ever bred in the school of Epicurus'.[15] In neoclassical art, the impact of Homer and Ossian is at times almost indistinguishable. But this was after a couple of Hume's compatriots had done Trojan work, as it were, in elevating Homer.

The *Enquiry into the Life and Writings of Homer* published anonymously in London in the mid-1730s by Professor Thomas Blackwell of Aberdeen University presents a view of its subject which modern scholarship finds entirely unsound. But the book remains an important milestone in the development in Scotland of the overwhelmingly influential view of history implicit, forty years later, in Adam Smith's *Wealth of Nations*.

Like Pope, Blackwell falls into circular theorizing. Homer is wonderfully 'natural'. Hence we infer that he is truthful. We can infer from Homer what conditions were like in Homer's Greece. The knowledge which we thus assume of that Greece enables us to guarantee that Homer tells the truth about it. Homer lived in an age of transition. The Greeks had at first lived crudely on land and as pirates at sea. The age of Agamemnon, when Troy was taken, had been produced by advancing wealth and the rise of strong kings in walled cities, but constant warfare had continued. Homer, born well after Troy's fall, could still behold 'Towns taken and plundered, the Men put to the Sword, and the Women made Slaves. He beheld their despairing

Faces and suppliant Postures; heard their Moanings o'er their murdered Husbands.'

Homer could also see cities blessed with peace and the founding of orderly colonies. Life was still simple, though, manners still natural. Our pleasure in Homer arises from his 'Representation of *natural* and *simple Manners*: It is irresistible and inchanting; they best show human Wants and Feelings; they give us back the Emotions of an *artless* Mind . . . Goodness and Honesty have their Share in the Delight; for we begin to love the Men and would rather have to do with them, than with more refined but double *Characters*.' Eighteenth-century man, cut off by the refinements of commercial civilization from nature, has to 'unlearn' his 'daily way of life' in order to write poetry 'in the higher Strains'. Blackwell quite seriously alleges that 'one and the same Kingdom' cannot be 'thoroughly civilised, and offer proper Subjects for Poetry . . . A People's Felicity clips the Wings of their Verse.'[16]

Blackwell justifies Homer's gods and goddesses as representations of natural feelings and powers present in the universe. His handling of the mythology which came to hand is consistent and apt, in contrast with Virgil's later 'improprieties'. Homer grew up (must have grown up – we are into a circular argument again) close to Troy, as an Ionian settler, and his copious detail convinces us that 'every tittle of what he says is true'. The actual Trojan war was 'a prodigious Rendezvous of the bravest Inhabitants of a free Country, wide and warlike; and engaged in a violent struggle of Passions and Arms, with another of more effeminate Manners. The Effect was, that it afforded him *real historic characters* for his MODEL.' All the Greek leaders are brave, but in different ways: '*Achilles* is fierce and impetuous, *Ajax* steady and firm, *Diomedes* gallant and open, *Ulysses* cautious and bold . . .' Concentrating on the most exciting part of the long siege, Homer is able to show the passions in action – love, ambition, pride, friendship, virtue, revenge. What over-genteel people object to in Homer is his '*too great Truth*' in representing the heroes as they naturally were.[17]

Blackwell's conclusion is Panglossian: Homer is the best of all possible poets because (as we infer from the evidence, chiefly, of his poetry) he grew up in exactly the right time and place, the best of all possible transition periods. An Irish gentleman, Robert Wood, who caused some stir by his report on the Ruins of Palmyra, published in 1753, also visited the Troas, presumed scene of the *Iliad*. He went even further than Blackwell in his claims for Homer's essential accuracy, as sociologist, historian, geographer. For Blackwell, a stay-at-home scholar, it was Homer's self-evident truth to *human* nature which was decisive proof of his accurate historicity. Wood the traveller felt able to claim that Homer's truth to topography was clinching. 'In the great province of Imitation he is the most original of all Poets, and the most constant and faithful copier after Nature.' On the Ionian coast you can still see the West Wind as described by Homer. Wood purges Homer of all taint of superstition. As an accurate observer of physical nature, he entertained 'pure and sublime notions of the Divine Nature'; Homer was almost more of a Christian than a deist, but like deists he subscribed to the true religion 'universal, of every country, and co-extensive with creation'. His use of a mythology ideal for poetical purposes is like Shakespeare's dealings with fairies. But there are, Wood concedes, 'disgusting pictures' in Homer. Unless you judge him by the standards of the 'Heroic Age' rather than those of present times, 'the courage of Achilles must appear brutal ferocity'.[18]

What Wood, following upon Blackwell, was able to do was to locate heroism in history. My first point was that the Homeric hero, like the Wild West hero, was a kind of necessary fiction, counter-factual. Wood asserts that Homer was, really, the best of all possible historians. He trotted round the plan of Troy noting its topography and – here Wood rounds on the ancient tradition that Homer wrote long after the siege – perhaps collected 'circumstantial accounts' from 'those who were eye witnesses of the siege . . . or at least from their children'. Writing about half a century, Wood reckons, after Troy fell, Homer's vividness derives from eyewitness accounts . . . 'Every sketch of this great Master is an exact transcript of what he had either seen, heard or felt.'[19]

However strained and naive Wood's views seem to us, they carried authority in his day. In effect, they proved that the bravery, devotion to cause and country, and acceptance of divinely proposed destiny – that is, in the cases of Hector and Achilles, death in battle – shown by the Homeric heroes *according to the standards of their time* could be regarded, not as fictions like those of Renaissance Romance, but as qualities present in human nature *in our own time* which might be relocated in present-day warfare. However, berserk, murderous rage could be cast off from the heroic ensemble, as belonging to the crude past. Men could surge out from the artificial, luxurious trammels of commercial civilization, and, purified by correct religious principles, assert their true heroic natures.

The Scottish artist Gavin Hamilton, whose long domicile in Rome as painter, archaeologist and art dealer made him a crucial figure in the development of European neoclassicism, knew Wood well, and painted him, together with his friend Dawkins, as the bold rediscoverers of

Palmyra. Hence one might expect him, as he purified 'History Painting', set it on a new course or, rather, put it back on Poussin's rails, to emphasize, perhaps, the somewhat ferocious character of battle as we find it in Homer. No. What he did with Homer helps to explain how nineteenth- and twentieth-century people have devised representations of war which they can accept as consoling them for its horrors and losses.

Beside Wood's ideas, Hamilton knew Blackwell's. Neither was a practitioner of, or heavyweight theorist in, the visual arts. The master theorist of neoclassicism was Johann Joachim Winckelmann. Writing in rococo Dresden, dissatisfied, like Jean Jacques Rousseau, with the superficiality and corruption of modern civilization, Winckelmann, in 1755, produced a pamphlet of *Reflections Concerning the Imitation of the Grecian Artists in Painting and Sculpture*. It fixed a notion of Greek art as especially beautiful, noble and pure which endures to this day.

'The imitation of the ancients', Winckelmann declared, 'is the only way of excelling in the sublime and elegant arts of Painting and Sculpture: and we may say of their productions, what has been said of Homer, that the more we study them, the more we must admire them.' Artistic theory commonly held that painters should imitate not just nature as it was, but 'nature in its most striking and perfect appearances'. And to such '*select nature*', the Greeks added something extra, an '*ideal beauty*' of which the model could not be found in the visible external world, existing only in the human mind, but, accordingly, 'natural' to humanity. Winckelmann believed that the ancient Greeks had been especially beautiful people, because of an excellent climate, devotion to 'manly exercises', strict diet, light, unconfining costume and the absence amongst them of smallpox, venereal disease and rickets. Hence artists, in the *Gymnasium* and elsewhere, could see very beautiful forms and were 'encouraged to go yet further than real nature, and to make a new step towards perfection, under the guidance of those very principles which Nature had furnished them with'. Theirs was not mere undirected fancy: 'Nature was their home and they never lost sight of it.' They combined all the best bits from visible nature. This is immensely convenient for the modern student. He can see the best of nature gathered together in antique sculpture. After studying the antique sufficiently, he can go ahead to imitate the nature around him with the idea of perfect nature in his mind.[20]

The year after Winckelmann wrote his pamphlet, Gavin Hamilton returned to Rome, where he had studied in his youth. Here, for the rest of his life, he was originator and middleman in the transmission of neoclassicism. His own paintings combine an obsession with accurate detail comparable to the very different work of Dutch genre painters with conceptions of ideal beauty derived from antique models. They are 'naturalistic', as Duncan Macmillan has pointed out, not in the sense that they show life as we know it, but because there is nothing ostensibly superhuman in them; the gods do not appear. The grandeur of Hamilton's heroic figures belongs entirely to nature. Starting in 1759 Hamilton painted a cycle of big works on Homeric subjects. Though these were sold to different private purchasers, a set of engravings from them, widely circulated, made them, together, a reinterpretation of the story of the *Iliad*. Crucially, for the purposes of my argument, killing in battle does not feature. Hamilton came closest in *Achilles' Revenge on the Body of Hector* (1766) but even here the moment is in effect static; the victorious hero rears in triumph over his adversary as mourning commences in Troy. As a whole, the sequence matches the theme of the wrath of Achilles – beginning with *Achilles Parting with Briseis*, the girl Agamemnon takes away from him – with what Macmillan calls 'a pathetic counterplot of the story of Hector and Andromache which provides a gloss of Hamilton's own on Homer's narrative'. The grief of women is strongly emphasized. A story of rampant male passions, energies and appetites is refracted so that tender, even domestic values are foregrounded.[21]

In a letter to his patron Sir James Grant, who commissioned four works on Homeric subjects, about his painting *Achilles Lamenting the Death of Patroclus*, Hamilton writes, characteristically, that he is

> desirous to know your own sentiments of a performance where the generous passions of benevolence and compassion have so great a share . . . That compassion gives an inward satisfaction you can feel better than I describe; if you are touched with this sentiment on looking at the picture the painter has succeeded and I am happy.[22]

The noble theme is to evoke noble emotions in the spectator, who will feel good as a result, will feel 'inward satisfaction'.

Generous emotion, while noble and satisfying in itself, tended, however, to expand into the public arena. Thus the emphasis on innate human benevolence in the Scottish school of moral philosophy with which Hamilton grew up provided important intellectual reinforcement for those who sought, as the century wore on, to abolish the slave trade. For some, it could be a very short step indeed from enthusiasm for

Winckelmann's aesthetic concepts to argument and then action against an *ancien régime* seen as corrupt, unnatural and life-denying. Important though the relative chasteness and simplicity of Hamilton's compositions were in setting neoclassicism on its way, his followers tended more and more towards greater simplicity, stripping the Homeric hero down to nakedness and pure line. David's great paintings on Roman themes, which are held very plausibly to have helped inspire the French Revolution, elicit our admiration for public-spirited action with compositions almost excruciatingly taut.

A more complex pain is represented in *Philoctetes*, by James Barry, an Irish painter who joined Hamilton's circle in Rome. Bitten by a serpent on his way to Troy with the Greeks, Philoctetes, the great archer, languished in agony on Lemnos, till the heroes sent for him and, cured, he performed the crucial deed of slaying Paris with an arrow. Barry painted it in Rome, in 1770, under Winckelmann's influence, but also under that of his fellow Irishman Edmund Burke's theories on the role of the 'sublime' in art. The background of stormy sky emphasizes the subject's noble anguish. The hero's pain, we believe, is not just physical; he is kept out of the action at Troy by his injury, on which he broods. Seven years later, Barry produced an etching in which his composition is adjusted so that both the wildness of the sky and the weight of Philoctetes' brooding are intensified. He dedicated this print to the politician Sir George Savile, who, like Burke, defended the revolt of the thirteen American colonies.[23]

There is no innate consonance, however, between the Homeric conception of the individualistic hero – profoundly obsessed with personal fame, proving his prowess by the extent of his loot, notching up in battle victim after victim while accepting his own violent death as part of the pattern in which his aristocratic superiority is guaranteed – and the Bible-toting Yankee rifleman or Rousseau-quoting sans-culotte who rises up in 1776, in 1789, to make what we call the democratic revolution. The problem had been faced in the fifth-century Athenian democracy where Homer's works were the basis of all education, ineluctably involved with dominant ideology.

' "It would be crude", Lorna Hardwick argues, 'to say that the poems were democratised.' Rather, the common citizen was inducted into the aristocratic sphere. The whole Athenian people, as venturers, colonists, fighters, had heroic status above other peoples. The concept of good death, by which the hero's destiny is fulfilled, was extended to the deaths in battle of common soldiers. In Athens, 'the traditional elements of the aristocratic funeral were accorded to all the war dead; a public funeral which followed a prolonged *prothesis* (public display of the corpse), and *ekphora* (carrying to the burial) by wagon, and in which funeral games followed the funeral oration.'[24]

Public memorials to the dead, however, included names but not patronymics – aristocratic families, it seems, guarded the right to emphasize their own stature in public and private monuments where patronymics were very much to the point. The imagery of democratic revolution drew much more from republican Rome than from the plains of Troy. Ossian, not Homer, was Napoleon's favourite reading. The poems and novels of Walter Scott provided models of the hero for emergent European nationalisms which were far apter than Achilles and Ajax. In Victorian Britain the Greek classics were an important inspiration for the elite. Winckelmannesque concepts of Greek purity and superiority informed the rigorous regimes and incessant sporting activity of the Victorian public schools. But even though Marx himself, notoriously, subscribed to the cult of Greek super-excellence, the world-view of William Morris (who was keener on Nordic heroes) and that of the emerging labour movement had no place for Achilles. Nor, really, did popular imperialist ideology. One of the problems, surely, was that Homer's Trojans were far too sympathetic. Hector, fatalistically prepared to die in defence of his city, his wife and his little son, is intrinsically far more attractive to most of us than wifeless, marauding Achilles whose noblest motivation is possessive love for one other male person, Patroclus, only. You had to be a jolly clever chap with a degree from Balliol or Kings to cope with the ambivalencies and complexities of Homeric epic. It was probably easier if you were American. It is not for nothing that a recent history of the US Civil War is called *The American Iliad*. Like Achilles and Hector, Grant and Lee spoke the same language, shared broadly the same religious world-view, deployed the same weapons. Shooting down Sudanese or Zulus in Africa with modern guns was really impossible to assimilate with Homer meaningfully.

Hence, it was the Great War, the First World War, which provided the first context since the late eighteenth century in which heroic values could be inspected and reworked by British writers and artists. The Germans were almost exactly like us. In Frankfurt, as in Birmingham and Bordeaux, Andromaches, as it were, grieved for dead Hectors. From Leipzig, as from Liverpool, men brought up to admire the projection of the human form established in Greek sculpture entered killing fields in which less perfect human forms were blown to bits. The madness of huge Ajax, the cowardice of Paris were replicated by thousands upon thousands of ordinary citizens unable to cope with the mud, the rats, the screaming of shells, the screaming of wounded friends.

This was a war in which individual heroism in action, except in the marginal case of the men who flew fighter planes, was in effect impossible. And yet it produced a new sort of hero, the war poet. Wilfred Owen, Second Manchester Regiment, died just before the Armistice. He had insisted on going back to the front after his time as a shell-shocked psychological invalid in Britain, to endure and suffer with his comrades. His last letter to his mother, dated 31 October, from a smoky cellar packed with soldiers, ends:

> I hope you are as warm as I am; as serene in your room as I am here; and that you think of me never in bed as resignedly as I think of you always in bed. Of this I am certain you could not be visited by a band of friends half so fine as surround me here.[25]

Human solidarity is the great theme of Owen's poetry. He goes beyond the indignant rejection of hypocritical heroics in the verse of Sassoon, the undermining of any notion of heroism in Rosenberg's great poems, to affirm the Christ-like moral stature of the sacrifice of the common soldier. If his own stature seems to grow year after year it is because he is part of a magnificent modern myth which is substantially his own creation. It incorporates anger over the waste of young lives in imperialist war with assertion of the dignity and value of all lives lost. It has eclipsed and made seem ridiculous, even nasty, the 'forever England' heroics of Rupert Brooke, poor man, who never saw battle, whose Winckelmannesque image of young volunteers as 'swimmers into cleanness leaping' was utterly belied by the filth of the trenches. In the summer of 1968, when I impulsively gave my well-worn copy of Owen's poems to a young student from Dubček's Prague, met in London, whom I have never seen since, I felt I knew what Owen meant by the 'eternal reciprocity of tears'.

It is not so far from Gavin Hamilton's ideology, in fact, and the *Iliad* can be read so as to support very strongly the weight of 'reciprocity of tears'. I will come back to this. Meanwhile, I borrow from Lorna Hardwick the point that the ways in which we have remembered the British dead of our twentieth-century world wars recall the ideological accommodation of Homeric heroism in Athens in the fifth century BC. We mourn the Unknown Soldier whom Owen made known to us. The dead listed on our memorials are not nameless, but they are undis-

tinguished. Images, often friezes, or frieze-like, in the neoclassical
tradition, decorate the larger monuments, like Albert Toft's bronze
statue of a young man, memorial 'To the Heroic Dead', which Lorna
Hardwick singles out; it adorns the Birmingham Hall of Memory. The
message, as Dr Hardwick points out, is that death in battle, as for the
Homeric hero, has been good death.[26] 'They shall not grow old, as we
that are left grow old', to quote Laurence Binyon's poem 'For the
Fallen', written in honour of the Great War's young heroes:

> As the stars that shall be bright when we are dust,
> Moving in marches upon the heavenly plain,
> As the stars that are starry in the time of our darkness,
> To the end, to the end, they remain.[27]

Heroism in action, displaced from the real battlefield with its
literally indescribable (Keegan shows this) horror and chaos, has been
redistributed. The *possible* hero of the twentieth century is the general
or air chief marshal, who can be shown acting, not alone, but according to his own will. As heroes, Dowding and Patten, Montgomery and
Rommel actually have a lot going for them. They were indeed
remarkable men with admirable qualities, including courage. But their
virtues are dialectically inseparable from the habitual vices of the
political world in which they perforce contended. They are better, we
feel, than politicians, though perhaps not better than that archetypal
fighting politician Churchill. However, they cannot replicate the
Homeric, or for that matter the Arthurian, or Wagnerian, hero.

Those who can do so are film actors. Your actual combatant, even
your fighter ace or your Desert Rat VC, is too visibly one of us, a kid
with parents, a man with a trade or profession, to achieve Achillean or
Hector-like aura. But Errol Flynn, or John Wayne, or Richard Todd, or
Lee Marvin, persons whom we know to be actors, can act out epic roles
in modern warfare. The camera, following their individual actions, can
carve an *aristeia* out of the confusion of battle.

As I was writing this, an Open University student, Don McGilp, who
had been working on Homer with me, happened to send me a
photocopy of something he published in the Aberdeen *Press and
Journal* years ago. A former RAF man, Don McGilp was brooding
about the meaning of Armistice Day:

The majority of us have a curiously ambivalent attitude towards the subject of war. One supposes that the average man in the street shuns war – unless it becomes necessary to defend his freedom.

But the same man may well be on his way to see one of the war movies that seem to proliferate these days. There is something about men at war that stirs the imagination; that has glamour attaching to it.

Whether it is reading an account of a swash-buckling, kilted colonel leading his pipes and drums into a beleaguered Middle-eastern city, watching John Wayne storm the beaches at Iwo Jima or Richard Todd blow up dams in the Ruhr – it all takes our fancy.

Don McGilp ended by calling for 'the re-education of public taste. Or is war always to be regarded as the catharsis that purges the world of its evils?'[28]

I would like to follow this with two points. First, as I have stressed, the hero was never real. The hero is always super-real, a factually speaking impossible combination of attributes and hardware, ideology and athletic prowess. Hence many of us can wisely transfer our hero-worship to sport, a transfer implicit in the New Guinea example with which I began. When a great rugby full-back – J. P. R. Williams, Serge Bianco, Gavin Hastings – surges up field knocking opponents over we witness a Homeric *aristeia*. When Maradona or Gascoyne beats five men and scores, the cunning of Odysseus is matched. When Botham or Kapil Dev starts hitting sixes, Ajax has his modern counterparts.

But, second, unless one embraces pacifism completely, the concept of a Good Death in a noble cause remains indispensable. Let us consider, for a moment, the recent case of the Bomber Harris statue. This was seen, not least by the fliers of Bomber Command itself, as redressing a notorious, wicked snub. Churchill insisted that Bomber Command hammered German cities nightly. It was the only form of direct attack available to Britain until D-Day. It was supposed to cripple German war industry, which in fact increased production as the bombardment went on. Casualty rates among air crew were appallingly high. Those who survived have lived ever since with traumas impossible to submerge. However futile their effort, the sacrifice was magnificent, and I hope nobody believes that the cause of defeating Nazism was a bad one. Yet after the war Harris alone, among British commanders, was denied a peerage. Apart from *The Dam Busters*, which commemorated a raid on an industrial, not human target, the post-war film industry also shunned Bomber Command.

These men deserve to be remembered. But a bust of Harris was probably the worst of all ways to remember them. The starkest possible slab of eternal granite, with the simplest possible inscription, would seem to me more suitable for these RAF dead who are fading into namelessness. Neoclassical values are, I submit still to the point. The appropriate emotion must be conveyed as starkly and simply as possible.

In my opinion, the greatest poetry written by UK citizens in the Second World War came from Scots who fought with the Eighth Army.

Hamish Henderson's *Elegies for the Dead in Cyrenaica* encompass, Homerically, Scots, Britons, Germans and Italians. A handful of poems in Scots Gaelic by Sorley Maclean, who was wounded in action, set the combat, with astonishing moral authority, in a world historical perspective. It was another imperialist war, Maclean believed. But, still, the Nazis had to be fought. And those who fought them bravely were heroes. Here is his poem, 'Heroes':

> I did not see Lannes at Ratisbon
> nor MacLennan at Auldearn
> nor Gillies MacBain at Culloden,
> but I saw an Englishman in Egypt.
>
> A poor little chap with chubby cheeks
> and knees grinding each other,
> pimply unattractive face –
> garment of the bravest spirit.
>
> He was not a hit 'in the pub
> in the time of the fists being closed',
> but a lion against the breast of battle,
> in the morose wounding showers.
>
> His hour came with the shells,
> with the notched iron splinters,
> in the smoke and flame,
> in the shaking and terror of the battlefield.
>
> Word came to him in the bullet shower
> that he should be a hero briskly,
> and he was that while he lasted
> but it wasn't much time he got.
>
> He kept his guns to the tanks,
> bucking with tearing crashing screech,
> until he himself got, about the stomach,
> that biff that put him to the ground,

mouth down in sand and gravel,
without a chirp from his ugly high-pitched voice.

No cross or medal was put to his
chest or to his name or to his family;
there were not many of his troop alive,
and if there were their word would not be strong.
And at any rate, if a battle post stands
many are knocked down because of him,
not expecting fame, not wanting a medal
or any froth from the mouth of the field of slaughter.

I saw a great warrior of England,
a poor manikin on whom no eye would rest;
no Alasdair of Glen Garry;
and he took a little weeping to my eyes.

I set the poem beside the important moment in Tolstoy's *War and Peace*, a novel dedicated to undermining conventional conceptions of heroic leadership and brilliant action, when Pierre at Borodino acknowledges the moral stature of Tushin, the pipe-smoking little captain, whose artillery men have been playing their part to ensure that Napoleon occupies Moscow at ruinous cost. Tolstoy told Gorky, 'without false modesty, *War and Peace* is like the *Iliad*'.[30] But it is an epic in which the peasant values of Russia, perhaps rather implausibly incarnated in the old general Kutuzov, triumph over the pseudo-aristocratic braggadocio of La Grande Armée. The French, as Kutuzov tells his troops at the frontier, when he is shown the captured colours of regiments defeated by General Winter, are human beings. 'But', he ends up, 'with all said and done, who invited them here? It serves them right for coming here, the buggers.' Just so, Sorley Maclean is in no doubt that the cause of the ordinary Englishman turned hero is the right one. His behaviour is favourably contrasted with the worthless aristocratic values of the stupid Marshal Lannes at Ratisbon, and even with that of heroes celebrated in Gaelic song. The resources of Gaelic song were largely devoted to such celebration. Maclean, as socialist and democrat, now applies them to a nameless Sassenach, apt hero for the People's War.

But in 'Death Valley', perhaps a still more powerful poem, Maclean's vision embraces the fate of a dead German soldier, face slate grey:

Was the boy of the band
who abused the Jews
and Communists, or of the greater
band of those

Led, from the beginning of generations
unwillingly to the trial
and mad delirium of every war
for the sake of rulers?

Whatever his desire or mishap
his innocence or malignity,
he showed no pleasure in his death
below the Ruweizat Ridge.[31]

Death, 'good death' or bad death, comes to all. Young or old, on both sides. I may seem to have spent a lot of time in effect bashing Homer, as a poet projecting an aristocratic ideology which was transmuted in Athens into an imperialist ideology, from whose work serious moralists in the eighteenth century could only draw acceptable values by misreading them on the basis of a false conception of how they were composed. But the *Iliad* is in fact an inexhaustibly moving work of literature. When Derek Walcott in *Omeros* appropriates the names and qualities of Achilles, Hector, Philoctetes and Helen and applies them to the vernacular life of his tiny West Indian island it is not in the interests of an epic view of battle. St Lucia, the Helen of the Caribbean, vied over by French and English who died like flies of yellow fever, then left, in the early nineteenth century, to the peripheral, almost history-less peace which it has enjoyed in Walcott's lifetime, is a place where wars are remembered, will never again be fought. But beauty and bravado exist everywhere. When Lluis Llach the great Catalan singer appropriates the words of the modern Greek poet Cavafy and tells us we must all seek Ithaca, he makes the quest of Odysseus, as others have done before him, into a model for universal human quest.

Owen did not go to a public school, and memorably rejected public-school classicism when he denounced 'the old lie – *Dulce et decorum est Pro patria mori.*' But the spirit of his masterpiece, 'Strange Meeting' can be seen as Homeric.

The last book of the *Iliad* is full, as usual, of supernatural elements which impede the modern reader when, deeply moved by it, she or he turns to the business of interpreting it. The corpse of Hector, left by Achilles in the Greek camp, is preserved by the gods from decay despite

Achilles's best efforts to deface it. When, from amongst the bitter grief of the Trojan royal family, Hector's aged father Priam bravely goes forth to beseech the body from Achilles, he is empowered to reach the Greek hero safely by the assistance of the god Hermes. Yet we 'naturalize' this strange meeting as Gavin Hamilton would have done: in our response to the emotions involved in it, we leave out the gods.

Entering unnoticed as Achilles finishes his dinner, Priam on his knees appeals to manslaughtering Achilles to remember his own father:

> '. . . one who
> is of years like mine, and on the door-sill of sorrowful old age . . .
> . . . I put my lips to the hands of the man who has killed my children.'
> So he spoke, and stirred in the other a passion of grieving
> for his own father. He took the old man's hand and pushed him
> gently away, and the two remembered, as Priam sat huddled
> at the feet of Achilleus and wept close for manslaughtering Hektor
> and Achilleus wept now for his own father, now again
> for Patroklos . . .[32]

When Achilles returns the body, he receives a rich ransom: the profit motive lurks everywhere in this book. But the 'reciprocity of tears' seems to control his actions as he dines with Priam (his second dinner) admiring the 'brave looks' of this 'godlike' old man, then promises to hold the Greeks back from attack until the eleven days required for Hector's funeral ceremonies are over. Pope's translation makes Achilles' response seem poised, even gallant:

> Alas! what weight of anguish hast thou known?
> Unhappy prince! thus guardless and alone
> To pass through foes, and thus undaunted face
> The man whose fury has destroy'd thy race . . .[33]

But Owen's 'Strange Meeting' comes closer to the sense which Homer gives – to the modern reader – of top men whose fates have been determined by the gods and have brought them into murderous opposition, now divested of considerations of status, reduced to the basic human situations of father and son, grieving together over common fate. In Owen's poem the speaker escapes from battle, as you will remember, to a 'sullen hall' in Hell where he confronts another who stares at him 'with piteous resignation in fixed eyes':

'Strange friend,' I said, 'here is no case to mourn.'
'None,' said the other, 'save the undone years,
The hopelessness. Whatever hope is yours,
Was my life also; I went hunting wild
After the wildest beauty in the world,
Which lies not calm in eyes, or braided hair,
But mocks the steady running of the hour,
And if it grieves, grieves richlier than here,
For by my glee might many men have laughed,
And of my weeping something had been left,
Which must die now. I mean the truth untold,
The pity of war, the pity war distilled.
Now men will go content with what we spoiled.
Or, discontent, boil bloody, and be spilled.
They will be swift with swiftness of the tigress,
None will break ranks, though nations trek from progress.
Courage was mine, and I had mystery,
Wisdom was mine, and I had mastery;
To miss the march of this retreating world
Into vain citadels that are not walled.
Then, when much blood had clogged their chariot-wheels
I would go up and wash them from sweet wells,
Even with truths that lie too deep for taint.
I would have poured my spirit without stint
But not through wounds; not on the cess of war.
Foreheads of men have bled where no wounds were.
I am the enemy you killed, my friend.
I knew you in this dark; for so you frowned
Yesterday through me as you jabbed and killed.
I parried; but my hands were loath and cold.
Let us sleep now . . .'

1993

References

[1] C. Dodwell, *In Papua New Guinea* (Yeovil: Oxford Illustrated Press, 1983), pp. 134–5.
[2] Homer, *Iliad*, tr. R. Lattimore (Chicago: University of Chicago Press, 1951), Books 3 and 4, pp. 100–19.
[3] Ibid., Book 21, pp. 418–24.
[4] E. S. Sherratt, ' "Reading the texts": archaeology and the Homeric question', in C. Emlyn Jones, L. Hardwick and J. Purkis (eds), *Homer: Readings and Images* (London: Duckworth, 1992), pp. 145–65.

[5] James M. McPherson, *Battle Cry of Freedom: The American Civil War* (London: Penguin, 1990), pp. 661–3.

[6] John Keegan, *The Face of Battle* (New York: Vintage, 1977), pp. 325, 329.

[7] Homer, *Iliad*, tr. G. Chapman (London: Dent, 1898), Book 21, p. 195.

[8] W. Shakespeare, *The First Part of King Henry the Fourth*, ed. P. H. Davison (Harmondsworth: Penguin, 1968), Act V, Sc. 4, p. 147, Act V, Sc. 1, p. 136.

[9] Voltaire, *Candide or Optimism*, tr. D Frame, in *A206 The Enlightenment: Texts 1*, ed. S. Eliot and K. Whitlock (Milton Keynes: Open University, 1992), pp. 315–16.

[10] M. Huband, 'Burundi bloodbath runs its course as the West looks on', *Observer*, 31 October 1993, p. 17.

[11] Lord Byron, *Don Juan*, ed. T. G. Steffan, E. Steffan and W. W. Pratt (Harmondsworth: Penguin, 1972), Canto VII, st. 80, p. 315.

[12] H. Honour, *Neo-classicism* (Harmondsworth: Penguin, 1968), p. 67.

[13] Homer, *Iliad*, tr. A. Pope (Edinburgh: J. Robertson, 1773), p. 400.

[14] A. Pope, 'Preface', in *The Iliad of Homer Books I–IX*, tr. A. Pope, ed. M Mack (London: Methuen, 1967), pp. 3–4, 8–9, 13–14, 18, 51, 68.

[15] David Hume, 'Of the authenticity of Ossian's poems', in *Essays Moral Political and Literary*, vol. 2, ed. T. H. Green and T. H. Grose (London: Longmans Green, 1875), p. 417.

[16] T. Blackwell, *An Enquiry into the Life and Writings of Homer* (2nd edn) (London: 1736), pp. 15–28.

[17] Ibid., pp. 300–1, 311–18, 327–8.

[18] R. Wood, *An Essay on the Original Genius and Writings of Homer* (London: T. Payne and P. Elmsly, 1775), pp. 4–5, 126–7, 177–80.

[19] Ibid., pp. 182, 216–9, 295.

[20] J. J. Winckelmann, *Reflections Concerning the Imitation of Greek Artists in Painting and Sculpture* (Glasgow: Robert Urie, 1766), pp. 5–6, 9–10, 35–6, 40, 43, 54, 61 etc.

[21] D. Macmillan, *Scottish Art 1460–1990* (Edinburgh: Mainstream, 1990), pp. 113–14. See also D Irwin, 'Gavin Hamilton: archaeologist, painter and dealer', *The Art Bulletin*, XLIV (2 June 1962), pp. 87–102.

[22] D. and F. Irwin, *Scottish Painters at Home and Abroad 1700–1900* (London: Faber, 1975), p. 101.

[23] William L. Pressly, *James Barry: The Artist as Hero* (London: Tate Gallery, 1983), pp. 52–3, 125–6.

[24] L. Hardwick, 'Convergence and divergence in reading Homer', in Emlyn-Jones, Hardwick and Purkis, *Homer*, pp. 232–4.

[25] Wilfred Owen, *Collected Letters*, ed. H. Owen and J. Bell (London: Oxford University Press, 1967), p. 591.

[26] Illustration to Hardwick, 'Convergence and divergence', p. 148.

[27] English Association, *Poems of To-Day: First and Second Series* (London: Sidgwick & Jackson, 1930), pp. 26–7.

[28] D. F. McGilp, 'Should we forget', *Press and Journal*, 9 November 1973.

[29] S. Maclean, *From Wood to Ridge: Collected Poems* (Manchester: Carcanet, 1989), pp. 209–11.

30 M. Gorky, *Reminiscences of Tolstoy*, tr. S. S. Koteliansky and L. Woolf (London: Hogarth Press, 1934), p. 57.
31 Maclean, *From Wood to Ridge*, pp. 211–12.
32 Homer, *Iliad*, tr. Lattimore, Book 24, p. 488.
33 Homer, *Iliad*, tr. Pope, Book 24, p. 476.

T. E. *Lawrence's* Seven Pillars of Wisdom

1

Seven Pillars of Wisdom is one of the major statements about the fighting experience of the First World War. But there is no doubt that what placed Lawrence himself, and then, in 1926–7, the abridged version of *Seven Pillars* published as *Revolt in the Desert*, so brightly in the public eye was the fact that his war seemed to be utterly different from the massacres in the mud which had characterized the Western Front. Britain, though getting off more lightly than Germany and France, had lost nearly three-quarters of a million young men, most of them in conditions like those so vividly evoked in the poetry of Owen and Rosenberg. There were lots of VCs, but in France and Flanders no epic heroes. Now here was a young man who had survived a sequence of campaigns which recalled the Peninsular feats of Wellington and his zesty officers, and the schoolboy sagas of *Boy's Own Paper* and G. A. Henty.

Dressed in beautiful, flowing, white Arab dress, with the golden dagger which proclaimed him an adopted *sherif*, descendant of the Prophet, Thomas Edward Lawrence had cantered on his camel through the clean air of limitless-seeming deserts. Unlike the Western Front, his had been a war of constant movement. He appeared to have proved, in spectacular fashion, that the British, uneasily aware that the USA and Germany had outstripped their country economically, deserved to hold the largest empire the world had ever seen because of the trust which they inspired in other races. For those who believed his tale, leading 'his' insurgent Arabs, united by him as no native could have achieved, over hundreds of rough miles to the capture of Damascus, Lawrence might have epitomized the spirit of the 'indirect rule' which the British practised in much of Africa and Asia. The wise and selfless Briton, ideally, advised a legitimate native ruler to the benefit of the latter and his people. If few Britons knew enough about the Empire to grasp this point fully, everyone could thrill to an exciting story.

It was told, with the help of moving pictures and the band of the Welsh Guards, to perhaps a million theatregoers in London, in 1919–20, by the American journalist Lowell Thomas, who packed out first the Royal Opera House then the even larger Albert Hall with his slide-lecture-cum-dramatic extravaganza. Before Lawrence insisted on withdrawing it from sale, for typically complicated reasons, *Revolt in the Desert* sold 30,000 copies in a few weeks in Britain – and 120,000 in the USA. It was replaced in the market by a hastily written biography, *Lawrence and the Arabs,* compiled by a friend of the hero, the poet Robert Graves. This was soon going at the rate of 10,000 copies a week. *Seven Pillars* had meanwhile circulated only in a very limited edition – four hundred expensively produced and lavishly illustrated copies for subscribers – and was already so valued that Graves, when hard up, had been able to sell his copy for over £300, the equivalent then of a year's middle-class income. When a popular edition came out very soon after Lawrence's mysterious death in a motorcycle accident in 1935, that too was an immediate best-seller, and the book has never since been out of print.

If at first Lawrence's story compelled the imagination because it seemed to transcend the grimness of an epoch of trench warfare and class warfare (the General Strike immediately preceded serialization of *Revolt in the Desert* in the conservative *Daily Telegraph*), we can now see *Seven Pillars* as quintessentially a product of the years 1919–26, in which Lawrence worked on it, for two reasons.

First, the text speaks of what it does not speak about: the losses on the Western Front. It is astonishing that commentator after commentator puzzling over the roots of Lawrence's guilt and self-loathing – which are given full expression in the complete text of *Seven Pillars* – fails to consider the impact on him of the deaths of his younger brothers, Frank and Will, on the Western Front in 1915. Nor can he have been insensitive to the passing of other young men whom he had known as schoolboy and student in Oxford. Survivors of a great disaster commonly experience guilt. Others had been taken – 'Ted' or 'Ned' Lawrence had been spared, to confront the possessiveness of a grieved mother.

There were other losses not related to the war which conditioned the gloom which invades Lawrence's desert romance. In September 1918, as Lawrence stood poised to enter Damascus at last, Salim Ahmed died, probably from typhus, at Karkamis in Syria, the place where Lawrence had organized an important archaeological dig before the war. 'Dahouin', as Lawrence called him, is the 'S.A.' of the dedicatory poem which introduces *Seven Pillars*. He had been Lawrence's young servant, and more, the most enjoyable companion of his life. Then, in April

1919, while Colonel Lawrence, CB, DSO, was in Paris aiding 'his' Arabs at the Peace Conference, his father was swept away in the great 'flu epidemic: also Thomas, but really, as Lawrence knew, Sir Thomas Edward Chapman, Bt., last of an old Irish line, who had lived 'in sin' with Lawrence's Scottish mother – a former servant, herself illegitimate – and could not pass his title on either to one of his daughters by his legal marriage, or to the oldest of his five illegitimate sons. (Ned was the second.) His father's change of name and decades of imposture, the bizarre discrepancy between his mother's true position and her strict Evangelical piety, and a frustrated sense of his own by-rights aristocracy, all help to explain complex patterns of self-dramatization, deceit and self-doubt in the 'English' Lawrence's literary masterpiece, as in his life.

But the national, indeed imperial, tragedy of the Western Front trenches is, as it were, the overarching absence in *Seven Pillars*. Early readers would probably think of 'S.A.' as a dead British soldier. The book, after so much free desert air – scalding or drenching, often, but free of gas and 'whizzbangs' – ends in a Flanders-like welter of stink amid corpses. Those who have accused Lawrence of lack of proper compassion for his Turkish adversaries (they include his recent, excellent biographer Lawrence James) should reconsider that penultimate passage in the 'hospital' in Damascus where Lawrence finds the Turkish sick, dead and dying with no medical assistance:

> The stone floor was covered with dead bodies . . . A few were corpses nearly fresh, perhaps only a day or two old; others must have been there for long. Of some the flesh, going putrid, was yellow and blue and black. Many were already swollen twice or thrice life-width, their fat heads laughing with black mouth across jaws harsh with stubble. Of others the softer parts were fallen in. A few had burst open, and were liquescent with decay.
>
> Beyond was the vista of a great room, from which I thought I heard a groan. I trod over to it, across the soft mat of bodies, whose clothing, yellow with dung, crackled drily under me . . .

This hideous carpet, and the liquid excrement puddling the floor of the 'great room' where sufferers from dysentery and typhoid are yet living, counterpart the corpse-strewn mud of the Western Front, from which Wilfred Owen had written of feet 'sore on the alleys cobbled with our brothers'. Terrible things have happened through the book. Lawrence has described Turkish atrocities and has been unable – or, one has to say, unwilling – entirely to gloss over the savage behaviour of his Bedouin allies on the rampage for loot or revenge. Aerial bombardment has visited the desert, with results foreshadowing the greater carnage of Guernica, Hamburg and Hiroshima. Whereas *Revolt in the Desert* ends on an upbeat – 'The clamour hushed, as every one seemed to obey the call to prayer on this their first night of perfect freedom' – *Seven Pillars* concludes with the Arab-garbed Lawrence, after he has done his best to clear up the 'hospital', being smacked in the face for his pains by an Australian medical officer who considers him the author of a situation which remains scandalous; then, after Feisal has been cheered into the city where he will before long reign as king, asking his commander, Allenby, for 'leave to go away', at odds with himself as ever, haunted by horror. The 'charnel house' hospital, though its victims are not necessarily 'casualties', gathers to a head all the intimations of disgust in life and dehumanization in death, which the preceding narrative has contained. This is not how exciting stories for boys, or escapist fantasies for adults, are allowed to end. It is as if Lawrence is claiming, for his own Passion in Arabia, some equivalence of moral status to those of his brothers, of the dead Owen, of his living friend Graves, on the Western Front.

The second respect in which *Seven Pillars* is of its time is its manifest Modernism. More obviously than his namesake D. H., who has often been claimed for Modernism, T. E. Lawrence wrote experimental prose and developed a narrative voice of extreme complexity. Though his admirer Graves came to voice an aversion to what now seems to be the mainstream of Modernism, Lawrence, very widely and deeply read, was open to all the influences affecting the heyday of Modernism in the English-speaking countries, and the observer who compared the effect of the brightly vari-coloured attire of his Arab bodyguard to Diaghilev's Russian Ballet may have been making a more substantial point than he imagined. (Though Lawrence's favourite composer, later, was Elgar, that great man's own threnody for the war dead, his cello concerto of 1919, was initially greeted with incomprehension.) Lawrence had enthused over the seminal poetry of Ezra Pound before the war, and his poem to 'S.A.' is an attempt at Modernist free verse. He shared an interest in Nietzsche with Yeats, and in Dostoevsky with MacDiarmid. The *Telegraph* readers who bought his book and imagined that Lawrence epitomized English leadership at its youthful best would mostly have recoiled from the idea that they were handling what is in effect the largest single contribution by an 'Englishman' to the movement of Modernism in English. (This is not to underestimate the achievement of an English woman, Virginia Woolf.) But the format of the subscribers' edition of *Seven Pillars* advertised its modernity, not least in the Pound-wise way it alluded heavily to the illuminated manuscripts of the Middle Ages. Lawrence (who spent a prodigious sum on the edition) commissioned illustrations from Modernist artists – Paul Nash, William Roberts, Eric Kennington. Renaissance traditions of fine printing were married with cubist and abstract imagery.

'Englishman' is in inverted commas because there has to be an element of self-conscious construction in the professed 'Englishness' of someone born in Wales to an Irish father and a Scottish mother. But Lawrence was more 'English' than the Pole Conrad, who died, mourned by avant-garde spirits, before the gestation of *Seven Pillars* was quite complete, and whose *Heart of Darkness* (1898) may be discerned as an element in its fabrication: one of the Lawrence voices is surely that of a Kurtz, a 'hollow man' enslaved in consciousness by the natives whom he has enthralled, unable to live with integrity in terms of Europe's self-proclaimed Civilizing Mission.

With Eliot's *The Waste Land* (1922), and its successor poem *The Hollow Men* (1925), Lawrence would have found much in common – indeed he wrote to a friend in December 1925, after reading Eliot's *Collected Poems,* that he was 'the most important poet alive'. He shared with the American a horror of the flesh, a deep repulsion from female sexuality. That the war had expressed a crisis in European civilization was understood by all early readers to be the concealed subject of *The Waste Land.* The poem, however ironically, represented a Grail-quest, eventually sublimated in a kind of oriental enlightenment, whereas in Lawrence's book Damascus is a surrogate Grail, which yields not redemption but perspectives of opportunist politicians and rotting Turkish soldiers.

The Irish poet Yeats had hardened his muse into Modernism in middle age, partly under Pound's influence, and his great sequences 'Nineteen Hundred and Nineteen' and 'Meditation in Time of Civil War', as well as other poems of the period from 1916 through the 1920s, powerfully express the attractions and penalties of violence at a point when Irish Home Rule was being achieved and nationalist allies were falling out. Like Eliot, Yeats generated images of purification and withdrawal from the world's corruptions, which were related to Lawrence's spiritual preoccupations: he wrote to a literary friend in 1931 that he thought Yeats's later poems 'wonderful'. With the *Ulysses* of James Joyce (1922), riotously carnal, chattily secular and up to date, it might seem that Lawrence's vision had nothing in common, until one remembers that he carried the *Odyssey*, along with Malory's *Morte*

D'Arthur, around the desert with him, and eventually translated Homer's epic (1932). Furthermore, he was self-consciously operating, like Joyce, on the frontiers of English expression. He commented ruefully before his limited edition of *Seven Pillars* was published that 'to bring it out after *Ulysses* is an insult to modern letters'.

On a more trivial level, his pranks and postures, both as writer and social creature, bring him strangely close at times to the flashy Modernism of the Sitwells – indeed, one can imagine Lawrence, the pseudo-Arabian dandy, featuring as a figment in Edith Sitwell's *Façade,* along with her 'allegro Negro cocktail shaker'. The very title of *Seven Pillars of Wisdom* should alert us to its Modernist character. It is wonderfully sonorous, unforgettable and, 'means' nothing, insofar as not a single passage in the text relates to it or serves to explain it. It just happened to be the title of a work of fiction which Lawrence had penned as what he later called a 'youthful indiscretion' and had burnt, incomplete, in November 1914, just before he joined the army. Such teasing – as in Eliot's notorious notes to *The Waste Land* and C. M. Grieve's reviews of the poetry of his alter ego, MacDiarmid – is definitive of the Modernist moment, the deep rejection of those sturdy, blinkered bourgeois values which had brought about the tragedy of the trenches. Lawrence's parents, as he had known since about the age of ten, had lived a lie of bourgeois respectability.

Equally characteristic of Modernism is the mixture, parodying and blurring of genres. We can now see *Seven Pillars* as a vast (and, it must be admitted, uneven) Modernist experiment. But the title suggests a philosophical meditation following the precedent of Nietzsche's *Thus Spake Zarathustra,* and a reader entering the book with that expectation would find certain chapters meeting it. It soon transpires, though, that *Seven Pillars* will offer ethnographic and topographical information much in the manner of a travel book – the most notable precedent being Charles M. Doughty's *Travels in Arabia Deserta,* an account of lone journeying in the 1870s, republished in 1921 with an enthusiastic foreword by its devout admirer, Lawrence. The narrative implicitly alludes, as it continues, to two old narrative forms, epic and romance. But most readers would have expected – most readers perhaps still expect – a 'true' or would-be true historical account of very important events from the point of view of a significant participant. On events in themselves exciting, the narrator brings to bear a wide historical perspective, and this can be read as an especially 'true' form of historiography – not the work of a dry-as-dust scholar moling his way through archives, but a vivid account by a wise man who was there. The most massive twentieth-century example of this genre would be produced by a hero-worshipper of Lawrence, Winston Churchill, in the form of a multi-volume history of the Second World War. Because controversy about *Seven Pillars* since 1955, when Richard Aldington published his indignantly debunking biography of Lawrence, has revolved not around the book's literary character and merits, but its many distortions of and inaccuracies about 'historical fact', it is best to get that matter clarified before returning to literary considerations.

2

Thomas Edward Lawrence, born in 1888, took a first-class degree in history at Oxford University. His initial interest in the Middle East, which he visited as a lone undergraduate, was in the castles of the Crusaders, European intruders into the Semitic world. As what we would now call a 'graduate student', at the ancient Hittite site of Karkamis, he later developed his skills as a leader of Middle Eastern people as the organizer, under academic seniors, of scores of labourers on the dig. He also worked more briefly in Egypt and Sinai. So when war broke out he was an obvious person to receive a commission as an officer in intelligence attached to the British GHQ in Cairo, centre of planning for the eastern war against the Turkish Empire, which had allied itself with Germany. Despite his eccentricities (which included not drinking alcohol, and holding socially aloof from most of the city's British community), he proved a significant asset. Whatever else may be controversial about Lawrence, there is no doubt that he had an acute mind and a great deal of practical ability, both organizational and, as it would prove, technical. He was clever at gathering 'intelligence', understood men of all nationalities quickly, and had an equally swift insight into the machines which made modern warfare very different from the combats of the Crusaders. For all his scholarly habits, and his basic ambition to be somehow a creative writer, he was more than a match in their own territory for most of the serious soldiers he had to deal with.

The British had blundered into trouble in Mesopotamia. A large force pushing north from Basra were besieged by the Turks in the town of Kut from December 1915. Attempts to relieve them failed. Lawrence was sent to Mesopotamia in April 1916 on a mission somehow to turn round the loyalties of disgruntled Arabs serving in the army of their Ottoman overlords. But this was not feasible, and while he was in the country, Kut fell, so that thousands of British and Indian prisoners passed into Turkish hands. The war was stalemated on the Western Front, and in the east the attempt to force a way to the Bosphorus through Gallipoli had failed disastrously. Under these circumstances, it seemed sensible to encourage the Arab revolt against Ottoman rule launched by Hussain, the Sherif of Mecca. His control of the Holy City of Islam conferred prestige on this descendant of Mohammed, and his four sons, trained in Western ideas, but also reared among Bedouin in the hinterland, might have the capacity to direct a serious revolt. Lawrence arrived in the Hejaz in October 1916. Despite his assertion in *Seven Pillars* that he attached himself to Ronald Storrs's mission on his own initiative when purportedly on leave, the truth was that he had an official remit, to collect intelligence about the Arab revolt, which after more than four months seemed to be getting nowhere. The extraordinary narrative of *Seven Pillars* – and the controversies surrounding it – begin there. Reading Lawrence's enormous book, it is hard to believe that his involvement with the revolt lasted only two years.

We can move from grand to little areas of controversy. First of all, was the Middle Eastern campaign merely a 'sideshow', as detractors of Lawrence have claimed? Yes and no. It is true that the Germans had to be beaten on the Western Front before the Allies ranged against them could claim victory. It is also true that, especially after the Russian Empire collapsed with the revolution of 1917, British statesmen worried desperately about the threat which the Germans, with and through their Ottoman allies, posed to the Suez Canal, the oil supplies of Mesopotamia – the Royal Navy had converted to oil in 1913 – and above all the Indian Empire. With the war going badly in both west and east, and fears that the French army would disintegrate, there was serious talk at the highest level of detaching in the west and concentrating, eastward, on imperial defence. India was economically vital to Britain, and its large army, sustained by Indian taxpayers, was the force which, along with the Royal Navy, enabled Britain to control the rest of its vast and heterogeneous empire. The Suez Canal was the means of passage to India, and a British army, under first Murray then Lawrence's hero Allenby, was grimly, if for a long time ingloriously, committed to defending it.

There was an important sub-plot involving the French, who had their own interest in the possible fragmentation of the Ottoman power. In 1916, the so-called 'Sykes-Picot' agreement between the British and French Foreign Offices divided the Middle East. The French would control as a 'protectorate' a swathe from the Lebanese coast through

Syria up into south-eastern Turkey and across to the upper waters of the Tigris and Euphrates. The British would have southern Meso- potamia. The position of Palestine would be determined by some form of international negotiation. The other Arab lands, mostly arid, would be under independent Arab control, though both Britain and France would have 'spheres of influence' in the north of the region. On this basis, the British were not wholly dishonest in flattering the Arab nationalist (or, rather, Hashemite-dynastic) dreams of Hussain and his sons. But Lawrence, fiercely anti-French, wanted Syria for the Arabs. Though Lawrence knew that Hussain in the Arabian Peninsula had a serious rival in ibn Saud, whose hegemony centred on Riyadh to the east of Mecca and who, by the mid-1920s, would prevail, his 'Arab nationalist' cause was, and would remain after the war, the Hashemite or 'Sherifian' cause. Indeed, it would be through his influence over Churchill, who brought him into the Colonial Office as adviser for a spell in 1921–2, that Feisal, extruded from rule in Syria, became king of Iraq and his brother Abdullah ruler of Trans-Jordan.

Allenby's successful push into Syria coincided with a turnaround at last in the Allies' favour in the west. For weeks in 1918, the German General Ludendorff's brilliant offensive had threatened to destroy France. But in the summer there was a French counter-offensive directed by Marshal Foch (whose military theories are a point of reference in *Seven Pillars*), and then, in September, the Germans broke in face of a determined assault by the British under Haig. The war ended suddenly, taking statesmen by surprise, and this was immensely to the short-term advantage of the British Empire, which could now consolidate its position as the main power in the Middle East, while the huge American army destined for the Western Front would not be in a position to win the war and dictate terms to Europe. The capture of Damascus, like Haig's success, seemed to show Britain still to be on top of the world.

Granted that serious issues were at stake in the Middle Eastern theatre, was the guerrilla-style desert warfare in which Lawrence engaged not just a sideshow beside the heavy push northwards, when it finally came in 1918, of Allenby's army? Lawrence's silly boast in *Seven Pillars* that he had personally blown up seventy-nine bridges, when in fact his tally was twenty-three, is an unimportant matter compared to the question: did blowing up bridges make any difference? The aim was to put pressure on the Turks to defend communications with Medina, where the line ended. The Turks were pestered, but not discomposed. Their army was well supplied with experts in railway repair, and there was an abundance of spare rails in Medina itself, assembled for a line to Mecca which had never been built. Pro-Turkish, or merely opportunistic, locals were always happy to sell food to the Medina garrison. Other Bedouin, who resented the railway because it had deprived them of a lucrative role in escorting pilgrim traffic southward, would certainly have harried the line without any encouragement from Feisal and Lawrence. However, high explosive was a bonus, and the capacity of Lawrence to rally locals on Feisal's side did put the Turks constantly on guard in a hostile 'countryside'.

Did the recruitment of local support depend, as the legend would have it, on Lawrence's personal diplomacy and magnetism? His charm, and his grasp of nuances in Bedouin life, must indeed have been useful. But the magnet which drew men to him was, frankly, money. At a time of considerable economic difficulty for the Bedouin, British gold was irresistible, and Lawrence had plenty of it to use at his own discretion. Furthermore, British efficiency in blowing up locomotives and capturing stations offered splendid chances of rich loot for those who tagged along with Lawrence. Loot secured, the clansmen headed off home. Read carefully, *Seven Pillars* does not ignore these factors. But they are swept under tides of rhetoric suggesting that Feisal's irregulars were 'preached' by Lawrence into disinterested support for the nationalist cause.

Whether or not Lawrence is 'accurate' in his account of this engagement or that is a relatively unimportant matter. Aldington, matching *Seven Pillars* against official histories, was an innocent writing two decades before John Keegan's masterly *Face of Battle* (1976) brought home to historians the point, which now seems obvious, that tidied up official reports of warfare, commonly a confused business, especially on modern battlefields, are most unlikely to deliver truth. If Lawrence's descriptions are plausible – and many soldiers have deemed them so – they do represent general 'truths' about conditions of battle.

The gravest charge against Lawrence is that in the interests of promoting his Hashemite-nationalist cause, he exaggerated the potency of 'his' Bedouin as auxiliaries and minimized the contributions of other whites, not only Frenchmen who served alongside him, but also the Australians who were in fact first into Damascus. The drift of his narrative is often to isolate himself, to make singular Lawrence the mainspring of the revolt and its momentum, whereas in fact he was always a British officer dependent on the goodwill of his superiors not only for the gold which sinewed 'his' war, but for the supplies, explosives, armoured cars and air support which made possible such successes as the revolt achieved.

Lawrence's general unreliability is clinched by the fact that we now know that the most dramatic single episode in *Seven Pillars* – our hero's flogging and sodomization in Deraa – simply cannot have happened. The dates given do not square with Lawrence's known movements. The Turkish governor who allegedly desired him was in real life, it seems, a notorious womanizer. It is incredible, sodomy or no sodomy, that such a person, in possession of a fair-skinned man at a time when there was a price on the head not only of Lawrence but of all stray Allied officers behind Turkish lines, would have let him escape quickly and easily. In any case, the most naive reader is likely to suspect the story because, after fearful lashings and beating, in a terrain where wounds do not heal easily, Lawrence is up and running, apparently fit as a flea, so quickly. Elsewhere he makes a great deal of his ailments; yet his lacerated back does not seem to bother him. We accept in movies that Humphrey Bogart's Philip Marlowe (for instance) may be beaten up heavily, after battering his own constitution with raw whisky, and still be capable of rapid calculation and activity. The Deraa episode is not inadmissible as art – it is a powerful piece of writing. But 'history' it certainly is not. It is a masochistic fantasy developed, perhaps unsuccessfully, for ideological and structural effect.

It prompts, however, a digression here about Lawrence's sexuality. If homosexual, it seems he was only latently so. His horror of physical contact with other people – of either sex – is as well documented as is his pathological misogyny. He certainly employed young men on a regular basis to flog him to the point of orgasm after the war, when he submerged himself in the RAF under the pseudonym, first of 'Ross', then of 'Shaw'. But masochism is not a specifically homosexual trait. As for the references to sex in *Seven Pillars*, they make Lawrence's crazy aversion to the idea that we are born from the bodies of women clear enough, and also his tolerance of Bedouin homosexuality. Idealization of male comradeship is prevalent. But the bourgeois British sent their sons to boarding schools where such idealization was institutionalized, and homosexual practises were not infrequent. The ancient Greeks, extolled as models of athleticism and nobility of mind, whose works were regarded as formative and fundamental in the higher reaches of education, had seen nothing wrong with homosexual love. The use which Lawrence makes of what might now seem homoerotic nuances (more than nuance in the case of Daud and Farraj, the two mischievous boy servants who are devoted to each other) was hardly extreme by the standards of Oxford and the British Establishment.

Amongst imperial heroes of the time, General Gordon, Baden Powell and Lord Kitchener had all been interested in boys. The one hero who had suffered for such interests was General Sir Hector MacDonald, 'Fighting Mac', who had committed suicide rather than face court martial for interfering with boys in Ceylon. But then, MacDonald was a crofter's son, risen from the ranks by merit, and other ranks, without the advantages of elite education, clearly could not put the correct Grecian gloss on their doings, which were therefore sinful rather than understandable. It is an immense point in Lawrence's favour that, having been awarded the CB and DSO, he refused his honours at the very moment when George V was about to confer them on him at Buckingham Palace, because, he said, they came from a government which had betrayed the Arabs; and before long he re-entered the king's service in the RAF at the bottom, where he was appalled by the coarse sex-talk of his low-born comrades, yet contrived to find virtues in these men, as they in him.

Richard Meinertzhagen gets approving mention in *Seven Pillars* as a cunning British political officer. Lawrence met him in Palestine in 1917, then again at the Paris Peace Conference. Lawrence was working on *Seven Pillars* and, in July 1919, showed him what he had written so far. Three days later, he turned up in his friend's room in a state of intense worry. 'He surprised me', Meinertzhagen wrote in his diary, 'by saying that little of his book was strict truth, though most of it was based on fact . . . He hated fakes, but had been involved in a huge lie – "imprisoned in a lie" was his expression – and . . . his friends and admirers intended to keep him there. He was now fighting between limelight and utter darkness.' He went on to confess his illegitimacy and his rape by Turks. That the latter had not happened suggests that Lawrence used the anecdote as a way of alerting others to his awkward sexual identity, a potential embarrassment to those who had made him a colonel and were boosting his heroic reputation.

One way of explaining his invention of the Deraa episode might be that it was a device for challenging the flatulent and hypocritical conceptions of all-male heroism to which Establishment and press would wish him to conform. 'Look – I have been buggered – I am unclean. Can't you see what fools you are, by your own professed standards of Church morality, to make an idol out of me?' Alternatively, of course, it could be argued that Lawrence is stoking up hatred against the Turks, helping to justify callous treatment of them – Lawrence James goes so far as to speak of 'war crimes' – by his Arab auxiliaries during the final push to Damascus. Like any large and powerful work of literature, *Seven Pillars* can sustain many interpretations.

3

Is the book a modern counterpart of medieval romance? Lawrence certainly went to war with a head full of such writings, but where the spirit of Malory prevails is in ironic melancholy. Malory's book after all is called 'The Death of Arthur'. Treachery undermines the king. The fellowship of the Round Table is finished. Lawrence was in touch with the group of devout imperialists, led by Milner, proconsul of South Africa, who produced a journal called *Round Table,* to which he contributed. That he did so suits the arguments of those who see him as essentially a committed agent of empire. He indeed acted that part on occasions, but no careful reader of *Seven Pillars* can doubt that the literary man inside him found Arthurian parallels deeply ironic. Besides, the scale and intellectual range of *Seven Pillars* go way beyond romance. It is a modern version of epic.

The epic of Homer which Lawrence chose to carry on his campaign was the *Odyssey. Seven Pillars* resembles that work only insofar as its protagonist steers through great difficulties towards a goal reached at last. But Damascus is certainly not like Ithaca, not Lawrence's home, and no Penelope awaits him there. *Seven Pillars* has much more in common with the *Iliad.*

Those who hear or read epic know the end of the tale already. There is no suspense. Achilles will kill Hector. Lawrence will enter Damascus. The strong feelings aroused by epic derive from detail of various kinds. One kind is found in catalogues of combatants. Lawrence confronts us with a stupendous number of Arab proper names, often bringing in this man or that as if we must have heard of him already, when we have not. If his primary aim had been to communicate historical fact about the revolt, he would have offered more ethnographic information and commissioned elaborate maps rather than expensive illustrations. A fully annotated edition of *Seven Pillars* would show us clearly patterns of activity among the desert clans, and pinpoint how Lawrence deploys and no doubt distorts them in his narrative. In the absence of such information his roll-calls are merely, but potently, suggestive:

In the afternoon Nuri Shalaan appeared, with Trad and Khalid, Faris, Durzi, and the Khaffaji. Auda abu Tayi arrived, with Mohammed el Dheilan; also Fahad and Adhub, the Zebn leaders, with ibn Bani, the chief of the Serahin, and ibn Genj of the Serdiyeh. Majid ibn Sultan, of the Adwan near Salt, rode across to learn the truth of our attack on Amman. Later in the evening there was a rattle of rifle fire in the north, and Talal el

Hareidhin, my old companion, came ruffling at the gallop, with forty or fifty mounted peasants behind him . . .

The impression is conveyed of a whole people excitedly in arms for the cause – ironically, at a moment when Lawrence himself is sick of it. There are similar accumulations of British names – 'In Cairo were Hogarth and George Lloyd and Storrs and Deedes' – likewise working to create an epic effect of momentous multitudinousness.

Detail superfluous to 'history', as that is conventionally written, is essential to epic. It generates a sense that the whole of life is somehow present and accounted for. Lawrence, as he makes clear more than once, kept a diary in the desert. If we believe his story, that he lost the first MS draft of *Seven Pillars*, together with most of his notes, at Reading railway station – and Robert Graves, for one, did not – then either his memory was supernaturally exact or he exercised imagination as freely as any fiction writer. However come by, we have smells smelt, water tasted, food eaten, wayfarers glimpsed. We learn an immense amount about the behaviour of camels in general, and also about that of particular beasts at particular moments. The most appealing strength of *Seven Pillars* is the way, when violent action comes along, Lawrence can integrate the knowledge he has given us, the sense impressions with which he has infected us, into narrative so vivid that it is as if we had been there.

But the most imposing arrays of detail relate to the hardest parts of the landscape. One way of justifying the minuteness with which Lawrence describes desert rocks could be to say the struggle of the reader to visualize what is presented matches the struggle of man and camel crossing them. But a reader not prepared to make the full effort will be left with a general sense of barren grandeur suitable to Lawrence's purposes. He wanted to write a 'titanic' book, and the naming of so many stones in itself creates an impression of titanism.

Another admirer of C. M. Doughty, Hugh MacDiarmid, began his great poem of the 1930s, 'On a Raised Beach', with a deliberately forbidding battery of stone-words:

> All is lithogenesis – or lochia,
> Carpolite fruit of the forbidden tree,
> Stones blacker than any in the Caaba,
> Cream-coloured caen-stone, chatoyant pieces . . .

and so on for twenty more lines before the poem's argument commences. The poem deals with life and consciousness on the edge, at the extreme, confronted with the obdurate persistence of stony matter in nature, contrasting that with human impermanence. ('There are plenty of ruined buildings in the world but no ruined stones.') Intention and effect owe a lot to Doughty, as a passage from *Arabia Deserta* will show. It will also illustrate Doughty's unique style, marked by punctuation which seems quite arbitrary, though the author may have had some secret system:

> Mild was the summer day's heat in all this Harra height, here 5000 feet above the sea level: the rarity of the air, was our shelter from the extremity of the sun, which now shone upon us only in friendly wise. We felt a light wafting breath in the higher denes; a tepid air streamed at large over this vast headland of the mountain. Somewhere in the lava soil we see yellowish loamy earth under the loose stones, tufa on it might be burned chalk-rock, which upon this Harra lies in few scales above the deep sandstone; and I have found it singed to ochre by the old lava's over-streaming. Such Harra land is more often a vast bed and banks of rusty and basaltic bluish blocks (*dims, róthm*, which after their crystalline nature are rhomboid;) stubborn heavy, as iron, and sounding like bell-metal: lying out eternally under the sand-driving desert wind, they are seen polished and shining in the sun . . . This Titanic desolation, seeming in our eyes as if it could not bear life, is good Beduin ground.

Reviewers of *Revolt in the Desert* commonly detected the influence of Doughty on Lawrence's style, though, as he himself privately protested, he eschewed Doughty's 'Scandinavian' syntax and recondite, archaic vocabulary. He rose to the challenge of out-Doughtying Doughty in the precision of his geological descriptions. The result is 'epic' writing of a peculiar kind: the Lawrentian protagonist is pitched against a titanic natural environment which is home to the Bedouin but deeply foreign to Europeans. One of Lawrence's voices in *Seven Pillars* exults over the wilderness; another yearns for the green fields of England.

4

It is easy to find in this complex book material to 'prove' that Lawrence was straightforwardly a racist. It is not just that his patience with the Arabs is often on the point of running out – even when he speaks lovingly of them, it is in racist terms categorizing, generalizing, demoting. To define his position more subtly, one might say that he is a prime instance of 'orientalism', the ideological vice which involves accepting, or constructing, an image of the oriental as opposite in every respect to Europeans whose European-ness is therefore defined as the negative of this presumed obverse. 'Orientalism' spawns pseudo-knowledge. After less than ten years amongst oriental people, Lawrence feels entitled to generalize authoritatively about them. His readers will believe him because he confirms their prejudices.

Lawrence's opinions about the Arabs were not simply, or even primarily, the result of direct observation. He was heavily conditioned by the views of Doughty, and another personal mentor, Wilfred Scawen Blunt. As Kathryn Tidrick has shown sharply in her study of British writers about *Heart Beguiling Araby* (1989), such key ideas as preference for the unspoilt Bedouin over the sophisticated, westernized Arab town-dweller, and belief that the Sherifians of Mecca were the right and natural leaders of the Arabs, came to Lawrence from these old men and their writings. A romantic Tory paternalism can be seen as Lawrence's base position, from which he despised modern bureaucracy and the corruptions of the modern, commercialized, high-technology western way of life.

But this is in fact the position taken by only one of the Lawrences present in the *Seven Pillars*. There is another Lawrence who delights in being driven round in a Rolls armoured car, is enchanted by the valour and success of a British pilot in a dogfight over the advance to Damascus, and sees that city, with all its modern ways, as the proper capital for an Arab state. There is a Lawrence conscious of more than one Lawrence within himself, along with Lawrences who are, on the one hand, wholeheartedly 'Arab', and on the other proudly and very self-consciously 'English'. There is a near-pacifist Lawrence wholly averse to killing, and a Lawrence who is cynically 'realistic' about massacring Turks. Shifts in style register moves from one Lawrentian identity to another. We have at one extreme the opaque, pretentious and often incomprehensible Nietzschean brooder, at the other the author of clean, sharp prose describing action and providing humorous accounts of Bedouin eating habits. The use of personae – masks – is a conscious device in Pound and Yeats and Eliot, permitting the expression of diverse and even contradictory points of view by the same author. One of the Lawrences sees himself as a play actor, and tells us so, but in fact all the Lawrences are acting parts. The text does not impose a single view – orientalist, imperialist, nostalgic or 'modern' – on us.

The use of 'we', 'our' and 'ourselves' in *Seven Pillars* is worth careful attention. The connotations of these simple words are extremely volatile. They often imply Lawrence's 'modest' wish to emphasize that he did not scheme and act alone. Thus in Chapter VI, 'We were not many; and nearly all of us rallied round Clayton . . .' 'We' here embraces the pro-Sherifians in British military circles in Cairo. By Chapter XV, after Lawrence has met Feisal, that straightforward British 'we' is expanding. 'We had let loose a passion of anti-Turkish feeling': this 'we' may – it should – include Feisal, his father and his brothers. By Chapter XX Lawrence, at Feisal's request, has assumed Arab dress. The 'we' who now improve the defences of Yenbo seem to include not only the British advisers, but the Egyptian troops and Feisal's Arabs. The 'we' who fill 'the valley to its banks with our flashing stream' in Chapter XXIII must be the whole of Feisal's force on the march, and the 'we' who form a 'merry party' in Chapter XXIV are all, bar Lawrence himself, Arab leaders.

But early in Chapter XXXII the words 'my' and 'us' imply in different ways a distance between Lawrence and his Arab comrades. When he talks about 'my Ageyl' he implies that he is uniquely, specially, paternally, the leader of these clansmen. When he avers that after a tricky ride 'the view from the crest compensated us', the 'us' seems 'royal', as in Queen Victoria's 'We are not amused.' Here and elsewhere Lawrence may seem to impute to Arabs his own feelings of awe at and delight in their terrain. Since he has absolutely no warrant for this, and mentions no equally sensitive British companion beside him, 'us' must be read as an aggrandizement of 'me'. 'For us', we are told in Chapter XLI, 'the rock shapes were constant speculation and astonishment.' Yet we learn in the next paragraph that Lawrence is riding beside the rugged old Bedouin warrior Auda, unlikely to be astonished by a landscape he probably takes for granted. Is this 'us' perhaps closely related to the 'we' of tourist guidebooks – 'Entering the church we see to our left . . .'? Does this 'we' include Lawrence's readers? In that case, in Chapter XLIII Auda denies 'us' the chance to enter the 'Great Nephud, the famous belts of sand-dune which cut off Jebel Shammar from the Syrian Desert', crossed by 'Palgrave, the Blunts and Gertrude Bell amongst the storied travellers'. Auda will not divert his march to serve Lawrence's touristical whim, growling that men only go to the Nephud 'of necessity, when raiding'. Reporting (or inventing) this, Lawrence comically subverts the cult of the Arabian picturesque which many of his passages staunchly serve.

It might also be taken to subvert the 'we' of Chapter XLV. Lawrence is still with Bedouin irregulars. Portentously, the Lawrence of this chapter asserts that, 'The long ride in company had made companions of our minds and bodies. The hazardous goal was in our thoughts, day and night; consciously and unconsciously we were training ourselves, reducing our wills to the single purpose which oftenest engrossed these odd moments of talk about an evening fire.' This implies commitment by the likes of Auda to Lawrence's 'goal', the independent Arab kingdom. As documentation of the revolt, this seems wholly unreliable. As a pointer to obsessiveness in one of the Lawrences, it is highly interesting – since it is, of course, this Lawrence who is 'reducing his will' to a single purpose and giving insufficient weight to the primary Bedouin motivations of cash and loot.

By Chapter LXV another Lawrence, an impatient English patriot, is irritated with 'his' Bedouin, 'who would never sit down for ten minutes, but must fidget and do or say something. This defect made them very inferior to the stolid English for the long, tedious strain of a waiting war . . . Today they made us [that is, Lawrence and his English colleague Stokes] very angry.' Later, in Chapter LXXXII, with several fellow countrymen now at hand, Lawrence enjoys 'English talk and laughter round the fire', over bully-beef and tea. 'For me it was a holiday, with not an Arab near, before whom I must play out my tedious part.' In the previous chapter, Lawrence has written explicitly of his 'divided selves' in relation to mind–body dichotomy. Politically and ideologically, also, his 'selves' are divided, and one of them believes that he shares with the Arabs, as he cannot with the British, something very important to him emotionally. The one new idea which Lawrence had about the Arabs, Kathryn Tidrick points out, was his notion that they regarded hardships as a due chastisement of the flesh, exulted in them, and shared his taste for physical degradation. It is this Lawrence, penitent, quasi-Christ, or both, who experiences fictitious flagellation in Deraa.

The last words of the narrative emphasize the theme of self-division. In Damascus, Allenby reluctantly agrees to let Lawrence go. 'And then at once I knew how much I was sorry.' Obsession with style largely explains why Lawrence put out *Seven Pillars* so slowly. He wanted to show perfected artistry and could not feel that his writing was good enough. But in relationship to the book's subject matter, his indecisiveness and restless inconsistency are virtues. What could have been merely a *Boy's Own Paper*-like tale of imperialist triumph, mock-modest but actually boastful about 'English' virtues, was saved by Modernist irony and self-subversion and bears impressive witness to human complexity. Lawrence's text could not be circumscribed by the racism and imperialism of his day, which it sometimes accepted and sometimes barged against. So it remains importantly alive – not a useful volume of historiography, not even a sound historical document, but a work of high literary aspiration which stands, as Lawrence hoped it would, in the tradition of Melville and Dostoevsky and alongside the writings of Yeats, Eliot and Joyce. One cardinal hero is perhaps Auda, the proud, angry, fighting man of the desert, unquenchably vital, essentially anarchic, a man to sing songs about. Another is certainly the manipulator of all the Lawrences, the protean author, who knows that he is not like Auda at all, not an Ahab, not Prince Hamlet (nor was meant to be), but an aesthete with a very bad conscience.

1997

Writing in the Sky: Battle of Britain Memoirs

1

A Battle of Britain fighter pilot might write a passionate, confused book about his experiences, publish it in 1942, see it become a best-seller, then within months die in a crash while training. That was Richard Hillary's *The Last Enemy* – perhaps the most celebrated memoir of the battle. Or he might make his personal story part of a carefully researched survey of the battle, beginning with its First World War antecedents, and covering the events of the summer of 1940 from many angles, with an admirable attempt at a historian's objectivity. Peter Townsend's *Duel of Eagles*, published in 1970, is that book. Or, in the aftermath of the war when his heroic stature was still taken for granted by everyone, he might let a vivid professional writer produce something between a ghost-written memoir and a fictionalized biography – this was *Reach for the Sky*, Douglas Bader's story as told by Paul Brickhill, published in 1954 and, as a notable best-seller, soon turned into a successful feature film.

But, however it came out, the tale would include dogfights. Bader's third person features in my first extract:

'Break 'em up,' yelled Bader and swept, firing, through the front rank of the bombers. He pulled up and veered behind a big Dornier turning away left, fired and fired again. A flash burst behind the Dornier's starboard engine, and flame and black smoke spewed from it. Suddenly he was nearly ramming it and broke off. Hell, aircraft of broken formations darting everywhere in the blurred and flashing confusion. In front – 400 yards away – another Dornier seeking cloud cover between the 'cu-nims'; he was catching it rapidly when his eye caught a Spitfire diving steeply above and just ahead. It happened fast. The Spitfire pilot clearly did not see the bomber under the long cowling; he dived straight into the middle of it and the Dornier in a burst of flame split and wrapped its broken wings round the fighter. Tumbling fragments glinted above the crumpled mass as the two aircraft fell in burning embrace.[1]

Is the following Hillary or Townsend?

One after the other we peeled off in a power dive. I picked out one machine and switched my gun-button to 'Fire'. At 300 yards I had him in my sights. At 200 I opened up in a long four-second burst and saw the tracer going into his nose. Then I was pulling out, so hard that I could feel my eyes dropping through my neck. The sky was now a mass of individual dog-fights. Several of them had already been knocked down. One I hoped was mine, but on pulling up I had not been able to see the result. To my left I saw Peter Pease make a head-on attack on a Messerschmitt. They were headed straight for each other and it looked as though the fire of both was striking home. Then at the last minute the Messerschmitt pulled up, taking Peter's fire full in the belly. It rolled on its back, yellow flames pouring from the cockpit, and vanished.[2]

Townsend or Hillary?

We were still climbing, trying to reach the bombers. Keep well away from those fighters! Not easy, though, with them sitting on top of us, able to strike as they pleased. Better move out towards the sun. But a dozen Me 110s now pinned us down. Every time they dived out of their defensive circle, I called, 'Leave them alone,' and wheeled the squadron towards them to shake them off our tails.

Then the inevitable – down came the Me 109s and it was each one for himself. When my Me 109 came, firing, I whipped round and caught him doing that fatal turn across my sights. Tighten the turn, nose up a little, and I had him. The Me 109 staggered, like a pheasant shot on the wing. A big piece flew off, maybe the hood. A plume of white smoke trailed. I had a split-second impression of the pilot, seemingly inert during those last dramatic moments. Then the aircraft stalled and dived to earth near Hastings.

This time I had the feeling I had killed a man, but there was no time for remorse. If it was him this time, it could be me the next. In the mounting frenzy of battle, our hearts beat faster and our efforts became more frantic. But within, fatigue was deadening feeling, numbing the spirit. Both life and death had lost their importance. Desire sharpened to a single, savage purpose – to grab the enemy and claw him down from the sky.[3]

I let Townsend, in the third extract, run on longer because, remarkably, it is the career RAF officer, a fighter pilot since 1935, not Hillary, the intellectual, the 'long-haired boy' who joined up straight from university in 1939, who describes himself as momentarily flicked by the painful apprehension that Messerschmitts carry human beings like himself and reflects that his own purpose was 'savage'. Hillary, writing far closer to the event, describes himself as rationalizing his first kill as a noble deed:

> My first emotion was one of satisfaction, satisfaction at a job adequately done, at the final, logical conclusion of months of specialised training. And then I had a feeling of the essential rightness of it all. He was dead and I was alive; it could so easily have been the other way round; and that would somehow have been right too. I realised in that moment just how lucky a fighter pilot is. He has none of the personalised emotions of the soldier, handed a rifle and bayonet and told to charge. He does not even have to share the dangerous emotions of the bomber pilot who night after night must experience that childhood longing for smashing things. The fighter pilot's emotions are those of the duellist – cool, precise, impersonal. He is privileged to kill well. For if one must either kill or be killed, as now one must, it should, I feel, be done with dignity. Death should be given the setting it deserves; it should never be a pettiness; and for the fighter pilot it never can be.[4]

Townsend applies what we are prone to think as 'normal' human criteria in ethics, and mundane compassion. Hillary is arrogantly antinomian. The fighter pilot transcends normal human criteria. 'Impersonality' is a privilege.

Commenting on this passage, the American scholar Samuel Hynes, who has surveyed Battle of Britain memoirs, generalizes that 'Hillary was right about one thing – in a fighter pilot's war, death is impersonal . . . it's not a man you kill but a machine.' This he perceives in those countless passages where it is 'it', a Dornier or Messerschmitt, which plummets blazing, not the persons or person in 'it'. Brickhill, writing for Bader, has a Dornier 'embrace' a Spitfire.[5] One might justify this usage by pointing out that incessant death did not bear much talking about and pilots were notoriously laconic about even close friends who did not return from combat, but were said to have 'gone for a Burton' (beer). Or one might conclude that Townsend's adjective 'savage' expresses quite fairly the brutalization implicit in fighter combat, and foregrounded in Derek Robinson's powerful novel *Piece of Cake*, published without public outcry and with much success in the 1980s.

Bomber planes could not be beautiful. But the main fighter planes of 1940 – especially Spitfires – had the visual appeal of clean, interesting lines while remaining human in scale, like large toys. They appealed to boys. They appealed to women. In the nature of it, several generations in Britain remembered, or grew up with, two indelible visions of the

Battle of Britain. One is from the pilot's cockpit. Film camera or prose description gives us the image of the Messerschmitt attacking, as it were, ourselves, like an immense wasp. Our paranoia is the pilot's. Our relief as the enemy hurtles blazing groundwards is his. Or, from the ground, we saw, we still see, we still imagine, the spectacle of 'our boys' *duelling* (and the title of Townsend's book impresses this notion even more strongly than Hillary's sentences of intellectualization) with equally matched adversaries above our rooftops: a gallant show, perhaps leaving behind some of those vapour trails across clear blue skies which still haunt many people whose memory falsely tells them that the weather that summer was exceptionally fine.

Whatever happened happened very quickly. A British fighter had only fourteen seconds' worth of bullets. It happened in confusion. Footballers interviewed on TV these days will often admit that they did not know how they scored this or that goal until they saw the action replays. The discrepancy on the British side between pilots' claims for kills in 1940 and actual German planes destroyed is long proven beyond a peradventure to be based on misperceptions in the heat of battle. There are obvious reasons for assuming that the somewhat sensationalist Brickhill, and Hillary, who is self-consciously writing 'literature', are not likely to be telling us *exactly* what happened. But I think even the experienced and conscientious Townsend can hardly be trusted as an exact reporter. Dogfights happened *somewhat* as writer after writer describes them. The main plot is variable, the sub-plots are numerous. But we know that dogfights happened *like that* because we have known it since we first saw it on newsreel or read about it in childhood or watched certain feature films. So we believe each writer in turn. However, so far from projecting an epic vision of individual deeds of daring, the basic plot of the dogfight assimilates each pilot with every other, and every burst of combat with every other such burst. The protagonists, contrary to what Hillary affirmed, are not men with freedom to express personal quiddities, but Spitfires, Hurricanes and those Messerschmitt cowboys of the air herding dark, sluggish cattle with udders full of death: Heinkels, Dorniers. Yet, because we believe it without question to be true, we can comfortably associate the basic plot of the dogfight with ideas of 'chivalry', duels, 'knights of the air', derived from discourses within Western culture in general and British culture in particular, originating long before humans could fly and wildly inappropriate to what actually went on over Kent and Sussex in August and September 1940. There was in fact more scope for individual self-expression, and even for chivalry, in certain phases of infantry warfare. In the air, in a fighter, it was kill or be killed – or run away. There were only those three possibilities, unless one throws in the option to strafe or not to strafe enemy aircrew parachuting down or helpless in lifeboats in the Channel.

Fighter planes were designed for defence, but also for attack. Ordered to strafe, their pilots had no choice except possible charges of insubordination. Peter Townsend, who interleaves the Luftwaffe's experiences with that of his own RAF, muses on the role of the Messerschmitt pilots in France during the Dunkirk evacuation:

> As for us the enemy was until then a *thing*, not a person. They shot at an aircraft with no thought for the men inside it. But now they had the job of ground-strafing as well. Sensitive, highly strung Paul Temme said, 'I hated Dunkirk. It was just unadulterated killing. The beaches were jammed full of soldiers. I went up and down at three hundred feet "hose-piping".' Cold-blooded, point blank murder. Defenceless men, fathers, sons, and brothers, being cruelly massacred by a twenty-four-year-old boy.[6]

Even in defence, the results of fighter activity might be casually murderous. German bombers crashed on English houses, or jettisoned their bombs at random as they fled. The great air ace Robert Stanford-Tuck (twenty-seven confirmed kills by January 1942) was pursuing a Junkers 88 over south Wales one evening, fired at it long range, failed to hit it, but saw its bombs dropped. Next morning he received a call from his father that his brother-in-law, stationed under canvas with the army in Wales, had been killed the previous night. Tuck checked. Only one stick of bombs had landed on Wales. Only one man, a soldier, had been killed.[7]

2

There were immediate reasons why civilians should idealize the pilots of the Battle of Britain. Also, the airmen themselves shared in a 'heritage of discourses' involving English chivalry which provided potent pretexts for idealization. And both civilians and airmen were susceptible to the very recent mystique attached to aviation itself.

To be resoundingly obvious, civilians saw that these men were fighting to save Britain from conquest by an exceptionally brutal enemy. Sometimes very young indeed, commonly undertrained for the job, they elicited pathos as well as admiration. Whether all the civilian

population always loved all of them is doubtful. An RAF man
venturing among London shelterers in the autumn of 1940 was liable to
get a hostile reception – why was he not up in the sky out there
defending the people? There is the curious case of the pilot found still
in the cockpit of his aircraft in the mid-1990s during routine civil
engineering excavations in Hove. He had crashed into this populous
place in 1940 and had literally been blotted out. One suspects that in
the general fear and commotion no civilian could be bothered to
inspect the crash, let alone rush to his aid. Now at last he has been
interred in a regular way with appropriate honours.[8] Army conscripts
resented the superior sex appeal of the 'Brylcreem Boys' of the air, and
may have transmitted their prejudices to others. But that same appeal
confirmed that these were indeed the young men of the hour, as
Churchill said they were.

All literate Britons, in and out of uniform, were affected by
interacting myths and discourses involving heroic combat, some as old
as the presumed King Arthur, others originating as recently as 1914–18.
In the context of a truly decisive battle, these were easily sufficient to
explain the mystique of Douglas Bader, and of other aces who had not
had his distinction of losing their legs in a peacetime air accident.
Fused with certain preoccupations of the literary intelligentsia between
the wars, they grounded the cult of Richard Hillary.

It would be tedious to rehearse the oft-told tale of how, spurred by
misreadings of Walter Scott, and more accurate readings of Alfred
Tennyson, the British Victorians had saturated their culture with misty
notions of chivalry. Christian soldiers marched to war, and Sir
Galahad's strength was as the strength of ten because his heart was
pure. The iconography of the Pre-Raphaelites penetrated the school
chapel and the Sunday school and there cohabited with imperialism.
Growing up just after the Second World War, as I did, it was still
impossible to avoid the presence of such a mix in school textbooks and
the minds of the older teachers. John Mackenzie's researches have
suggested that, so far from declining and falling, imperialist ideology
was still at its climax in 1939–45.[9] John Buchan's immensely popular
First World War spy thriller *Mr Standfast* (1919) had concluded with
an exciting, if historically baseless, episode in which the crippled
Afrikaner air ace Peter Pienaar had saved the Allied side from defeat in
France in 1918 by taking on the gallant German aviator Lensch and
bringing him down at the cost of his own life. Though Pienaar, a
former big-game tracker in his fifties, hardly conformed to type, it was
easy to assimilate the 'knights of the air' with the conception of the

ideal imperial hero, gallant, young and presumed pure, invoked by so many public and private memorials for the fallen of wars from the Crimean to Flanders, suggested by prints in school halls representing Sir Galahad or Spenser's Red Cross Knight.

The notion of a knightly chivalry of the air was potent throughout Europe. Flying, as George L. Mosse, documenting this, has remarked, signified the conquest of the sky, an intimation of eternity, which pointed back to the pre-industrial ages, to innocence and Arcadia. In 1914–18 all pilots of whatever nationality ranked as officers, all were volunteers, none were conscripted. While von Richthofen had been a passionate hunter in peacetime, the British probably went further than anyone else in assimilating air war with the imperialist cult of team games.[10] The young officer in Henry Newbolt's oft-quoted poem 'Vitaï Lampada' rallies the ranks when the sands of the desert are sodden red, the Gatling's jammed and the colonel's dead, by invoking the spirit of the cricket field – 'Play up, play up and play the game.' There were sacred and secular versions of sportsmanship to be invoked in 1940 in connection with the Battle of Britain. The famous newsvendors' placards which displayed Spitfire kills as if they were cricket scores might suggest idealized versions of Hutton opening the England innings against furious fast bowlers, or Compton joyously smiting Australia's best, to name the rising young heroes of the day. Or they might, closer to reality, suggest the changing-room atmosphere of the fighter base, with men such as Bader stomping about swearing at the Huns. Bader, before he lost his legs, had been tipped to play for England at rugby football. Hillary, twixt and tween, recalls early in *The Last Enemy* the exploits of an undistinguished, unofficial rowing eight from Oxford University which turned up in Germany in 1938 to compete for General Goering's Prize Fours. Spurred on by German insults directed at their decadent race, they came through to win by the slimmest of margins. 'Looking back,' Hillary wrote, 'this race was really a surprisingly accurate pointer to the course of the war. We were quite untrained, lacked any form of organisation and were really quite hopelessly casual.'[11] British improvisation on ground and air, as Hillary misconstrued it, was superior to inflexible Luftwaffe tactics because of joyous traditions of youthful sportsmanship.

But more technically minded watchers, and later, readers, among the British public were enthralled by the very new traditions of manned flight and air warfare. The Spitfire itself was romantic enough, without invoking knightly jousts or Wally Hammond's fabled cover drive. When Neville Chamberlain flew to Munich to see Hitler in 1938, his choice of transport must have seemed to his older compatriots as disturbingly innovative as the release of Prosecutor Starr's report on President Clinton through the Internet did to such oldies in 1998. Though civil aviation had made progress before the Second World War, and transcontinental flights were available, few people in Britain had yet been in the air. Until the advent, well after the war was over, of the package holiday and the big passenger jet, flying remained outside normal experience and retained glamour, if no longer mystery.

In his famous book *Sagittarius Rising*, published in 1936, Cecil Lewis describes how in 1915 he bluffed his way into the Royal Flying Corps as a sixteen-year-old schoolboy. Barely old enough to register the fact when the Wright brothers made the first successful flight in a heavier-than-air machine at the end of 1903, Lewis could 'hardly remember a time when [he] was not air-minded'. At prep school he made gliders out of paper and studied the pages of *The Aero* and *Flight* magazines. By the age of thirteen, befriending a fellow fanatic, he was obsessed with making serious model aeroplanes:

> But, in spite of this passion for 'aeronautics' – as they were then called – it never occurred to me that I might be actively concerned in them. That I myself might fly a real full-sized aeroplane was beyond the bounds of the wildest possibility. Then came the War . . . The opportunity opened, and the onlooker became participant.

Training with the RFC in France enhanced Lewis's love of planes and flying and introduced him to the concept of the dogfight:

> Follow my leader with Patrick gave me my first taste of aerial fighting, getting your nose and your guns on the enemy's tail and sitting there till you brought him down. It was a year later before I actually did any, but, from the first, the light fast single-seater scout [fighter] was my ambition. To be alone, to have your life in your own hands, to use your own skill, single-handed against the enemy. It was like the lists in the Middle Ages, the only sphere in modern warfare where a man saw his adversary and faced him in mortal combat, the only sphere where there was still chivalry and honour. If you won, it was your own bravery and skill, if you lost it was because you had met a better man.
>
> As long as man has limbs and passions he will fight. Sport, after all, is only sublimated fight, and in such fighting, if you don't 'love' your enemy in the conventional sense of the term, you honour and respect him. Besides, there is, as everybody who has fought knows, a strong magnetic attraction between two men who are matched against one another. I have felt this

magnetism, engaging an enemy scout three miles above the earth. I have
wheeled and circled, watching how he flew, taking in the power and speed of
his machine, seen him, fifty yards away, eyeing me, calculating, watching for
an opening, each of us wary, keyed up to the last pitch of skill and
endeavour. And if at last he went down, a falling rocket of smoke and flame,
what a glorious and heroic death! What a brave man. *It might just as well
have been me . . .*

So, if the world must fight to settle its differences, back to Hector and
Achilles! Back to the lists! Let the enemy match a squadron of fighters
against ours. And let the world look on! It is not as fanciful as you suppose.
We may yet live to see it over London.[12]

Reading or re-reading this in 1940, one might have imagined that Lewis
had been exactly prophetic. That was how journalists and speech-
makers conceived the Battle of Britain – a 'duel of eagles' in the air
between gallant young men of both sides.

Yet in fact the battle was not like that. Nor was Achilles, if you read
the *Iliad* carefully, quite the model that a humane person, after due
consideration, could have proposed. Leaving his tent to avenge
Patroclus, he performs as a serial killer, ruthlessly attacking a defence-
less Trojan boy away from the battle. When he drags the dead Hector
behind his chariot, his triumphalism disgusts all decent sentiment.
Lewis was in fact a humane man, not a gung-ho warrior. His notion
that wars might be decided by competing fighter squadrons represents
a desire to return battle to the olden days of chivalry when supposedly
champions in single combat could settle matters (an idea which harks
back to times when warfare, for a settled tribal group, might have a
ritual, ceremonial character). But even the air battles of the First World
War contradicted Lewis's idealized vision of air combat, as his own
pages show clearly enough. Formations of scores of fighters had engaged each other in confused combat. Of one tussle involving relatively
few planes, Lewis remarks, 'It would be impossible to describe the
actions of such a battle.'[13]

When he heard that the matchless Don Bradman of serial killers,
Baron Manfred von Richthofen (eighty kills), had at last been felled,
probably by ground fire as, like insensate Achilles, he flew low over the
British lines in pursuit of a helpless victim whose guns had jammed, the
British ace Mannock remarked, unchivalrously, 'I hope he roasted all
the way down.'[14] The British decision to bury him themselves with full
military honours was a rather touching attempt to assert the Arthurian
view of aerial warfare, more formal than Adolf Galland's invitation to
Douglas Bader, grounded and imprisoned in France, to join him for tea,

with an assurance that he would not be interrogated, while the Germans were preparing to receive a replacement metal leg from England for that British Hector.[15] Mannock himself (credited with seventy-three kills) was a leader in the air already anticipating the anti-individualistic ethos of Leigh-Mallory's 'big wings' in 1940. 'Always possessed by an exemplary caution, to avoid unnecessary risks he would painstakingly manoeuvre to secure the best possible position from which an attack could be launched in strength.'[16] Albert Ball (forty-one victims), granted a posthumous VC, and a statue in his home town, Nottingham, was in contrast adored for his recklessness. Lewis, who was with him on his last sortie, summarized his ethos: 'Absolutely fearless, the odds made no difference to him. He would always attack, single out his man, and close. On several occasions he almost rammed the enemy, and often came back with his machine shot to pieces.'[17] And this Ajax did not last very long. Meanwhile, his fellow knights of the air had meaner tasks to perform. A young American flying with the RAF wrote in his diary in August 1918, 'Yesterday we did ground strafing down south. That's my idea of a rotten way to pass the time . . . All the machine guns on the ground opened up and sprayed us with tracer and a few field guns took a crack at us, but we got through somehow and dropped our messages [bombs] and shot up everything we could see on the ground.'[18]

'Everything we could see' included people. The memoir-writing of the fighter pilots of 1940 was prefigured in descriptions from the 1914–18 war when allegedly knight-like single combat with visible honoured adversaries had been the norm. It is understandable that cricket-loving public opinion in 1940 should gratefully swallow, in days of great peril, the idea that their prime defenders were 'knights' or 'duellists' of the air. But why did leftish literary intellectuals, whose formation between the wars had involved bitter scepticism about modern mechanized combat, accept Hillary's book in 1942, as most seem to have done? And how could Hillary himself believe what he wrote?

I think the 'Romance of the Air' holds the answer. W. B. Yeats, mourning the death of his friend's son Major Robert Gregory, serving with the RFC in the First World War, had contributed, in 'An Irish Airman Foresees His Death', a short poem which many knew by heart:

> Nor law, nor duty bade me fight,
> Nor public men, nor cheering crowds,
> A lonely impulse of delight

> Drove to this tumult in the clouds;
> I balanced all, brought all to mind,
> The years to come seemed waste of breath,
> A waste of breath the years behind
> In balance with this life, this death.[19]

No one could have been less like a heroic aviator than the unphysical national bard of Ireland. Yet Yeats hit unerringly on formulations which represented the spirit of aviation as it developed between the wars. Cecil Lewis expresses this spirit in a notable passage. He is utterly disgusted with the carnage on the Somme: 'a sort of desperation was in the air. The battle had failed. The summer was over. The best men had gone.' He goes up alone on patrol 'one dreary grey morning' and rises above the clouds into a private heaven:

> Here it was still summer . . . A hundred miles, north, south, east, west. Thirty thousand square miles of unbroken cloud-plains! No traveller in the desert, no pioneer to the poles had ever seen such an expanse of sand or snow. Only the lonely threshers of the sky, hidden from the earth, had gazed on it. Only we who went up into the high places under the shadow of wings![20]

After him into the air went the epic long-distance fliers of *entre deux guerres* – Alcock and Brown, then, solo, Lindbergh, Amy Johnson and Beryl Markham, who wrote in her memoirs, published in 1942, and extolled as a masterpiece by Ernest Hemingway, about how she learnt to fly in Kenya:

> After this era of great pilots is gone, as the era of great sea captains has gone – each nudged aside by the march of inventive genius, by steel cogs and copper discs and hair-thin wires on white faces that are dumb but speak – it will be found, I think, that all the science of flying has been captured in the breadth of an instrument board, but not the religion of it.
> One day, the stars will be as familiar to each man as the landmarks, the curves, and the hills on the road that leads to his door, and one day this will be an airborne life. But by then men will have forgotten how to fly; they will be passengers on machines whose conductors are carefully promoted to a familiarity with labelled buttons, and in whose minds knowledge of the sky and the wind and the way of weather will be extraneous as passing fiction.[21]

The French writer Antoine de Saint-Exupéry, born in 1900, a year after Lewis, had been a pioneer pilot in the early, dangerous days of airmail post, pitting himself with such legendary fliers as Jean Mermoz and Henri Guillaumet against the air over the Sahara and the peaks of the Andes. His prizewinning novel of 1931, *Vol de Nuit* ('Night Flight'), had been filmed by Hollywood, starring Clark Gable. Friendly with intellectuals in advanced Parisian literary circles, and respected by them, well-grounded in Nietzsche and Proust, he extended in his memoir, *Terre des Hommes* (1939) – a major best-seller as *Wind, Sand and Stars* in the United States and Britain – his religious sense of what flight meant: how it lifted men up and taught them wisdom which could be brought to earth and translated into fraternal action. 'No sum', he told his readers, 'could buy the night flight with its hundred thousand stars, its serenity, its few hours of sovereignty.' Writing of the almost unbelievable heroism of Guillaumet, who, not fearing death but for the sake of wife and friends, trekked back to the world of men after crash-landing in the remotest Andes, Saint-Exupéry rhapsodizes:

> He is among those beings of great scope who spread their leafy branches willingly over broad horizons. To be a man is, precisely, to be responsible. It is to know shame at the sight of poverty which is not of our making . . . It is to feel, as we place our stone, that we are contributing to the building of the world.

George L. Mosse comments that though Saint-Exupéry 'professed himself a democrat, in reality [he] emphasized the metaphysical dimension of pre-industrial virtues, attacked the acquisition of material goods, and implicitly exalted an elitism just like that of the wartime pilots.'[22]

3

Independently, the so-called 'Auden generation' of young British writers, not fliers themselves, had made the airman a favourite motif. As Sebastian Faulks points out in his interesting recent biographical study of Richard Hillary, they were haunted by the memory of an Italian anti-Fascist poet called Lauro de Bosis, who flew in a light plane from Marseille to Rome in October 1931 to drop political leaflets and never returned. 'A man', Faulks observes, 'was to make his point, alone, then die. His action should preferably be politically motivated, but there was a possibility that action itself could redeem.' It was not only in France that currents were tending towards the existentialism so fashionable in the years immediately after the Second World War. The Anglo-Irish poet Cecil Day Lewis, not to be confused with the airman-author of *Sagittarius Rising,* hailed Auden himself in one poem as 'Wystan, lone flier, birdman' and produced a verse narrative 'singing' of two Australian war veterans called Parer and McIntosh, who flew from England back to the Antipodes in a written-off DC 9. Faulks further notes the significance for the Auden generation of T. E. Lawrence, 'of Arabia', who turned away from his army colonelship and public adulation to enlist in the RAF as a mere 'aircraftman'. Lawrence was an intellectual who questioned his own motives in those actions which had made him a hero, and became more truly heroic by renouncing public applause.[23]

Hillary was a well-read young man, certainly aware of the latest literary fashions. He was a fluent and effective writer who could certainly, had war not come, have fulfilled with success his ambition to be a journalist. He was fitted to make his name by a book which combines elements very potent in 1942. First, there was his relatively straightforward narrative of the training, then the engagement in action, of a young Battle of Britain pilot. To this he added quasi-political musings, using a real comrade, Peter Pease, whose deeply English Christian idealism fascinates him, and an imaginary fellow student from Oxford, David, a conscientious objector working on the land who, after the Battle of Britain in which Peter Pease has died, has come to question his own decision and thinks he will join up for military service. In his windy concluding paragraphs, lone survivor of his fraternity of young pilots, the narrator sees that what he must do is write, about them, and for them, so as to justify 'at least in some measure, my right to fellowship with the dead, and to the friendship of those with courage and steadfastness who were still living and who would go on fighting until the ideals for which their comrades had died were stamped for ever on the future of civilisation'.[24]

These elements alone would have provided the material of a brief book of great interest, most likely, to the Ministry of Information. What made, and still makes, *The Last Enemy* seem exceptional is the heroic young killer's presence throughout the book as victim of battle, angrily unresigned to his status as martyr. The book begins with his agony. On 3 September 1940, flying out of Hornchurch, Hillary emerges from 'a blur of twisting machines and tracer bullets' to find a Messerschmitt below him; he attacks, hits the German plane – 'him' – with a two-second burst, then, 'like a fool', lingers to 'finish him off' with another three-second burst. As the German spirals downward in flames, Hillary himself is hit by an assailant he does not see and his cockpit becomes 'a mass of flames'. He barely manages to parachute into the North Sea and his face and hands are horribly burnt. Later, we will learn of the painful months in which the pioneering plastic surgeon Archibald McIndoe gave him new eyelids and lips and released, though not completely, his clawed hands. There had been nothing in previous writing about war to prepare readers for this epic of medical science, in which Hillary is only one among hundreds treated.

How Hillary might have described the Battle of Britain had he survived without such mutilation we can barely guess. After the war was over, he might not have been attracted to the ideas, proto-existentialist, or quasi-'Résistencialist' à la Saint-Exupéry, or merely gaseous, which most readers now will find an impediment to their pleasure in a fascinating narrative – though at least they also cut across the Mills-and-Boonish possibilities inherent in Hillary's close relation-ship, after she visits him in hospital, with the fiancée of his now-dead friend Peter Pease. I think it is unwarrantable of Sebastian Faulks to set Hillary's life in a triptych of 'fatal Englishmen' flanked by the tragic young painter Christopher Wood, who killed himself, and the brilliant post-war journalist Jeremy Woolfenden, who died aged thirty-one of alcoholism. It was indeed tragic that Hillary insisted on rejoining the RAF to fly after the success of his book, like Wilfred Owen gratuitously returning to the trench life which he had exposed so fiercely in his poetry and T. E. Lawrence abdicating from public admiration. Hillary was not fit to fly and his fatal crash was so predictable that it tempts thoughts about suicide. But unlike Wood and Woolfenden, Hillary had objective reasons to be confused and depressed, which would have applied whether or not he had been 'English'. A notably attractive young man – he is said to have lost his virginity at sixteen – he was now disfigured. He was doomed to represent, in public, as long as he lived, the fate of his comrades who had died in the Battle of Britain. He would not have had to be alert to the more morbid strains in Western philosophy to experience at times an intense 'death wish'. The guilt of the survivor alone has been enough to drive people mad.

A facile reading of Hillary's text makes him into an appropriate sacrificial martyr for a Just War which is also a People's War. The 'last of the long-haired boys', he seems to represent an insouciant, privileged pre-war generation of Oxbridge *jeunesse dorée* who perish in the Battle of Britain. Cynical about political ideals, he finds ideal-ism. Arrogantly contemptuous of the masses, he finds that his fate has merged with theirs. In a brilliant but invented episode, he is caught in a

London air raid and takes refuge in a pub. The next-door house is hit. Despite his painful hands, Hillary helps dig out a dead child and a middle-aged woman, whose face 'through the dirt and streaked blood' is 'the face of a thousand working women'. He gives her brandy from his flask. She reaches for her child, weeps, utters her dying words: 'Thank you, sir . . . I see they got you too.' In great distress, Hillary now realizes that the Battle of Britain, as Peter Pease had 'instantly recognised', was a crusade against evil.[25] A cascade of rhetoric which surges from this fictional incident to the book's conclusion implies that the woman's death, mingling with memories of Peter, has inspired him directly to write what the reader has just read.

In fact, Hillary had read a sample to a publisher during his convalescence, but finished the book only after a trip to the United States. The Ministry of Information thought he might be useful for propaganda there and arranged his discreet attachment to the Air Mission in Washington. But his horrible appearance convinced the embassy that they could not send him forth to inspire US factory workers. Unable to do anything useful, bar four anonymous broadcasts, the frustrated Hillary turned back to his book. In New York he met Antoine de Saint-Exupéry. This amiable, physically ungainly man, highly intelligent yet childlike, had lived in the USA in exile since 1940, well supported by his fame and spellbinding all who met him with his card tricks. He represented the spirit of aviation in person, and Sebastian Faulks suggests that Hillary imbibed sentiments from him which made him scorn life and insist on returning to the air. (As did Saint-Exupéry himself. Over-age, and physically hampered by old injuries sustained in air crashes, he died in 1944 flying for the Free French air force, probably shot down by a German fighter above the Mediterranean between Nice and Monaco.)[26]

Be that as it may, it is the dissonance between proto-existentialist conceptions related to flying and the book's virtually propagandist conclusion which gives *The Last Enemy* some permanent interest. Hillary wears the mask which McIndoe has given him. He projects the antinomian, potentially arrogant, spirit of aviation, relates it to the personal arrogance for which he chides himself, and so exposes it to question. But, reciprocally, his self-projection as outsider calls into question vapid propagandist banalities. It is the thought-provoking inconsistency of the book which makes it valuable.

He might well question the notion of the flyer as independent knight-errant. He jauntily describes how, after his squadron of Spitfires has broken up in a series of dogfights, with plenty of ammunition left, he roams the skies, finds no Spitfires, but attaches himself as 'arse-end Charlie' to a squadron of Hurricanes. Suddenly he is raked by fire. Going down in a spin he tries to warn the Hurricanes, but his radio has been shot away. He finds the whole experience 'most amusing'.[27]

Reading this made Peter Townsend angry. In *Duel of Eagles* he describes a Hurricane patrol from Croydon in late August 1940:

> At eighteen thousand feet a lone Spitfire joined us. It was a foolish, almost criminal act. Our wave-lengths were different and thus we could not communicate. And, end-on, a Spitfire could be taken for an Me 109. 'Watch him very closely,' I called to our tailguard, our 'arse-end Charlies'.
>
> The controller's voice was faint. A blood-red, sinking sun stained the blue-grey haze. With the thin voice of the controller calling 'Bandits in your vicinity,' we turned aimlessly here and there and craned our necks, searching uneasily in the treacherous light . . .
>
> It was the 'Ace' who noticed the Spitfire had changed into an Me 109. 'Look out, Messerschmitts!' he yelled, and each of our sections slammed into a left hand turn, but not before the square wing tip of an Me 109 flashed by just above my head. Straightening out, my heart sank. To starboard, Hammy's Hurricane was heeling slowly over, wreathed in flame and smoke. Then it tipped downward into a five-mile plunge to earth. Only Nigger Marshall got in a shot at the Me 109. It dived abruptly into the haze, but its destruction was never confirmed.
>
> Was Richard Hillary in that Spitfire? The height and position agree. It was only after he 'managed to pull himself together and go into a spin' that he thought of warning the Hurricanes – impossible anyway on his wave-length even if his radio had not been shot away. Hillary crash landed 'in the back garden of a Brigade cocktail party.' The timing agrees, too.
>
> Whoever it was, we felt bitter about the Spitfire. Had it kept on the flank where we could see it, Hammy might never have died. 'If this Spitfire pilot can be identified, I would like these facts brought home to him, because his . . . action contributed to the loss of one of my flight commanders,' I wrote in my combat report.[28]

The 'lonely impulse of delight' was, it seems, as treacherous a motivation in combat as the mythology of 'the knights of the air' is to the writing of sensible history about the Battle of Britain. Townsend emphasizes that, ideally, effort was selfless and collective. And participants in aerial warfare ought to know rather more about the proper functions of an arse-end Charlie and the technology of radio communication than Hillary, it seems, had bothered to learn.

2000

Notes and References

[1] Paul Brickhill, *Reach For the Sky: The Story of Douglas Bader* (London, 1954), pp. 220–1.
[2] Richard Hillary, *The Last Enemy* (London, 1942), pp. 130–1.
[3] Peter Townsend, *Duel of Eagles* (London, 1970), pp. 361–2.
[4] Hillary, *Last Enemy*, pp. 121–2.
[5] Samuel Hynes, *The Soldier's Tale: Bearing Witness to Modern War* (London, 1998), p. 127.
[6] Townsend, *Duel*, p. 229.
[7] Laddie Lucas, *Out of the Blue: The Role of Luck in Air Warfare, 1917–1966* (London, 1987), pp. 100–2.
[8] *The Times* (26 October 1996; 3, 10, 11, 26 November 1996).
[9] John Mackenzie, *Propaganda and Empire* (Manchester, 1984), pp. 231–6ff.
[10] George L. Mosse, *Fallen Soldiers: Reshaping Memory of the World Wars* (New York, 1990), pp. 120–2.
[11] Hillary, *Last Enemy*, p. 21.
[12] Cecil Lewis, *Sagittarius Rising* (London, 1966), pp. 7–8, 45–6.
[13] Ibid., p. 176.
[14] Nigel Steel and Peter Hart, *Tumult in the Clouds: The British Experience of the War in the Air, 1914–1918* (London, 1997), pp. 320–2.
[15] Brickhill, *Reach*, pp. 290–4.
[16] Steel and Hart, *Tumult*, p. 324.
[17] Lewis, *Sagittarius*, p. 73.
[18] Neville Duke and Edward Lanchbery (eds), *The Crowded Sky: An Anthology of Flight* (London, 1964), pp. 151–2.
[19] W. B. Yeats, *The Poems*, ed. D. Albright (London, 1994), p. 184.
[20] Lewis, *Sagittarius*, pp. 147, 149–50.
[21] Beryl Markham, *West with the Night* (London, 1988), pp. 163–4.
[22] Antoine de Saint-Exupéry, *Wind, Sand and Stars*, tr. William Rees (London, 1995), pp. 21, 29; Mosse, *Fallen*, p. 123.
[23] Sebastian Faulks, *The Fatal Englishman: Three Short Lives* (London, 1997), pp. 197–200.
[24] Hillary, *Last Enemy*, p. 221.
[25] Ibid., pp. 209–16.
[26] Faulks, *Fatal Englishman*, pp. 163–6; see Curtis Gate, *Antoine de St-Exupéry* (London, 1970).
[27] Hillary, *Last Enemy*, pp. 132–4.
[28] Townsend, *Duel*, pp. 362–3.

Mr Wu and the Colonials: the British Empire's Evacuation from Crete, 1941

On the night of 30–31 May 1941, Brigadier Howard Kippenberger, with the 20th New Zealand Battalion, was determined that whoever got left behind on Crete, it would not be the 230 men he had selected to go. Around the tiny beach at Sphakia, off which Royal Navy vessels waited to take up evacuated Commonwealth troops, a mob of stragglers, chancers, deserters and men whose luck had run out surged with such energy as was left them after their trek across high mountains with scant access to food or water. The cordon keeping them away from the ships was provided by survivors of the 22nd New Zealand Battalion, who had fired the first shots in the battle for Crete on 20 May, just eleven nightmarish days before. They were determined to get off themselves, and they had orders to shoot if necessary. Grimly, Kippenberger counted his men through, grieving for the scores of soldiers he had had to leave behind – though these got away next day.[1]

On 31 May/1 June, Colonel Bob Laycock, of the Commando formation called, after him, Layforce, had ordered his brigade headquarters to embark after squaring the officer in charge of the beach. With him went his intelligence officer, Captain Evelyn Waugh. Layforce had airily been told to push their way through the rabble to join their leader. They could not do it, and men who had fought bravely as rearguard to the Commonwealth retreat across Crete fell into German hands next day.[2]

That the British evacuation from Crete marked a major military setback was never seriously denied. News of it came at a bad time for British morale. Would Britain be the next target for airborne invasion? The latest German air raids had been especially heavy, notably on London, where Churchill had wept over the ruins of the House of Commons. People were not to know that the Luftwaffe was going east for Barbarossa, Hitler's attack on the Soviet Union, nor that, far from coincidentally, the fact that as many as 18,000 Commonwealth troops were taken off Crete while 12,000 remained alive as prisoners could be attributed to an easing off of the daily attentions of the Luftwaffe there too. Churchill himself was downcast and highly critical in private of Wavell, the British commander in the Middle East, and Freyberg, who had led the force on Crete. News on 22 June that the Nazis had struck towards Russia lifted a pall of gloom and, in the new phase of war, Crete was comfortably forgotten, except by relatives of men killed or taken prisoner there. But there was never any attempt to romanticize it as a smaller version of the Dunkirk evacuation exactly one year before. The evacuation, as John Keegan has put it, was 'a shaming culmination to a benighted battle'.[3]

After the war was over, numerous able writers on the British side picked at the scab. The British official historians were cautiously defensive; a Panglossian line emerged that holding Crete would have involved a deleterious diversion of forces from the desert battle against Rommel, so that the forced evacuation had been a blessing in disguise. The honest and acute author of the official New Zealand history, Dan Davin, was freer to be critical – after all, ultimate responsibility for the debacle rested with Wavell, who had failed over several months before the battle to supply and reinforce the British garrison properly, and Churchill, who had insisted on Crete's defence when this had simply not been practical. The Poms had let the Kiwis down. However, several later authors of a string of detailed books about the battle have inclined to think that Crete might have been held quite easily if this, that or the other strategic or tactical decision had been taken.[4] After all, as was finally admitted, the Bletchley code-crackers had supplied Wavell and, through him, Freyberg, a fortnight before the battle, with ULTRA information, derived from slips by Luftwaffe ENIGMA operators, which revealed exactly, in detail, the plan of campaign which the Germans actually followed.[5]

My purpose here is not to attempt fresh judgement on the battle, but to consider front-line morale on the Commonwealth side insofar as this can be reconstructed from first-hand accounts and from secondary sources using these. 'Mr Wu' was the pet-name accepted by Evelyn Waugh in his correspondence with Lady Diana Cooper, wife of one of Churchill's ministers, whom he in turn jokingly identified with 'Mrs Stitch', an all-powerful society hostess in his fiction. Their lifelong platonic friendship epitomizes Waugh's fascination with the British ruling class into which, as the son of a literary man, he, most painfully and regrettably, had not been born. A sergeant-major had called him 'Wuff' and play with his name – pronounced 'Wauch' in Scotland, whence, via his grandfather, it had come – was one of the smallest amongst many tribulations suffered by this talented but unhappy man in the course of war service almost from the start until very near the finish, volunteered for despite quite advanced age – he was thirty-six in 1939.

In his trilogy *The Sword of Honour,* published between 1952 and 1964, the protagonist Guy Crouchback's war matches his creator's closely. The fall of Crete is the subject of some fifty virtuoso pages in *Officers and Gentlemen,* the second part of the trilogy, which was published in 1955 after Waugh had the chance both to influence – since Davin consulted him – and to read the official accounts of the battle. The novel's details relate very closely, incident by incident, to a long 'Memorandum on Layforce' written by Waugh after his taste of action on Crete. Hence we have in Waugh's novel first-hand testimony adjusted to secondary sources. He could not have taken his fiction far beyond well-known facts even if he had wanted to. His description of the state of affairs in Crete is remorselessly pessimistic. Now that the trilogy is regarded as a modern classic, it is bound to determine what many readers know, or think they know, about the battle.[6]

The other significant writer on Crete in May 1941 was Dan Davin, a subaltern in the New Zealand Division. His two quite striking short stories about the battle are unimportant compared to the massive volume, *Crete,* which he contributed to the New Zealand series of official war histories. Published in 1953, the year when his fellow countryman Hillary scaled Everest, this must be regarded as the 'classic' historical account.

Waugh attached himself to the class of Englishmen who saw 'colonials' from the dominions as absurd provincials, earnest, ill-mannered and ignorant of the necessity of social hierarchy. On Crete, he was not attuned to be aware that the New Zealanders, by their actions, were writing national epic. As viewed by Davin, and others among or close to the New Zealand Division, Crete was a grim story but not a negative one. The New Zealanders, volunteers to a man, had been gallantly blooded in the rout which had driven the Commonwealth forces out of Greece. Now they bore the brunt of exceptionally ferocious fighting in Crete. Superbly trained in advance, they emerged awesomely battle-hardened by their reverses – 'reverses', as Davin says, 'the more readily assimilated because the fighting man and his officers rightly believed that they were not due to their own failings in the field'.[7] A quarter-century before, New Zealanders had suffered through British blunders in the agony of Gallipoli. Now, not so far away, they rubbed in the point that, especially with the bayonet, they were the best soldiers in the world – a claim which Rommel himself endorsed as they helped thrust his Germans back in the Western Desert, on to Sicily, up to Monte Cassino, where the doughty Kippenberger lost both his feet, finally to Trieste, where they pre-empted takeover by Tito's Yugoslav partisans.

One man's, Waugh's, account of morale on Crete as shameful must be balanced against the testimony of others to the exceptional courage and steadiness of many, perhaps most, of the New Zealanders. Perhaps in these different perceptions we seem to have in little the contrast between a rising nation and a decaying imperial ruling class.

On 6 April 1941, Hitler sent German forces into Greece to cut short the Greeks' successful resistance to his ally Mussolini's attempted invasion and check the British, who had depleted their forces in North Africa to send support to their valiant ally. He had to secure his southern flank in advance of invasion of the Soviet Union. Operation Marita was swiftly successful. Within three weeks the swastika flew over the Acropolis. Of the Commonwealth contingent, 12,000 were left behind, dead or in captivity. Those who were evacuated arrived in Crete without most of their equipment. Even blankets and cooking utensils were in short supply.

The island was idyllic in spring. Men relaxed after their campaign, bathed, drank wine and enjoyed the friendship freely offered by the local population. But Crete would be hard to defend. It was 152 miles long, 35 miles wide at greatest, and its population of something over 400,000 was mostly settled on the northern coastal plain with concentrations at Canea, the capital, in the west, and Heraklion, the main port, further east. The only serious road on the island ran along this coast, where there were now airfields at Malame, Retimo and Heraklion. The harbour at Suda Bay, near Canea, could handle only two ships at a time. From the autumn of 1940, the British had garrisoned Crete, but it was over 400 miles from Egypt, no fighter cover was normally possible, and supplying troops on the island was awkward and, if the Luftwaffe intervened, very risky for the Royal Navy. Lack of sustained attention from headquarters in Cairo was compounded by the fact that six different commanders, in as many months, were in charge on Crete before, on 30 April, Wavell handed it over to the reluctant General Freyberg of the New Zealand Division. Inadequately armed before the influx from Greece – which included thousands of Greek soldiers without rifles – the British force was now encumbered with drivers without vehicles, gunners without guns, and scraps of units.

Defeat could subsequently be attributed to any one of several key shortages. The RAF flew a few Hurricanes and Gladiator biplanes against the Luftwaffe, but removed the last half-dozen, after constant attrition, on 17 May, leaving the sky open to dive bombers and low-flying Messerschmitt fighters. Anti-aircraft guns were in short supply. So, crucially, was wireless equipment – a lack exacerbated as telephone lines were severed in the fighting. Twenty-three inferior tanks were insufficient. Even entrenching tools were in short supply.

To the *in situ* Creforce of 5,200 men were added about 20,000 from Greece, about half of these of little or no military significance, and nearly 3,500 reinforcements from Egypt. The grand total was imposing, but they faced attack by crack German troops with total control of the air.

Hitler had been listening to those who wanted to use the airborne army created for Goering's Luftwaffe by General Kurt Student. It had been deployed in support of ground attack in Norway and the Netherlands, fanning wild fears in Britain. Now what could it achieve against islands? Malta, the most valuable target, was strongly defended, and Hitler approved Operation Merkur against Crete. Twenty-two thousand soldiers were committed, most to descend by parachute or glider. An airforce of 280 bombers, 150 Stuka dive-bombers and 200 fighters was in support. Though the techniques of German parachuting were crude and contributed to appalling losses, such men as survived would be well armed and supplied. The aim was to capture the island's three airfields starting from Malame in the west, and roll back and squeeze the Commonwealth defenders along the north coast road.

Despite having softened up the defence with days of continuous air attack the Germans still failed to capture a single airfield on 20 May. Retimo and Heraklion remained in Commonwealth hands till the end of the battle, so the British and Australian troops defending them were never defeated and never went into retreat. Those at Retimo, however, became prisoners, and many of the soldiers from Heraklion were lost at sea after the navy had taken them off. The decisive fighting was in the west of the island. Crucially, on the night of 20 May, the New Zealander Colonel Andrew VC, commanding the defenders of Malame airfield, withdrew his men after expected reinforcements had failed to come up. The Germans had suffered so heavily that they expected defeat, but next day were able to seize and use the airfield. A belated Commonwealth counter-attack on 22 May failed. Growing steadily in strength, the Germans drove east as planned. Canea was subjected to an air raid reminiscent of Guernica. The Commonwealth defence got so tangled and confused that any coherent account of what happened is intrinsically suspect. By 26 May, Freyberg was convinced that the island was untenable. A stream of men south over the White Mountains, which rose to 8,000 feet, had begun, heading for the tiny harbour at Sphakia. The road stopped short several kilometres from Sphakia village and the last ordeal was to scramble down a goat track to the little beach. Rearguard fighting continued to the end, but the traffic from 26 May was all one way.

No one ever denied that the spectacle was pitiful, though the Latin phrase *via dolorosa*, which features in several accounts including Freyberg's, attempts to accord the trek such sacred dignity as might be attributed to exhausted men who had done their best against odds. The road was steep, footwear disintegrated, wells were few, food hard to come by, dysentery rife. That the navy, operating only at night, was able to take off 18,000 men makes the Dunkirk evacuation seem almost a dawdle. Why did the Germans not find some way, easy surely, of cutting the road off and the British to pieces?

Davin's description of the *via dolorosa* can stand for many grim accounts:

> The natural savage grandeur of the mountain road was overprinted with the chaos of war. Every yard of the road carried its tale of disaster, personal and military. The verges were strewn with abandoned equipment, packs cast aside when the galling weight had proved too much for chafed skin and exhausted shoulders; empty water bottles; suitcases and officers' valises gaping their glimpses of . . . pullovers knitted by laborious love in homes that the owners might not live to see again; steel helmets buried in the dust . . .[8]

Most men – though not brave Captain Waugh – were wary in the daylight, hiding in gullies and caves and groves from the Luftwaffe. Even at night, fear was intense. Kippenberger, leading the 4th New Zealand Brigade in relatively good order, on a gruelling night-march to a new rearguard position, stopped, unsure of which fork to take, and turned his torch on a map. From the bank above voices chorused, 'Put out that fucking light!' As Kippenberger recalled it, deadpan, 'a man rushed up and kicked the torch out my hand. I stood up and seized him by the throat, throttled till he started to choke, and threw him down. I then stated that if there were any more such talk I would open fire.' Silence followed.[9]

The Cretan debacle remains controversial not because of the indisputably humiliating retreat to Sphakia, but for other reasons. It was, as Len Deighton has put it, 'history's only defeat by an unsupported parachute army'.[10] The word 'unsupported' is literally true because the

Royal Navy smashed an ancillary German attempt to land men and equipment from the sea. Student's men suffered such heavy losses – 4,000 dead, 220 out of 600 transport aircraft knocked out – that Hitler would never permit another such operation.[11]

The Cretans, furthermore, were the first people conquered by the Nazis to start resistance against the Germans from the moment they arrived. Formed by centuries of militant resentment of Turkish rule, traditions latterly revived in recalcitrance against the reimposition of monarchy in Athens prompted extraordinary heroics, not just by ill-armed men but by women and children, priests and monks. At the village of Platanias, a New Zealander saw dead parachutists. 'That they had fallen to the villagers was gruesomely obvious. These Cretan women were already widowed from the fighting in Albania [against Mussolini], and they made short and ghastly work of any German who fell into their hands.'[12] The Germans responded in a style which came to typify their conduct in eastern theatres of war.

Resisted by locals at Kastelli, they revenged themselves on 27 May by shooting about 200 hostages in the town square. While the British, in this savage little campaign, disposed unceremoniously of Germans who attempted to surrender,[13] the systematic German atrocities against civilians, which continued during years of occupation, were of a different order of barbarity. This point may be taken either to supplement or to modify Omer Bartov's implication, in his study of *Hitler's Army*, that the barbarization of German soldiery originated on the Eastern Front.[14] What he describes happened spontaneously on Crete – a self-righteously brutal response to a hostile population deemed to be savages themselves – though Hitler had so admired the spirit shown by the Greeks against Mussolini, and so idealized these descendants of classical heroes, that he had ordered, before his campaign against them began, that all Greeks taken prisoner should be released as soon as an armistice was signed.[15] It seems that *übermenschen* became *untermenschen* in the minds of German soldiers as soon as they first saw a German corpse with eyes pecked out by crows and assumed that vengeful villagers had torn them out.

It does seem that if the British had done more to arm the Greek soldiers evacuated to the island, and had furnished local people with weapons, the German attack would probably have failed. In this case, Wavell's lack of attention to the island before the attack might make him seem the author of defeat. Other candidates for that title include Andrew, who made the fateful decision to withdraw at Malame on 20 May when the Germans thought themselves beaten; Brigadier Hargest, who failed to support Andrew timeously; and Freyberg, held to have misread an ULTRA message for his eyes only so as to reinforce his own obsession that he must position men to defend the beaches against a main thrust by the Germans from the sea. No one blames Admiral Cunningham, whose Royal Navy ships were grievously knocked about by the Luftwaffe as they defended the island, reinforced it, and finally took troops off it.

But it is hard to hold anyone on the spot truly culpable granted the conditions under which the Commonwealth troops fought the battle. Leaving aside the smoke rising from Suda Bay and bombed Canea, the stench of corpses in the sun and the stink of wounds assailed by flies, the lack of efficient communication by telephone and wireless and inability to use in daylight what little transport was available made co-ordinated command impossible. On 26 May, Brigadier Puttick, commanding the New Zealand Division, had to walk four miles to Freyberg's headquarters, then four miles back, delivering an essential message. The Luftwaffe dominated proceedings completely. As the first British official historian says, 'It is difficult to think of any instance in the history of warfare where a force has been so pinned down and paralysed at *every level*, from the rifleman in his slit trench . . . to the staff officer at Force Headquarters waiting for information that does not arrive or planning movements that will not be carried out . . .'[16]

Tolstoy would presumably have welcomed news of this reduction nearly to absurdity of evidence to support his view, in *War and Peace*, that generals do not really control battles. Had the morale of the half-starved Commonwealth troops disintegrated completely, the enormous condescension of history might have been prevailed upon to forgive them. Lieutenant Roy Farran, a twenty-year-old British tank commander, was horrifed at Malame when the commander of his lead tank was killed just ahead of him. His own machine soon packed up in a bamboo field, under a 'swarm' of Messerschmitt 109s. 'The terror of the aeroplanes', he would write, 'had turned me into a frightened, quivering, woman . . . I lost my head. I was so afraid that I could have burrowed into the ground.'[17]

But, as Farran should have known, Cretan women were amongst those on the island who remained uncowed by the endless snarl of planes. So was Captain Waugh. Different men, different units, reacted very differently to the same conditions. One case in point, already alluded to, involves Colonel Bob Laycock, a dashing, intelligent, upper-class soldier whom Waugh admired almost unreservedly.

Layforce had been sent from Egypt to reinforce Crete in a gesture by Wavell too little and too late. The first contingent, without their commander, turned up in Suda Bay on the night of 23–4 May. Laycock and Waugh, detained by shipping difficulties, arrived with the rest on 26–7 May. Freyberg already knew that the battle was lost. Layforce consisted of commandos, recruited for daring strikes by sea against enemy-held coastlines. On Crete its members were consigned to rearguard infantry duties remote from their training and aspirations. However, they seem on the whole to have performed these effectively. They were, bar Germans, the freshest troops on the island.

As 'last on', they were to be 'last out', even though Freyberg insisted on priority for fighting units. On 31 May, the last night of evacuation, they were listed to embark after the New Zealanders and Australians who were with them in the rearguard, before only the Royal Marines. But Laycock and his staff flitted precipitately, admittedly in conditions when order had broken down, with no senior staff officer present. Though only a handful of his Layforce men managed later to push through the increasing chaos on the beach and get out of Crete, and Layforce itself was soon disbanded, Laycock's career was unimpeded. He rose to be a general, to head Combined Operations Command, to be knighted. Before he died in 1968, his affable and distinguished personality had predisposed inquisitive historians not to pry too zealously into a scenario where he had not only disobeyed orders – 'Layforce to embark after other fighting units but before stragglers', as Waugh had noted – but abandoned brave subordinates to their fate.[18]

Others, who had fought longer and harder, reacted differently to the painful moment when it became clear that the navy could accept little more battering and thousands would have to be left on Crete. Kippenberger protested vehemently when told that he must leave his second in command on the island and only agreed to get off when told that Freyberg had expressly ordered it. He agonized in detail over which seventy-six of his 306 men should stay, and succumbed, changing his mind when a deputation of subalterns came to him asking to remain themselves in place of the officer he proposed to leave in charge, who, as they pointed out, was married.[19] On 29 May, Freyberg himself had been most reluctant to leave before his rearguard, but if he had been captured, ULTRA could have been compromised, and he bowed to orders and necessity.[20] At much lower level, men sacrificed themselves. Michael Woodbine Parish, a very young gunner acting as General Weston's liaison officer on a motorcycle, had no romantic illusions – he later wrote that Waugh had 'clearly portrayed' in his novel the 'shameful' retreat to the south coast. He was ordered by Weston himself to embark, but volunteered at Sphakia to carry rations up to the Maoris in the rearguard. The Maoris got away, but Woodbine Parish was taken prisoner.[21]

Evelyn Waugh's original view that the war was or should be a crusade against the Nazis and their wicked Soviet allies had been challenged by the boring and at times farcical time he had spent in khaki. In 1955 he would still feel able to dedicate *Officers and Gentlemen*

TO

MAJOR-GENERAL
SIR ROBERT LAYCOCK

that every man in arms should wish to be

but the night of 31 May in Sphakia seems to have completed a long process of disillusionment.

Like his protagonist in *The Sword of Honour*, Guy Crouchback, Waugh had been captivated by the old-fashioned traditions of the Royal Marines, who became the 'Halberdiers' in his fiction. But he never rose above, and sometimes fell below, the rank of captain which he soon achieved. In August 1940 he embarked with the Marines on an abortive attempt to capture Dakar from the Free French. Influence in high places – he knew Churchill's crony Brendan Bracken – helped secure his transfer to the Commandos, where he mingled with aristocratic clubmen whose arrogant, casual, expensive ways he partly idolized, partly laughed at. His second chance of participation in glorious warfare came when 8 Commando, stationed in Egypt, raided Bardia along the coast. It was supposed to be full of Italians. There were none there.

If Dakar and Bardia had been farcical, Crete was something worse than that. When Laycock asked him on the ship which took them back to Egypt how he had found his first battle, his reply was, 'Like German opera – too long and too loud'. He wrote to his wife afterwards:

> I have been in a serious battle and have decided I abominate military life. It was tedious and futile and fatiguing. I found I was not at all frightened only very bored and very weary . . . The thing about battle is that it is no different at all from manoeuvres with Col. Lushington [of the Marines] on Bagshot heath – just as confused and purposeless.[22]

From disillusionment, Waugh went on to suffer petty vexation, quarrelling with and sneering at superiors in a succession of desk jobs.

There was a very bitter moment in 1943 when Laycock, ordered to take his Commando to Italy, left Waugh behind. Eventually he was seconded for six grim months to the British Military Mission in Croatia headed by his old drinking companion Randolph Churchill, the great man's son. When VE Day came Waugh, some weeks out of uniform, mused: 'I remember at the start of it all writing to Frank Pakenham that [the war's] value for us would be to show us finally that we are not "men of action". I took longer than him to learn it.'[23]

If Waugh was not a 'man of action', his physical courage, bordering on death wish, determined his reactions to the Cretan disaster. Arriving at the very moment when defeat had been acknowledged as inevitable, he was the harshest possible judge of the behaviour of exhausted men who had been fighting Germans. He became tired himself, though not as tired as they were, and suffered hunger like them, but he still could not allow for the effect of many days under bombardment and strafing on the nerves of commanders and men. His 'Memorandum on Layforce' records instance after instance of what he took to be cowardice. The 'first indication' is the arrival on the ship which brought Waugh with Laycock into Suda Bay of a 'stocky, bald, terrified' naval commander gibbering with weariness and panic. 'My God it's hell . . . Look at me, no gear. Oh my God, it's hell. Bombs all the time. Left all my gear behind.' Shortly afterwards, on land, they met Lieutenant-Colonel Colvin, whose crack-up would provide Waugh with the model for Major Hound's in his novel, but who 'did not seem particularly nervous that night', and then Freyberg – 'composed but obtuse'.

After they reached Layforce headquarters, Laycock sent Waugh forward to give Colvin his orders. 'At one point in our journey, General Weston popped out of the hedge. He seemed to have lost his staff and his head.' He reproved Waugh for producing a map to show him where Laycock was. 'Don't you know better than to show a map? It's the best way of telling the enemy where headquarters are' – a remark baffling in its inconsequentiality. Weston tried to hitch a lift from Waugh back to Laycock, but Waugh insisted on going forward to find Colvin. 'I used to command here once', Weston said wistfully. Waugh's habitual insolence towards superior officers – probably the main reason for his frustrations in the army – was never more cruelly and successfully applied.

Back in Egypt Colvin's obsession with discipline had plagued the unorthodox Waugh. Now Waugh found him a total wreck – hunched under a table in his headquarters in a farm building 'like a disconsolate ape'. When the Luftwaffe took their usual break for lunch, Colvin emerged, and 'still looked a soldierly figure when he was on his feet'.

But as the aeroplanes returned he lay rigid with his face in the gorse for about four hours. At night, in a panic, while Laycock was absent, Colvin ordered Layforce headquarters to withdraw and took men on an all-night march through mobs of retreating stragglers. 'All the officers', Waugh noted cynically, 'seemed to have made off in the motor transport.' Colvin marched insensately on. 'Nothing but daylight would stop him. The moment that came he popped into a drain under the road and sat there.' Waugh found Laycock and brought him to Colvin, 'still in his drain'. Laycock relieved him of his command – 'You're done up. Ken will take over from you.'[24]

Laycock, polite to this unfortunate officer, showed a consideration which Waugh refused to concede. Colvin was obviously shell-shocked. When Laycock was negotiating his flit from the island, General Weston, who had at first charged him with the task of surrender next day, changed his mind – 'it was foolish to sacrifice a first-class man' – and allotted the role to Colvin. What became of Colvin is not clear. He may have embarked with Laycock, who sent the surrender instruction back to George Young, still with the Commando rearguard. The editor of Waugh's diaries thought that, like Hound in the novel, he 'disappeared'.[25]

Waugh was consumed with guilt over Laycock's flit and his connivance in it. This may explain his obstreperous mood when he returned to Egypt. He went to see his friend and future biographer Christopher Sykes, who had a job at GHQ, Cairo, and when Sykes asked about Crete, overboiled with anger:

> He said that he had never seen anything so degrading as the cowardice that infected the spirit of the army. He declared that Crete had been surrendered without need; that the officers and men were hypnotised into defeatism by the continuous dive bombing which with a little courage one could stand up to; that the fighting spirit of the British armed services was so meagre that we had not the slightest hope of defeating the Germans; that he had taken part in a military disgrace, a fact that he would remember with shame for the rest of his life.

As Sykes notes, such extreme views, repeated to others, 'including people he met for the first time', can have done his prospects in the army no good at all.[26]

In *Officers and Gentlemen*, begun eleven years later, Waugh of course refracted what had become his settled view of the battle through his fictional characters. Colvin became Brigade-Major Hound – less senior, rather more sympathetically observed. Laycock was eliminated, since his fictional counterpart Colonel Backhouse breaks his leg in transit to Crete and takes no part in the battle. Something like Laycock's flit, though, is attributed to Ivor Claire, a Household Cavalry officer serving with the Commando who deserts his soldiers at Sphakia and is spirited from Egypt to India by the resourceful Mrs Stitch lest word of his disgrace might ruin him. Guy Crouchback has grown especially fond of Claire – he is outrageously effete, but a wonderful horseman, and seems possessed of spiritual depth. He is shocked and shamed by Claire's desertion, but connives in the shielding of him by the aristocratic Mrs Stitch, defending one of her own class against rule-bound vulgarians. Guy himself, left behind on Crete, escapes with ad hoc company in an open boat and barely survives a terrible crossing to Egypt. (In historical fact, hundreds managed to get off in similar ways.) His sacrificial courage clearly relates to Waugh's wish that he himself had stayed honourably behind rather than going with Laycock, just as his disillusionment with Claire echoes the shattering of Waugh's own hopes of a chivalric, crusading war in the company of choice, aristocratic, spirits.

Walking through the chaos of Crete, Crouchback at one point encounters his old comrades, the 'Halberdiers', now in the rearguard. Royal Marines were actually on the island, but commanded by Weston whom Waugh despised – this is a dreamed-up encounter. The Halberdiers are shining lights of stiff morale, completely cool under bombardment. Guy wistfully asks to be taken back – after all, he points out, they have incorporated a company of New Zealanders, who, Colonel Tickeridge has told him, 'rolled up and said please may they join in our battle – first class fellows'. After Tickeridge replies, 'No can do' – Guy is under a different command – Guy watches the Halberdiers execute a withdrawal in which 'everything' is done correctly, before he plods on to rejoin his Commando.[27]

So Waugh, in his artistic resolution of his Cretan experiences, did acknowledge that not all morale was bad, and, in a brief but telling reference, recognized the special qualities of the New Zealanders.

Perhaps the New Zealanders did so well because Crete, as a terrain, was less alien to them than it was to their Commonwealth comrades-in-arms.[28] In the Antipodes, New Zealand lay in Mediterranean latitudes. Its people depended on agriculture and livestock, like the Cretans, and unlike the urbanized British and Australians. New Zealand's mountainous terrain, especially rugged in South Island, perhaps made the White Mountains which were crossed to get to Sphakia seem not quite so daunting to its soldiers.

The first attacks on Crete on 20 May, in the western sector, were borne almost entirely by the New Zealand Division – 'the Div' as its members called it. Four battalions of Hargest's 5th Brigade were stretched along about five miles of the north-west coast. Some three miles to the east, there was the newly improvised 10th New Zealand Brigade, of which more later. The 4th New Zealand Brigade was towards the outskirts of Canea. So New Zealanders were first in the fighting, and virtually the last off in the navy's evacuation ships. In between, two of them won VCs.[29]

Correspondingly, questions of blame for the defeat revolve mostly around New Zealand commanders. Bernard Freyberg was a huge man physically, VC with DSO and two bars in the First World War, when he had been copiously wounded. Churchill described this durable hero as the 'Salamander of the British Empire'. He was perhaps, as Waugh thought, 'obtuse', and suffered from an incapacity to deal sternly with faulty subordinates, but he communicated, as one historian puts it, his own 'Homeric gusto' to the infantry he led. Waugh saw him at dusk outside the cave in the gorge above Sphakia where had set up head-quarters, 'saying goodbye to New Zealanders who were leaving that evening. Some had photographs of him which he signed.' Cultivated, somewhat romantic, brilliant at training men, Freyberg had a 'relaxed attitude towards formal discipline'.[30]

However, he was not so popular with his senior subordinates. He was not quite a real New Zealander. Born near London in 1889, he had been taken to New Zealand as a small child, had trained as a dentist and territorial soldier there, but then departed, as a ship's stoker, to see the world. After his First World War heroics, he had settled in Britain as a professional soldier, deeply aggrieved when he was retired on health grounds in 1937. When the New Zealand government in 1939 accepted his own offer of his services and put him in charge of their volunteer expeditionary force, 'the Div', he was an Anglicized outsider coming in above Brigadier Puttick, who had played a leading part in forming and training the force. On that fateful 20 May, Puttick commanded in the Malame area. Under him there was Brigadier Hargest of 5th Brigade, like Freyberg a Gallipoli veteran, but latterly a Conservative MP in the New Zealand parliament. Freyberg had tried to have him rejected in 1939 as too old and without recent military experience, but political pressure had prevailed. Brigadier Inglis was, like Kippenberger, a lawyer in peacetime – 'quick thinking', but also 'pugnacious and opinionated' – the Judas who eventually spoilt Freyberg's reputation with Churchill when he got to London soon after the Cretan disaster.[31]

All these men, though, had one thing in common with Freyberg. They had distinguished themselves in the trench warfare of 1914–18 and were not quite able to adjust to a new style of war in which air power might be decisive and mobility was imperative. As Dan Davin tells us, such veterans receded from senior positions as 'the Div' fought on, so that 'in its prime' in Africa and Italy it was 'officered by men in their twenties and thirties, at least at battalion level'.[32]

However, the way 'the Div' had been raised guaranteed that even in Crete there was rapport across the ranks. New Zealand had a population of only 1,630,000 people, including 90,000 Maoris. Commitment to the British cause was total. The smallest of the dominions rationed its copious supplies of home-grown food so that Britain might be fed, agonized over the Mother Country's ordeal in 1940, and committed the same proportion of its expenditure to the war effort, becoming, on a par with Britain, the most heavily mobilized of all combatant countries. Nearly a tenth of the population entered the armed forces, 50,000 served overseas. Proportionately, more New Zealanders were killed in the war than from any other part of the Empire.[33] Under this overarching, national dedication, 'the Div' fostered local loyalties.

'The Div' had three brigades, each with three battalions. The Maori battalion was attached to any one of these as occasion prompted. It was subdivided into units approximately corresponding to 'tribal' areas. In each brigade, likewise, the first two battalions were drawn from the Auckland and Wellington areas of North Island and the third from South Island. As Davin writes:

> The territorial divisions thus described became more difficult to maintain as the war went on, but to the end – at battalion level especially – they were an important factor in pride and morale: officers and men in a given unit tended to know each other from civilian life – from school, the office or factory, university, the rural district, work or the playing field – or a combination of any of these. Since men and officers alike were drawn from an egalitarian population, social class as a distinction or sanction barely existed . . .

Ties to New Zealand, so many thousands of miles away, remained strong: 'the troops were as zealous to sustain their standing in the eyes of family and friends back in, say, Southland, as a provincial Rugby football side would be or the All Blacks [NZ national rugby team] on tour.'[34]

Whether or not primary group loyalties are seen as always, in general, everywhere, the main reason why soldiers keep on fighting in such a hell as Crete became, there is no doubt that in the particular case of 'the Div' they were crucial. The closeness between Freyberg, Kippenberger and their men made strict, formal discipline inappropriate. Thinking of John Keegan's 'triad' of factors in morale, 'coercion' was relatively unimportant compared with the 'inducement' of sustaining local and family traditions of service and courage. If 'narcosis' featured, the adrenalin-rich rush of pride, comparable to the emotions experienced on and around the rugby field, could be as potent as drugs or alcohol. The very fact that New Zealand was a small nation paradoxically made for big courage – and there were, in Keegan's parlance, some very big men providing inspiration to others in 'the Div'. They did not come bigger than Freyberg or cooler under fire than Kippenberger.[35]

Sandy Thomas, a junior officer on Crete, thought his platoon there

a grand crowd – wonderful company for the past year since I, a very raw second lieutenant of twenty years had welcomed them all into the mobilisation camp at Burnham, New Zealand. Most of them were from my district and were either miners, bushmen or farmhands. There were also those who, like me, had been country bank clerks, or shop assistants.

Such men, Thomas noted, did not take kindly to being told to withdraw from the Malame area.

They had seen so many of the enemy dead that their morale was quite unshaken by the terrific air attacks by day. Man for man they considered that they could lick the German despite his superior weapons and equipment. Their fathers had made a name in the first war for ruthless and invariably successful night attacks.[36]

New Zealand troops made fun of the Luftwaffe, capturing the coloured strips used by the Germans to signal supplies from the air, and collecting for their own use what was duly dropped. High spirited when cheerfulness was in order, they stuck by each other when things got bad. In a characteristic cameo, three New Zealand sappers are on the road to Sphakia. The officer, Phil, has bad feet, torn to shreds by walking, and tries to order the other two to leave him behind to his fate. They refuse. As Sapper Trethowen recalled, 'We had been through a lot together and we were staying together.' The three eventually embarked at 12.45 a.m. on 1 June, amongst the very last to go. Whatever his failings as politician or brigadier, Hargest, like Freyberg and

Kippenberger, was loath to accept evacuation ahead of some of his men. As his 5th Brigade marched as best they could down the rocky path to Sphakia to embark, it was seen that 'All had shaved. They wore helmets and haversacks. Every man carried a weapon.' Lesser mortals 'got on their feet to watch them pass. There were murmurs in the darkness, "It's the New Zealanders, the New Zealanders." '[37]

The young English tank officer Roy Farran had experienced early in the battle that awe which New Zealand morale eventually evoked in many outsiders. As he took his tank up towards Galatas on 20 May, after the airborne attack had started, he 'passed several New Zealand positions, where the troops stood up and gave us the "thumbs up" sign with a grin. Just to look at their confident, smiling faces was good for the spirit.' Later that day, told to cooperate with New Zealanders in an attack on the Galatas cemetery, he hid his tank among trees and walked down to 19th Battalion headquarters to report to Colonel Blackburn for orders.

> I had some difficulty in finding him, firstly because we were interrupted by an air raid, and secondly because he was out in the forward defence lines potting at a sniper. I ran along to him with my head ducked, bullets whistling all round, until I noticed that ducking did not quite seem to be the fashion in this part of the world. With a tremendous effort, I tried to appear brave and walked up to him. He muttered, 'Just a moment,' out of the corner of his mouth, and only turned when he had brought the sniper tumbling from a neighbouring tree.

Later in the campaign, he watched Maoris falling back with the Germans close behind, 'but not a shadow of fear showed on their smiling, copper faces. As they passed my tank, they winked and put up their thumbs. Some fifty yards behind the rest came two Maoris carrying a pot of stew across a rifle.'[38]

At Galatas again, on 25 May, Farran was able to help New Zealanders stage a counter-attack which would figure in history books as a little epic of spontaneous group heroism. About four that afternoon, Farran was ordered to take his two tanks up to cooperate with Kippenberger, currently in charge of the improvised New Zealand 10th Brigade, whose headquarters had been in Galatas.

Around the events which followed, the first British official historian, Buckley, felt entitled to deploy purple prose unsuitable for other parts of his sorry story. The New Zealanders, 'men of English blood from the land of the Southern Cross', matched, he said, the spirit of Alfred the Great's Saxons against the Danes at Ethandune, with that heroism 'that has so often snatched victory from defeat'.[39] Unfortunately, Kippenberger snatched no more than the briefest of respites, if that, from ongoing defeat, and his own quite dry account should take precedence as we try to imagine the counter-attack.

His 10th Brigade represented in microcosm the higgledy-piggledy, patchwork character of the whole Commonwealth force in the west of the island at this time. When battle had been joined on 20 May, he had had under his command 2,300 Greek troops in two battalions whom he thought were mostly useless. The 20th New Zealand Brigade numbered 650, but could not be used without approval at divisional level. The New Zealand Divisional Cavalry, 190 men, were untrained in infantry work, though well disciplined. There were one and a half platoons of New Zealand machine-guns, and one battery armed with three Italian 75s without sights. There was, finally, the First Composite Battalion of 750 men, gunners and members of service corps mobilized as infantry, but no good, Kippenberger thought, except in defence. By 25 May, many of these men were coming round to the opinion that they had done enough fighting. Generally ill-equipped, the brigade had only about six digging tools per company.

A picturesque young Englishman, Michael Forrester, an officer in the Queen's Regiment attached to the Greek Mission, had turned up on a visit and decided to stay for what he called 'the party'. He had managed to rally many of the Greeks and on 22 May had led a charge of about a hundred Greek soldiers and Cretan villagers, including women and children, 'yelling like Red Indians', which had startled German attackers into precipitate retreat. But the Composite Battalion was demoralized, and General Puttick, in overall charge of the sector, decided on 23 May that the still battleworthy 18th Battalion should reinforce Kippenberger.

On 25 May, the Germans attacked the 18th in front of Galatas. The village was lost. A first counter-attack by a force including the padre, clerks, batmen and 'everyone who could carry a rifle' failed. The 20th Battalion, now ordered up, found the Composite Battalion 'nearly all gone', and, as the Germans continued to press, 'suddenly the trickle of stragglers turned into a stream, many of them on the verge of panic'. Kippenberger rallied them in person, 'shouting "Stand for New Zealand!" and everything else I could think of', and managed to place many under the nearest officers and NCOs – 'in most cases the men responding with alacrity'.

In the new line which he constructed on a ridge to the west of Galatas, the band of the 4th Brigade stood next to the Pioneer Platoon of the 20th Battalion, the Kiwi Concert Party of entertainers intended to relieve the *longueurs* of army life, and A Company of the 23rd Battalion. The 20th Battalion was to extend this line. Kippenberger's memoirs state that he ordered Farran to go into the village to reconnoitre and blaze away. In Farran's own account, the young man, bitter about signs of impending defeat and anxious to help the New Zealanders whose wounded he had seen, bandages on heads, arms in slings, as he drove up, 'asked permission to go in first, alone'. Two more companies of the 23rd arrived while Farran's tanks were shooting up the village. Kippenberger told the commanders that they would have to retake the village, with the two tanks. 'Stragglers and walking wounded were still streaming past. Some stopped to join in.' So did a noted New Zealand sportsman, Carson, a brave officer now leading only four men. When Farran reappeared his lead tank had two wounded men in it. Volunteers were asked for to replace them, and the chosen two were taken off for ten minutes' training.

Then came the charge, in gathering darkness. The tanks set off downhill, followed by the ad hoc infantry, who began running and shouting in a 'terrifying crescendo'. Kippenberger listened to the din, augmented by gunfire. By the time it was clear what had happened in the village, 'we had lost', he notes drily, 'both tanks, Farran was wounded and in each company some thirty men were hit. Two of the subalterns who had led the charge, Sandy Thomas and Rex King, were badly wounded . . .' So, far from feeling triumphant over the recapture of Galatas, Kippenberger felt 'more tired than ever before in my life, or since'. He walked to report and consult at Brigade headquarters, where the commanders agreed that Galatas must now be abandoned, and everyone brought back before morning to the line established by Kippenberger on the Daratsos ridge.

Next day it turned out that the Composite Battalion had retreated, 'for its own reasons'. The game was clearly lost, and Kippenberger was 'unashamedly pleased' to get Freyberg's order to move towards Sphakia.[40]

So the recapture of Galatas achieved, at the time, nothing of consequence. As years wore on, though, it came to encapsulate the improvisational flair, raw courage and volunteer morale of 'the Div' on Crete. The outsider Farran's account, published in 1948, turned it into pure Hollywood.

Farran claims that 'about three hundred' New Zealanders volunteered to replace the wounded men in his lead tank. Later, lying with wounds on his legs and right arm in the inadequate shelter provided by a low stone wall, he prays for the New Zealanders to arrive. 'They came up the main street in a rush, but were met by a hail of machine-gun bullets on the corner. Several went down in a heap, including the Platoon Commander. I shouted, "Come on New Zealand! Clean 'em out New Zealand!" '

The wounded platoon commander was Sandy Thomas. Someone, according to Farran, called out that Germans were on the roof. Farran saw Thomas 'lift himself up on his elbows and take careful aim with his pistol. The German machine-gunner came tumbling down the slates on to the street below. It was an astonishing shot in such a light and at such a range.'[41]

Astonishing, indeed, if it happened. One suspects that memories of screen westerns had got mixed up in Farran's mind with events in Galatas. He and Thomas should have published the same story, since both were captured by Germans in the improvised field station and both were flown to Athens for treatment, successful in both cases, of gangrenous wounds; they confabulated in transit. But Thomas's account, published three years later, while equally filmable, is quite different.

He and his comrades, suddenly ordered up to Galatas, sheltered from a lone German aeroplane and first saw Kippenberger from the ditch where they had flung themselves, 'a slight figure, pipe in mouth, standing unconcernedly on the road in contempt of danger'. Rapidly drawn into the brigadier's plan of attack, they found themselves lined up on a terrace just 200 yards from the village. 'It occurred to me suddenly', Thomas writes, 'that this was going to be the biggest moment of my life.' As the infantry followed Farran's tanks, 'the whole line broke spontaneously into the most blood-curdling shouts and battle cries. The effect was terrific. One felt one's blood rising swiftly above fear and uncertainty until only an inexplicable exhilaration, quite beyond description, remained.' Elsewhere, Thomas, quoted by Davin in his official history, analysed that epic yell as a composite of Maori-style *hakas* chanted as rugby matches commenced by school and college teams throughout New Zealand. An NCO, also quoted by Davin, described it as 'the most ungodly row I ever heard. . . cat-calls and battle cries, machine-guns, rifles, hand grenades all going on at once'.

As the New Zealanders surged on yelling and firing at random, a tank, Farran's lead, flew back towards them in retreat. 'The shouting stopped. From the turret a frenzied man screamed, "Let me through . . . For cripes sake run for it – the place is stiff with Germans." ' This may have been one of the eager volunteers, though Thomas does not say so.

Thomas, threatening the driver with a revolver, got him to turn the tank round. 'The maniac in the turret' leapt out and began to flee through the ranks. Thomas knew the effect on morale could be disastrous and that his 'duty as an officer' was to shoot him, but he could not bring himself to do it, and was relieved when a private soldier did the job for him and 'looked grimly around his friends. No one said anything [Thomas goes on]. We just all moved on again, quieter now, but I think the better for that.' The tank sent back soon stood wrecked by the village square, its driver dead. Thomas decided, seeing this, that 'Action, quick action was essential. I decided to charge . . .' As one man the New Zealanders marched across the square and were soon in hand-to-hand combat with the Germans. When someone shouted, 'Look out, that bastard on the roof', according to Thomas he fired along with several others at the helmeted form above which was dropping a grenade. This wounded Thomas in the back at the same time as his thigh was hit by a bullet . . . But he did remember hearing Farran in his 'very English voice' calling out, 'Good show New Zealand . . come on New Zealand.'[42]

Davin's official account inevitably smooths discrepancies into a single heroic flow. From a letter by Captain Bassett written soon afterwards, he conjures up the 'big man' figure of 'that great lump of footballing muscle William Carson, with a broad grin, licking his lips before the counter-attack and saying, 'Thank Christ I've got a bloody bayonet.' Davin salutes the brief affray as 'one of the fiercest engagements fought by any New Zealand troops during the whole war'.[43]

When peace came, after Mr Wu had returned to his writing desk, the surviving members of 'the Div' went back to their rugby clubs. Their war stories barely interconnected with his. New Zealanders had not been immune to onsets of strange behaviour under Luftwaffe attack such as had appalled Waugh in Colvin and Weston. By 27 May, Kippenberger saw the strain telling on his officers. As German fighter planes harried them, one 'continued digging until he could not climb out of his pit'. Another 'appeared walking very fast, with odd automaton-like steps and quivering incessantly. He made a great effort to control himself, offered cigarettes to Jim [Burrows, second in command] and me, and continued his move at high velocity.'[44] To reduce the story of Crete to a straight contrast of colonial courage and British cowardice would be absurd. But Dan Davin's countrymen could pull pride from defeat. Evelyn Waugh's, convinced by his account, will think of it as silly, sorry show. It ain't what you see, it's the way that you see it.

Notes

1   Major-General Sir Howard Kippenberger, *Infantry Brigadier* (Oxford, 1949), pp. 76–8.
2   Evelyn Waugh, *The Diaries of Evelyn Waugh* (Harmondsworth, 1979), pp. 509–10.
3   John Keegan, *The Second World War* (London, 1989), p. 171.
4   The first British official account was in a popular series: Christopher Buckley, *Greece and Crete, 1941* (London, 1952: 1977 edn cited here). Then came Major-General I. S. O. Playfair's version in *The Mediterranean and the Middle East*, Vol. 2 of the UK Military Series of War Histories (London, 1956). The official Australian account had appeared in Gavin Long, *Australia in the War of 1939–45: Greece, Crete and Syria* (Canberra, 1953). Dan Davin's volume in the *Official History of New Zealand in the Second World War . . . Crete* (Wellington, 1953) is by far the fullest, representing the relative importance of this campaign for the smallest of the Dominions. An early unofficial account was by Alan Clark, *The Fall of Crete* (London, 1962) – strongly opinionated. John Hall Spencer, *The Struggle for Crete* (London, 1962) incorporates views supplied to the author by Colonel Laycock. Ian McD. G. Stewart, *The Struggle for Crete* (Oxford, 1966) has become the standard account, though he could not discuss ULTRA. Of the most recent books, Antony Beevor, *Crete: The Battle and the Resistance* (London 1991) gives overdue emphasis to the role of the native population, and Callum MacDonald, *The Last Battle: Crete, 1945* (London, 1993) makes a very able summary of the accumulated knowledge of the subject.
5   See Keegan, *The Second World War*, pp. 163–4.
6   Waugh's 'Memorandum' is printed in the *Diaries*, pp. 489–517. His *Letters*, ed. Mark Amory (London, 1980), cast only a little further light on his experience. An early biography by Waugh's friend Christopher Sykes, *Evelyn Waugh* (London, 1975), established the view that the novelist was disqualified as field officer by the hatred which he roused in his men. This had been suggested by John St John's little memoir, *To the War with Waugh* (London, 1973). Martin Stannard's scholarly *Evelyn Waugh*, vol. II, *No Abiding City* (London, 1992) suggests a more complicated view. Selina Hastings's excellent *Evelyn Waugh: A Biography* (London, 1994) draws further perceptions from 'interviews, letters and advice' from scores of people, many of them friends of Waugh. The *Sword of Honour* trilogy was published in one volume by Penguin in 1984. Though this does not in fact correspond to the conflated version devised by Waugh himself (London, 1965), differences do not affect the Crete episode.
7   Dan Davin, *The Salamander and the Fire: Collected War Stories* (Oxford, 1986), p. x.
8   Dan Davin, *Crete* (Wellington, 1953), p. 402.
9   Kippenberger, *Infantry Brigadier*, p. 72.
10 Len Deighton, *Blood, Tears and Folly: An Objective Look at World War II* (London, 1993), p. 223.
11 Keegan, *The Second World War*, p. 58.
12 W. B. Thomas, *Dare to be Free* (London, 1951), p. 19.

[13] See for example Roy Farran, *Winged Dagger: Adventures on Special Service* (London, 1948), pp. 89–90.

[14] Omer Bartov, *Hitler's Army: Soldiers, Nazis and War in the Third Reich* (Oxford, 1992), *passim*.

[15] Keegan, *The Second World War*, p. 158.

[16] Buckley, *Greece and Crete*, pp. 184, 210, 245.

[17] Farran, *Winged Dagger*, p. 96.

[18] Hastings, *Evelyn Waugh*, pp. 427–30, gives a careful account from Waugh's point of view. Beevor, *Crete*, pp. 219–23, reckons that General Weston, left behind by Freyberg to command the rearguard, was 'collared' by Laycock after the clear order recorded by Waugh had been given, and persuaded to allow Layforce Brigade HQ to leave. As Beevor says, Laycock, undoubtedly a brave man, cannot be accused of personal cowardice. But he did want to be sure of getting off the island.

[19] Kippenberger, *Infantry Brigadier*, pp. 74–5.

[20] MacDonald, *The Lost Battle*, p. 289.

[21] Michael Woodbine Parish, *Aegean Adventure, 1940–43* (Lewes, 1993), pp. 71–2. I owe this reference to Dr Jeremy Crang.

[22] Sykes, *Evelyn Waugh*, p. 216; Waugh, *Letters*, p. 152.

[23] Sykes, *Evelyn Waugh*, p. 202.

[24] Waugh, *Diaries*, pp. 499–504.

[25] Ibid., pp. 508–9; Beevor, *Crete*, pp. 219–22.

[26] Sykes, *Evelyn Waugh*, pp. 215–16.

[27] *Sword of Honour*, pp. 356–60.

[28] I owe this point to an Edinburgh University undergraduate, Harry Acton.

[29] Playfair, *The Mediterranean and the Middle East*, pp. 131, 144.

[30] Buckley, *Greece and Crete*, p. 167; Waugh, *Diaries*, p. 507; MacDonald, *The Last Battle*, pp. 139–43; *Freyberg: Churchill's Salamander* by Laurie Barber and John Tonkin Covell (London, 1990) is an important study.

[31] *DNB*, 'Freyberg' – the biography is by Christopher Sykes; Stewart, *The Struggle for Crete*, pp. 113, 120, 123–04; MacDonald, *The Lost Battle*, pp. 157–8, 298–9.

[32] Davin, *Salamander*, p. ix.

[33] I. C. B. Dear (ed.), *Oxford Companion to the Second World War* (1995), pp. 796–801.

[34] Davin, *Salamander*, pp. viii–xi.

[35] See John Keegan, 'Towards a Theory of Combat Motivation', in Paul Addison and Angus Calder (eds), *Time to Kill* (London, 1997), pp. 3–11.

[36] Thomas, *Dare to be Free*, pp. 8–9, 16.

[37] Buckley, *Greece and Crete*, p. 220; Spencer, *The Struggle for Crete*, pp. 287, 293; Davin, *Official History of New Zealand*, p. 452; Stewart, *The Struggle for Crete*, pp. 467–8.

[38] Farran, *Winged Dagger*, pp. 87–8, 91, 98.

[39] Buckley, *Greece and Crete*, p. 239.

[40] Kippenberger, *Infantry Brigadier*, pp. 49–69.

[41] Farran, *Winged Dagger*, pp. 99–101.

[42] Thomas, *Dare to be Free*, pp. 21–30.

[43] Davin, *Crete*, pp. 297–316.

[44] Kippenberger, *Infantry Brigadier*, p. 71.

Scottish Poets in the Desert

Why did the poets come to the desert?

The first line of Edwin Morgan's poem 'North Africa', from *Sonnets from Scotland*,[1] poses a question which permits obvious and not-so-obvious answers. Scottish poets were naturally impelled towards the desert, but did not have to go there. In the 1939–45 war against Hitler, Scotland's history was largely written, for weal or woe, by the 51st Highland Division – Seaforths, Camerons, Gordons, Black Watch. Its contingent in France, not brought out through Dunkirk in 1940 but rounded up by the victorious Germans at St Valéry, became prisoners of war (an event perversely commemorated by street names in Ullapool, and perhaps elsewhere.) Reorganized, the 51st was in North Africa in 1942 to assist mightily in the 'turning point' defeat of Rommel at El Alamein and the subsequent pursuit of the Germans to Tunisia, then on to Sicily and Italy. Retrained in the flatlands of south-east England to take part in the D-Day invasion of 1944, the 51st performed ingloriously in that utterly different terrain, the *bocage* country of Normandy. An English commander noted that they were 'extremely swollen-headed. They were a law unto themselves; they thought they need only obey those orders that suited them'.[2] Jock bloody-mindedness was brilliantly projected by James Kennaway through his wonderful portrayal of an ex-ranker promoted to acting colonel in his novel, set post-war, *Tunes of Glory* (1956). Jock Sinclair, a former army piper himself, is in his element as his comrades sing. 'Like all drunk men, they got round to the sad tunes, and they sang all the Jacobite songs with sweating vigour: *The Skye Boat Song, Will ye no come back again?, Charlie is my darling, my darling.* They returned for a second time to *We're no awa' to bide awa'* and *I belong to Glasgow.*'[3] What Kennaway, who did his National Service first in the Cameron, then in the Gordon Highlanders, seems to have sensed powerfully was the extent to which the 51st, at El Alamein and onwards to Italy, had become the incarnation not only of the fierce and proud ('swollen-headed') Scottish military ethos but also of Scotland's piping and song tradition.

So the poets 'came to North Africa' to serve with the 51st. But not all of them. Some could not go, some did not want to. Taking the men seated in Sandy Moffat's fictitious collective portrait, *Poet's Pub*, MacDiarmid was too old to fight, though not for war work in Scotland, Mackay Brown too unfit, Iain Crichton Smith too young, and MacCaig was a conscientious objector. Like W. S. Graham, not depicted by Moffat, Goodsir Smith stayed in Scotland, though he wrote impressive poetry about the war.

Morgan's sonnet goes on: 'They learned the meaning of an oasis . . .' Born in Bombay, educated in Edinburgh, Norman Cameron (1908–53) before the war had lived in Mallorca with Robert Graves and worked as an advertising copywriter in London. His job as a wartime propagandist took him to North Africa. 'Green, Green is El Aghir', one of numerous much-anthologized items among his slender output, is not a 'war poem', on the face of it, but a witty poem about the pleasure of reaching, after the desert, a town with water. Italy later yielded him three 'war poems' in a mode common among young British versifiers in uniform – wry, understated, at a distance from the big battles. (See, for other examples, the compendious anthologies produced by the Salamander Oasis Trust, founded in 1976 by writers who had participated in the *Oasis* anthology published in Cairo in 1943: *Poems of the Second World War*, Dent, 1985 and *The Voice of War*, Michael Joseph, 1995.) Several other Scottish poets encountered the desert more painfully than Cameron.

> They learned . . .
> the meaning of heat, fellahin's phrases,
> tents behind the khamsin-blasted dannert.
> We watched Maclean at the Ruweisat Ridge
> give a piercing look as he passed by
> the fly-buzzed grey-faced dead . . .

It is not surprising that Sorley Maclean (1911–96) published only six 'war poems' related to his service with the 51st Highlanders in the desert.[4] Wounded twice already since his arrival in Egypt in December 1941, he suffered injuries to feet and heels when a landmine exploded near him at El Alamein on 2 November 1942, which took him back to Scotland for prolonged hospitalization and ended his soldiering. Yet several of these few poems rank, not only (as even Lowland Sassenachs may infer) with the most powerful ever written in Gaelic, but also, in Maclean's own translation, as the strongest short poems about the Second World War by any writer from the north-west European archipelago, and they are fit to bear comparison with the work of such major participant-poets as the American, Jarrell, the German, Bobrowski, the Russian, Slutsky, the Greek, Elytis and the Hungarian, Radnóti. What Maclean has in common with these writers (and the best English 'war poet', Keith Douglas), is the capacity to focus on particular events very sharply with a vision informed by irony and a sense of 'tragedy' as the Athenians had understood that term. Maclean brings three 'histories' together – that of a war fought needfully against Fascism and Nazism by a British Empire which MacLean detested, that of the Scottish Gaels, saturated in military tradition, and that of Scottish Calvinism, which had come to overlap so largely with Gaeldom.

Maclean had been in emotional and intellectual crisis when he joined the army in 1940, and this continued until 1944, when he met Renee Cameron, whom he married. A hopeless love for an Irish woman had been followed by a tortured affair with a Scottish woman. These were sterile except insofar as they helped to produce the poetry of *Dàin do Eimhir* (1943), his first solo book. Furthermore, his position on the war itself was a lonely one. Though much influenced by Marxism he could not go along with the Communist Party's initial rejection of Britain's cause as simply 'imperialist'. Nor was he convinced by the pacifist gestures of certain people in the Scottish National Party. Joy Hendry suggests that North Africa brought him relief, after many months of training in Britain. 'He became concerned with the plight of the ordinary soldier, irrespective of nationality, forced to fight in a war the origins of which were so remote from him and outwith his control.'[5]

'Going Westwards', with 'a shame on [his] shoulders' which he identifies with that of his entire Gaelic people, Maclean observes the 'innocent corpses of the Nazis':

> There is no rancour in my heart
> against the hardy soldiers of the Enemy,
> but the kinship that there is among
> men in prison on a tidal rock

But 'this is the struggle not to be avoided' and Maclean goes on westward, conscious that he shares the 'ruinous pride' and extreme courage of

> . . . the big men of Braes,
> of the heroic Raasay MacLeods,
> of the sharp-sword Mathesons of Lochalsh . . .

In 'Heroes', still more obviously a masterpiece, Maclean describes the
valour of an ugly little English infantryman, slain fighting against
tanks in the heart of battle. One irony here is that his magnificent
courage inspires other men to face forward and die – 'if a battle post
stands / many are knocked down because of him.' 'Death Valley' is the
poem to which Morgan's sonnet alludes. It derives from Maclean's first
encounter with a German corpse. This mere 'boy' might have been a
committed Nazi, or was he

> . . . of the greater
> band of those
>
> led, from the beginning of generations,
> unwillingly to the trial
> and mad delirium of every war
> for the sake of rulers?

Maclean's wry conclusion displays ironic understatement of a kind
which Gaelic seems to release more readily than English. A linguist
points out that a 'very high degree of co-operation between speaker
and listener . . . is required in the comprehension of understatements'.[6]
One might say that it is the force of Maclean's understatements which
draws readers without Gaelic into his Gaelic mentality with a shock of
recognition, rather than incomprehension. The last lines of 'Death
Valley' are impossible to paraphrase and have to speak for themselves:

> Whatever his desire or mishap,
> his innocence or malignity,
> he showed no pleasure in his death
> below the Ruweisat Ridge.

Comparing this poem with Keith Douglas's justly famous encounter
with a German corpse, in 'Vergissmeinicht', one sees how the English
poet, gaining power over the reader's feelings by evoking the dead
man's girl-friend whose photo is found by him, loses the starker power
that Maclean achieves by setting dead youth in relation, abstractly, to
class, and both in apposition to state power. This fierce austerity relates

strongly to the Calvinist (Wee Free) traditions of his native culture, which MacLean rejected intellectually but continued to respect, and which command his most extraordinary war poem, titled, with supreme understatement, 'An Autumn Day'. Here, under the 'indifferent' sun, the speaker lies for a day, amid the 'snoring' of shells beside six dead 'men' (not 'comrades', nor in any way personalized, just 'men').

> One Election took them
> and did not take me
> without asking us
> which was better or worse:
> it seemed as devilishly indifferent
> as the shells.

The point of transition, frequently crossed, between Calvinism and atheism, has never been made clearer. If God exists, Calvinist logic insists, he must be arbitrary and virtually indifferent. Who can wish to believe in such a God? But the unsentimental rigour of the Calvinist mentality permits an unusually sharp appreciation of the cost of the Desert War. Were these six men, 'Elect', in fact lucky to die?

> We . . . swivelled our eye
> west through tank-strewn dune and strafed-out village
> with Henderson . . .

The war helped to make Hamish Henderson a writer unique in Scottish literature. He went into uniform from Cambridge University. He had visited Germany on behalf of a Quaker organization in 1939, and was familiar with German poetry. As an information officer with the Highlanders in North Africa, he interviewed German prisoners in their own language, to which he added Italian – he stayed on in Italy after the division had been withdrawn to take part in D-Day, and became the first to translate the Italian Marxist theorist Gramsci into English. But beside his 'high' intellectual concerns, he was passionate about folk music, and made it his business to see that his comrades-in-arms had topical songs. 'The 51st Highland Division's Farewell to Sicily', written on the island to a familiar pipe tune, preceded him back to Scotland, and later, as a folklorist taping singers in the north, he encountered it rendered by veterans who did not know he was the author. No one since Burns, Scott and Hogg had lived so fully on the interface between literary and folk culture.

Yet his first and only 'slim volume' of poetry, *Elegies for the Dead in Cyrenaica*, published by John Lehmann in London in 1948, requires a reader with some knowledge of ancient Egypt, alert to echoes of Homer, attuned to Goethe and Rilke, aware of Gaelic tradition. 'Ten Elegies' – two sets of five with an 'Interlude' – and the 'Heroic Song' in which they culminated were started in North Africa in 1942 and completed in Argyll in 1947. In his foreword to the first editon, Henderson wrote: 'It was the remark of a captured German officer which first suggested to me the theme of these poems. He had said: "Africa changes everything. In reality we are allies, and the desert is our common enemy".'[7] The book's title page is inscribed, 'For our own and the others.' Introducing a reprint nearly thirty years after the *Elegies*' first appearance, Sorley Maclean explained how they matched his own experience. Few civilian natives lived in the terrain where the British fought against Rommel and his Italian allies. This was a fast-moving war, backwards, forwards, backwards, forwards, wholly unlike the trenches of the 1914–18 Western Front. 'The combatants were as if abstracted from the real world to fight on a remote moon-like terrain, and in general the only bitterness against the "enemy" was when a soldier got news of deaths of his near and dear by civilian bombing at home.' He agreed with Henderson's statement, which he quoted, that the war seemed to be between 'the dead, the innocent – that wronged proletariat of levelling death in which all the fallen are comrades – and ourselves, the living . . .' (pp. 10–11). Henderson, precociously aware of Maclean's verse, had taken an epigraph, in Gaelic, from 'Death Valley'.

The *Elegies* together form the only long poem in English by a young 'soldier poet' to match in scale and seriousness (and erudition) Eliot's contemporaneous *Four Quartets*. One finds a Continental counterpart in Odysseus Elytis's *Heroic and Elegiac Song for the Lost Second Lieutenant of the Albanian Campaign*, likewise produced soon after the war's end by a poet with combatant experience. But Elytis is more sensuous, less systematically intellectual, marked by the impact, pre-war, of surrealism. Henderson's sonorous discourse blends conversational directness with slow measures evocative of (say) translations of Homer and Rilke's *Duino Elegies*. Close to the squaddies whose deaths he grieves, Henderson's speaker nevertheless maintains the over-vision and authority which inform his most quoted line – 'There were no gods and precious few heroes' – and the ancient-Athenian judgement later in the first Elegy 'that all / have gone down like curs into anonymous silence'. In the Third Elegy, 'Leaving the City', the evocation of Jocks trucking back to the desert to rejoin the 'proletariat / of levelling death', agents 'of a dialectic that can destroy us', is elevated by quotations from Cavafy.

Henderson, more expansively, explores the same paradox as Sorley Maclean – both are deeply sympathetic with German and Italian 'brothers', yet both feel the compulsion to fight, bravely, with honour, which in Highland tradition had so often attached itself to doomed clans and causes. The Fifth Elegy, 'Highland Jebel', with an epigraph from Hölderin, uses a term, 'the Grecian Gael', explained by Henderson in a note, as one employed occasionally by Scottish and Irish bards to refer to their own people, so that the cry 'Another falls for Hector' evokes not only the *Iliad*, but also the war cry of the 700 Macleans who died fighting for their chief at the fatal Floddenesque battle of Inverkeithing in 1651: *Fear eile airson Eachainn!* The 'Interlude' which follows, 'Opening of an Offensive', employs accents to mark stress, as in the poems of Hopkins, in an effort to suggest the fury of the British barrage. And even above this the yell of the bagpipes of the advancing Jocks is heard:

> . . . The shrill war-song: it flaunts
> aggression to the sullen desert. It mounts. Its scream
> tops the valkyrie, tops the colossal
>   artillery.
>
> Meaning that many
> German Fascists will not be going home
> meaning that many
> will die, doomed in their false dream
> We'll mak siccar! . . .

This necessary explosion of partisan ardour exhausted, the second half of the sequence reverts to wry meditation. The Sixth Elegy questions painfully whether the deaths of men in the desert were, as the top brass would have it, 'necessary':

> No blah about their sacrifice: rather tears or reviling
> of the time that took them, than an insult so outrageous.

The speaker now seeks words with the power 'to reconcile and heal'. In the Seventh Elegy 'Seven Good Germans' are vividly and ironically characterized – Henderson draws on his direct encounters with prisoners, and his first-hand knowledge of Germany and its culture and goes out with words from the song 'Lili Marlene', broadcast by German radio from Belgrade to the desert, which chimed with the yearning of soldiers of all nationalities, and generated a quasi-operatic version in Italian and a Tin Pan Alley best-selling disc in English. The remarkable Eighth Elegy takes us to Karnak and confronts the rich, hieratic, death-obsessed culture of ancient Egypt with the land's repeated subjection to foreign conquest –

> . . . the trampling migrations of peoples,
> the horsemen of Amr, the 'barbarians' of Cavafy
> and Rommel before the gates of Alexandria . . .

> . . . the Other, the recurrent
> the bearded
> the killer in the rhythmical tragedy
> the heir the stranger

At this point Henderson's Marxism is perilously close to dissolving into a view of history as cyclical rather than progressively dialectical. But there is in fact no way that he can fully reconcile his compassion for the Germans whose deaths Marxist orthodoxy deems to be 'necessary' with his own conviction that Fascism must be fought ferociously. The Tenth Elegy, voiced from a post-war return to the battlefield, exhorts that surviving soldiers should

> . . . inhabit that desert
> of canyon and dream – till we carry to the living
> blood, fire and red flambeaux of death's proletariat.
> Take iron in your arms! At last, spanning this history's
> apollyon chasm, proclaim them the reconciled.

This rhetoric expresses not a solution of the dilemma, but, in its hazy unconvincingness, impasse. So the 'Heroic Song for the Runners of Cyrene', with which the sequence concludes, must necessarily give emotive force to the Rilkean notion of 'early death' as transcendent. Henderson's note explains that Cyrene for him is 'a symbol of civilized humanity, of our "human house"' and that his symbol of the runners was suggested by the 'legend of the brothers Philaeni who competed against athletes from Cyrene'. He does not explain that this was more than an athletic contest. Cyrene and Carthage argued over the extent of their territories. It was agreed that at a stated hour two men should leave each city, and the boundary should be fixed where they met. When they did meet, deep in territory claimed by Cyrene, the Cyreneans asserted that the Philaeni had jumped the gun, overpowered them, buried them in the sand – and then, in honour of their self-sacrificial patriotism, raised two altars upon their graves. These were then acknowledged as the actual boundary of the Carthaginian dominions. It seems to me that this complicated old tale (from Sallust) may have influenced Henderson less than memories, perhaps unconscious, of 'The Song of the Ungirt Runners', the most famous production of Charles Hamilton Sorley, the one Scot to rank high among the martyred 'soldier poets' of 1914–18:

> We swing ungirded hips,
> And lightened are our eyes,
> The rain is on our lips,
> We do not run for prize.
> We know not whom we trust
> Nor whitherward we fare,
> But we run because we must
> Through the great wide air.[8]

Gladly, Henderson's Cyreneans run towards the arrows of enemies – 'the clash close at hand, O incarnate dialectic' –

> Each runs to achieve, without pause or evasion
> his instant of nothing
>
> they look for an opening
> grip, grapple, jerk, sway
> and fall locking like lovers
>
> down the thunderous cataract of day.

The German Romantic conception of the *doppelgänger,* the shadowing double – which can be related to Owen's great and simple line in 'Strange Meeting', 'I am the enemy you killed, my friend' – has been immanent throughout the sequence. Now the *doppelgänger* of these runners, running to meet them, is 'history' itself. So Henderson uses symbols to reconcile the proletariat of the dead with the Marxist dialectic and to those who still live in and with the history which the dead have made.

> *. . . and Hay saw Bizerta*
> *burn . . .*

George Campbell Hay (Deorsa Caimbeul Hay, 1915–84) will remain an enigma until (and perhaps after) the long-awaited complete edition of his poems in Gaelic, Scots and English is published. MacDiarmid had valued him before the war as a contributor to his periodical *Voice of Scotland,* and continued to praise his Gaelic verse during and after it. He coupled Hay with Sorley Maclean as a rising genius and after Hay's *Fuaran Sleibh,* with English translations, was published by Maclellan of Glasgow in 1947, MacDiarmid pronounced that it was 'unquestionably' the 'most important volume of Gaelic poetry for a century and a half.' (So much for *Dàin do Eimhir*: MacDiarmid, *The Raucle Tongue: Hitherto Uncollected Prose,* Vol. 3, Carcanet, 1998, p. 165). But, despite publication *in extenso* with Maclean (and William Neill and Stuart MacGregor) in Gordon Wright's compilation of 1970, *Four Points of a Saltire* (Edinburgh), Hay's work has never achieved wide public acclaim. His verse is commonly well-shaped but uningratiating, marked by fatalism and bitterness. It seems that war service in North Africa shattered him, and that in particular he could not get over his shock at the effect of the conflict on native Muslims. He responded to the Islamic world in a long poem *Mokhtar and Dughall,* written during the war in Gaelic and left incomplete, which was published in 1982, but remains fugitive. A short extract in the Oasis anthology *Poems of the Second World War* (1985, pp. 86–7) emphasizes, as Maclean or Henderson might have done, the community in death of the Muslim casualty with the Scot. 'Bizerta', the powerful Gaelic poem which struck Edwin Morgan, is a rare case where a poet of the Second World War concentrates his compassion on foreign victims of bombardment. On night guard, the speaker sees the distant Tunisian city burning, but cannot hear the screams and lamentation which he must imagine in 'the poor streets where, every window spews / its flame and smoke.'[9] The city's agony is identified with unmitigated evil.

> *Garioch was taken at Tobruk,*
> *Parched* Kriegsgefangener, *calm, reading Shveik.*

Morgan's German word here means simply 'prisoner of war'. If Hay, for whatever reasons, has been neglected, Robert Garioch Sutherland (1909–81) has been misremembered. Loved in Edinburgh as a satirical-comic writer in what he called 'artisan' Lowland Scots, a natural choice as 'Poet Laureate' for Radio Forth, Garioch has been seen rather differently by English editors who have anthologized his war poetry. He had made a small but distinctive mark on Scottish letters in 1940 when he had published *Seventeen Poems for Sixpence*, printed on his own handpress, in collaboration with his friend Sorley Maclean. He was captured by the Germans in mid-1942, before the 'glorious' turnaround at El Alamein, and was long confined in Italy. His verse from the war years, in Scots and English, not all reprinted in his *Collected Poems* (Macdonald, Loanhead, 1977; Carcanet, 1981), varies greatly in mode and mood. 'Letter from Italy', in deft octosyllabic couplets, with fluent traditional English diction, must commend itself to anthologists by its straightforward 'timeless universality' – the prisoner, beholding the stars, thinks of someone at home looking, like him, at the Plough – whereas 'Kriegy Ballad', revised by Garioch for the 1985 Oasis anthology (pp. 193–5) is a Hendersonian exercise in scatological 'folk-song', recording with jocularity the hunger and the discomforts in fulfilling bodily functions which were the lot of POWs:

> At Musso's show camp at Vetralla
> They gave us beds, blankets and sheets,
> They'd even got chains in the shit-house.
> But still they had no bloody seats.

'The Presoner's Dream', contributed by Garioch to Oasis and included in its 1995 anthology, is not in *Collected Poems*. It is a pleasantly half-jocular, half-eerie poem in 'artisan Scots' in which the captive, after eating a raw onion, has a nightmare about his home town, Edinburgh.

The production which, more than any other in his entire œuvre, might seem to establish Garioch as a 'major poet' transcending dry Lothian jest, is 'The Wire' – a long poem, ambitious, stark and very strong. Set in a POW camp, it is framed in *Collected Poems* by 'The Bog' and 'The Muir', which emblematically evoke Scottish landscape. The three together constitute Garioch's exploration of the essential human condition in its Scottish variant. The 'bog' is a clarty morass in which feet pine for stones, and Garioch's speaker dreams of bright foreign light. Meanwhile, German bombing planes pummel Scotland –

> The causey street we staund on shaks and shogs,
> freestane fowre-storey housses flee in air;
> real super-realism everywhere
> maks grand pianos mate wi clarty bogs.

The speaker now accepts the bog, finds that it does sustain his weight, and wrily notices in it 'colours braw as onie shroud' and a Scottish travesty of the legendary gold at the foot of the 'watergaw'. The 'muir' in the later poem, written well after the war's end, which follows 'The Wire' in *Collected Poems,* evokes Dante in a Highland setting – 'In Hell, the winds swack and the waters swaw / as on Loch Slapin.' While Paradiso would be 'Badenoch in simmer, wi nae clegs about', every Scot can recognize features of Inferno in the daily life around him. But in our faithless age,

> Nou that the Deil's awa, our skaith's the waur;
> for want of Hell, we tine the Warld alsweill.

What follows is an exploration, as if animated by MacDiarmid's call that poets should cope with science, of the intellectual consequences of the overthrow by Einstein and other twentieth-century thinkers of Newton's steady conception of the universe, intercut with references to the madness and visions of the poet Fergusson – 'gyte in Darien, / jummlin his heid wi thochts of Satan's den.' Hellfire, curiously, seems more real than the particles conceived by modern science. Pipe music and poetry give us solidity of identity. The tuneless howl of Fergusson's singing in the madhouse correctly estimated the human condition. War images flood in – futile manoeuvres by soldiers, the explosion at Hiroshima which proved that nuclear physics worked.

In the tradition of 'common sense' philosophy, Garioch asserts the ultimate supremacy of direct human apprehension, as the invisible forces discovered by scientists prove their causal effects in visible life:

> Licht isna quantum and it isna wave,
> just licht itsel, and naething mair nor less.

The poem ends with an evocation of the beauty of Badenoch – even with clegs about – and an affirmation of the spiritual superiority of human feeling to scientific knowledge. *Pace* MacDiarmid, Garioch has shown that Lallans is capable of handling the most advanced scientific ideas. He has also expressed as fully and strongly as any writer the 'post-Calvinist' mentality characteristic of twentieth-century Scottish intellectuals, still haunted by the logic of a dour creed and the riposte to it by the philosophers of the Enlightenment. MacDiarmid whored intellectually after strange Russian gods – Garioch asserts Scottish philosophical tradition.

'The Wire' presents a prison camp as emblematic. 'Ane endless muir' is in vision, a bleak, sunless mirage of autumnal Scotland, until the 'gossamer' seen everywhere proves to be barbed wire. Nightmare intensifies. Guards, 'cruel and persecuted, baith' stand always ready to shoot any prisoner who interferes, however accidentally, with the wire. The victim's body is devoured by guard dogs.

> Impersonal in uniform,
> the guairds are neither friens nor faes;
> nane ettles to propitiate
> nor fashes them wi bribes or praise . . .
>
> On this dour mechanistic muir
> wi nae land's end, and endless day,
> whaur nae thing thraws a shadow, here
> the truth is clear, and it is wae.

Some prisoners (here the emblematic, not 'realistic', character of Garioch's camp becomes quite clear) tether themselves so that they cannot blunder into the wire, yet, safe though they are, 'aye they ettle to gang free'. Others do 'stravaig' freely – 'their lives are short, but are their ain'. We are back in Edinburgh, by implication – repressed Morningside, reckless Rose Street. Just a few men – we might call them 'elect' – stand apart in 'orra ill-faur'd airts / on barren stretches of the muir', sustained by true vision, acknowledge despair, so attain 'inwart joy'. The camp is emblematic of all human life:

> I saw yon planet slawlie birl;
> I saw it as ane endless muir
> in daylicht, and I saw a few
> guid men bide still amang the stour.
>
> *Morgan ate sand, slept sand at El Ballah*
> *while gangrened limbs dropped into the pail*

Morgan, a conscientious objector, served in the Royal Army Medical Corps as a compromise. As stretcher-bearer and nurse in Egypt and Palestine, he was not spared horrors. It was over thirty years before they surfaced in *The New Divan* (Carcanet, 1977), by when the Cold War nuclear nightmare had supervened. This sequence of a hundred short and cryptic poems draws on memories of the Middle East which are hedonistic as well as disturbing. It evokes Islamic life, gives glimpses of a homosexual love affair, and offers generalized images of war (for example, poems 64, 66, 88 and 89). Only the penultimate poem (p. 56), as if releasing a hitherto secret key to the sequence, presents Morgan's RAMC experience with appalling directness:

> I dreaded stretcher bearing,
> my fingers would slip on the two sweat-soaked handles,
> my muscles not used to the strain.
> The easiest trip of all I don't forget,
> in the desert, that dead officer
> drained of blood, wasted away,
> leg amputated at the thigh,
> wrapped in a rough sheet, light as a child,
> rolling from side to side of the canvas
> with a faint terrible sound
> as our feet stumbled through the sand.
>
> . . . *Farouk*
> *fed Fraser memorandums like a shrike.*

The last poet named by Morgan is associated not with the desert, but with Egypt's corrupt and corpulent puppet King. After five other poets have been accorded tragic vision, and presumably activity of mind, the unpleasant implication is that Fraser is passive, like the nested nursling of a vicious bird. George Sutherland Fraser (1915–80) was a figure of some importance in British literary life from the 1940s through to the 1970s. He was a bellwether for the grotesque 'New Apocalypse' movement of the late 1930s, a fact which Ian Fletcher and John Lucas, the editors of the posthumous *Poems* of G. S. Fraser (Leicester University Press, 1981), chose not to mention, though it would have been a basis for his connection with Tambimuttu's *Poetry London* operation, which published his pamphlet *The Fatal Landscape* in 1943 and his first book, *Home Town Elegy*, in 1944. *The Traveller Has Regrets* appeared from Harvill Press in 1948. More than two decades passed before Fraser's third book, *Conditions,* was published by Byron Press (Nottingham) in 1969. What is curious about Fraser's œuvre is that he was at his most prolific during the war, which he spent in uniform, yet has very little to say about it directly.

Born in Glasgow, Fraser was educated at Aberdeen Grammar School after his father became deputy town clerk of that northern city. After taking a degree at St Andrew's he worked as a trainee journalist on

Aberdeen newspapers. When war broke out, he joined the Black Watch, but his physical ineptitude led to his transfer to the Royal Army Service Corps. This shipped him to Africa in May 1941. In Cairo, then in Eritrea, he worked on army publications, finally, in 1944, becoming a staff writer for the Ministry of Information in Egypt. This entirely honourable service gave him time and occasion to participate in the literary circles of wartime Cairo which included John Wailer, Terence Tiller and Lawrence Durrell, and played host to such soldier-transients as Keith Douglas.

Fraser never returned to Scotland. In London after the war, and through the 1950s, he worked as a freelance journalist and broadcaster. Young poets later associated with the Movement and the Group read at salons in his Chelsea home, and Donald Davie remarked that for years Fraser was arbiter of poetic taste to literary London. In 1958 he transferred to Leicester University, where he became lecturer in English and then Reader in Poetry. He remained a cosmopolitan, who had translated widely from Latin and from French, Italian and Spanish, had stayed with Pablo Neruda in Chile (1947) and sojourned in Japan as cultural adviser to the United Kingdom Liaison Mission (1951–2).

Some of his poetry of the 1940s harks back to Aberdeen – to granite, slates, gulls, and ineffectual dates in ballrooms with prudish girls. He had been a precocious, self-conscious, and (forgivably, of course) pretentious young poet in a city which he thought of, not without reason, as a provincial backwater. The war gave him a chance to become a citizen of the world. He remained fatally facile. The style of his early books melds Auden and Yeats, and echoes the long English poetic tradition, with only a debilitating looseness of imagery to recall his New Apocalypse phase. He prided himself on a 'good ear', but his metrical fluency was cage, not perch or eyrie. The combination of Yeatsian bardishness, Audenesque knowingness and vestigial-Aberdonian reluctance to be caught out posturing is inherently uneasy. Perhaps he would have written better if he had returned to Scotland. But what was there for him in Scotland, when he was demobbed in 1945? In London there was the new BBC Third Programme and the literary pages of august broadsheets. In Scotland . . .?

> In Glasgow, that damned sprawling evil town,
> I interview a vulgar editor,
> Who, brawny, self-made, looks me up and down
> And seems to wonder what my sort is for.
> Do I write verse? Ah, man, but that is bad . . .

> And, too polite, I fawn upon this tough,
> But when I leave him, O my heart is sad.
> *He sings alone who in this province sings.*
> I kick a lamp-post and in drink I rave:
>   With Byron and with Lermontov
>   Romantic Scotland's in the grave.[10]

The refrain, adapted from Yeats's 'September 1913', symptomatically transfers lament from a recently living political figure – O'Leary – to two long-dead poets. The notion that Lermontov's distant descent from a seventeenth-century Scottish mercenary called Learmonth made him part of Scottish tradition presumably came to Fraser from Mac-Diarmid, who had harped on this rather absurdly. Of course, Fraser was not in fact 'singing alone' in Scotland, and the next poem in *Home Town Elegy* is addressed to MacDiarmid. It is a curious and revealing item. It begins by acknowledging MacDiarmid's greatness and relating it to the older man's experience of poverty and adversity – whereas 'I am Convention's child, the cub reporter, / The sleek, the smooth, conservatively poised . . .' Several stanzas of encomium for the em-battled MacDiarmid follow – then this:

> Because my love was never for the common
> But only for the rare, the singular air,
> Or the undifferenced and naked human,
> Your Keltic mythos shudders me with fear.

> What a race has is always crude and common,
> And not the human or the personal:
> I would take sword up only for the human,
> Not to revive the broken ghosts of Gael.[11]

A strategy, if one can call it that, which begins with excessive self-abasement and ends with an assertion of moral superiority over MacDiarmid, whom Fraser suggests is racist, explains why the expatri-ate literary chatter of Cairo, dominated by English voices, diverted Fraser so effectually. It gave him a visa to the London milieu where the Movement emerged, distrustful of potent symbolism and grand political and aesthetic gestures – and where Fraser's own verse-writing withered.

A poem of the 1940s which was never collected by Fraser himself, addressed to John Waller, full of self-disgust and reference to death wish, evokes the ambience of literary Cairo under occupation by the Eighth Army, where males and females in military public relations mingle with Anglophile Egyptian intelligentsia, uneasily conscious that they are not where the action is – in a war which they did not start 'and cannot justify'. Lawrence Durrell sinks whisky at the bar. In breezes Keith Douglas, since dead in Normandy, with

> . . . shrewd and rustic eyes
> that had endured 'the entry of a demon':
> His poems spat out shrapnel; and he lies
> where all night long the Narrow Seas are screaming.[12]

The word 'rustic' strangely applied to Douglas (public school and Oxford) is a tell-tale tiptoe into pastoral mode – real life equals peasant life. The quotation from Douglas's most famous poem, 'Vergiss-meinicht', suggests Fraser's own incapacity to evoke battle, where he has not been, and the vague bombast of the valediction – which may translate as 'Douglas is buried near the French coast not far from the English Channel where war goes on with bombers heading across to Germany and reinforcements and munitions shipped across to the Western Front' – further emphasizes the speaker's distance from action. 'And the bar-propped / Exile has lost the courage to depart . . .': such distance, one might say, was painful, regretted, but sustained after the war as Fraser failed to confront the 'home town' sources of his sensibility.

But awareness of such 'literary scene' as there was in Scotland in the late 1940s might well have deterred able writers from returning. The Gaelic brought back MacLean and Hay, song retrieved Henderson, Lallans Garioch. With MacDiarmid ageing and decreasingly active, leadership of his 'Renaissance' had passed to Douglas Young – classicist, accomplished translator from modern languages, prominent figure in the Scottish National Party, and conscientious objector during the war. Though far from parochial in his vision, and gifted himself as a poet, Young conspicuously failed to measure up to the human crisis of the mid-twentieth century when he edited his influential collection *Scottish Verse 1851–1951* (Edinburgh: Nelson, 1952). Though he included all the poets just discussed, except for the so-far-unproductive Morgan, the only 'war poems' from 1939 to 1945 were an extract from an early (1943) version of what had since become Henderson's 'Interlude' in his *Elegies*, a trite 'Lament for the Gordons' by one David Martin, and a better, but still conventional, 'Coronach' for dead

Gordons by Alexander Scott, in Lallans. I have tried here to express my sense that Maclean, Henderson, Garioch and possibly Hay wrote out of war experiences poetry comparable in strength and seriousness with major work of the day from Europe – and for that matter with the late work of dead Yeats and with Eliot's contemporaneous 'Little Gidding'. This earthquake of achievement was not recorded by the inadequate instruments of Young and of Scottish poetry-reading and publishing circles. Scottish literary culture seems to have been gripped by Lallans faddists, elocution teachers and genteel poetasters. No doubt they cared with passionate sincerity for their own version of Scotland – but it seems that they felt no impetus to set it beside the landmines still littering the desert, the ruins of Europe haunted by displaced persons, the new and apocalyptic threat of nuclear war.

Consider *The New Athenian Broadsheet*, first produced, in Edinburgh, in 1947, to garnish that city's brand-new Festival of Music and Drama. Curious tourists would here have encountered, in Scots and English, poems evoking historic and rural Scotland, without a hint of its grim city tenements and its families grieving for recently dead soldiers. English literary circles had latterly produced Grigson's *New Verse*, Connolly's *Horizon* and Lehmann's *New Writing*. They would soon greet the *London Magazine* and Jon Silkin's *Stand*. All that Scotland's capital, in an era of purported cultural 'renaissance', could come up with was a huddle of verse which would have seemed comfortably old-fashioned even in Edward Marsh's Georgian *Anthologies*, three decades before.

The second, Christmas, number is an even more distressing object. The editor, based in the heart of Morningside, included poems by the dead Soutar and the living Goodsir Smith – but they were represented by verses not offensive to 'Georgian' sensibility. A poem by the vivacious Dorothy Parker was republished by permission – but a solemn little thing about Christ's Nativity, not something witty or political. One would not expect No. 3, 'Spring and Summer Poems', to be more challenging, and it was not. Certain prolific writers of feeble verse were making the broadsheet their own organ, and Scots, as in all its fifteen issues, was an instrument of easy pathos and hackneyed lyricism, not of intellectual or moral challenge. When MacDiarmid made his debut in issue No. 8, in July 1949, it was with a previously unpublished bairn's rhyme 'for a little boy in Linlithgow'. No. 14 (spring 1951) gives his 'The Sauchs in the Reuch Heuch Hauch' pride of place in an issue devoted to 'Poems [forsooth] for Choral Speaking': it had previously appeared in that reassuringly rural and genteel organ, *Scottish Field*.

Metaphorically speaking, Morgan's poets had returned from a literal desert to a literary desert. In the nineteenth century, Edinburgh had led the world in publishing. It had seemed as natural that Gladstone should unbosom his thoughts to the nation through the *Edinburgh Review* and that Blackwoods should publish George Eliot, as that 'Miles Franklin', pioneering Australian feminist fiction in the outback, should send her manuscript to the same Blackwoods. By the 1950s, this great publishing tradition was in terminal decline – Nelson's production of Young's anthology was one dying spasm.

In a review article published in *New Saltire* in autumn 1961, Edwin Morgan asked: 'When are the leading Scottish publishers going to do something about modern Scottish poetry? Every time a reviewer receives a batch of pamphlets by Scottish poets (they are usually pamphlets, not even 'slim volumes'; spineless staplings apparently doomed to ephemerality) he is made aware that there is something wrong with Scottish publishing and wishes he could bring about a change in the situation.' As he observed, it had been left to little printer-publishers – William Maclellan in Glasgow, Callum Macdonald in Edinburgh – to keep things going. In retrospect, Macdonald's founding of *Lines Review* in 1953 had been visionary, and a turning point. Had *Lines* existed in 1946 it could have been a showcase for the poets of the desert, and for Fraser. As it happened, Macdonald's journal outlived *New Saltire*, survived after *Scottish International*, a lively response to '1968 and All That', had perished, and was finally joined in the 1970s by equally tenacious periodicals – *Chapman*, the [initially *New*] *Edinburgh Review* and *Cencrastus*. *Lines* was given its quietus in 1998 not long before Macdonald's own death. It had printed verse by almost every considerable poet in Scotland, as well as much in translation. Macdonald had published collected volumes by Garioch, Crichton Smith and Derick Thomson, and many, many more books of merit. Now there were five other publishers in Edinburgh with respectable lists of new poetry books in print.

Yet perhaps we should not now regret that realization, represented by Sandy Moffat's *Poet's Pub*, that twentieth-century Scotland had produced great poetry by several highly distinctive hands, was delayed until the 1970s, until after Henderson's 'folksong revival' had transformed many Scots' sense of their own culture, Maclean's work had been tumultuously acclaimed in England and MacCaig had moved into his final, most distinctive phase. Reaching by difficult, very different routes the point where a Scottish public existed which was prepared to extol them simultaneously, the modern Makars, bar the glitch or blip, for a couple, of the New Apocalypse, had not been gathered into self-conscious cliques – 'Thirties Poets', 'Movement', 'Confessional Poets', 'Neo-Black Mountain School'. The local clique which had failed to contain them, of neo-Georgian Lallans-mongers, had passed, as Winston Churchill might have put it, into innocuous desuetude. The desert, Milne's Bar, and Macdonald Printers, Loanhead, had nurtured remarkably diverse, sudden and hardy blooms.

1999

Notes

[1] Edwin Morgan, *1984: Collected Poems* (Manchester: Carcanet, 1990), p. 446.
[2] Carlo D'Este, *Decision in Normandy* (London: Harper Perennial, 1994), p. 273.
[3] Edinburgh: Canongate, 1988, p. 140.
[4] Sorley Maclean, *From Wood to Ridge: Collected Poems in Gaelic and English* (Manchester: Carcanet, 1989), pp. 205–15.
[5] R. Ross and J. Hendry (eds), *Sorley MacLean: Critical Essays* (Edinburgh: Scottish Academic Press, 1986), p. 29.
[6] Maria Dossena, 'Diminutives in Scottish standard English', *Scottish Language* 17, 1998, p. 34.
[7] Hamish Henderson, *Elegies* (Edinburgh: EUSPB, 1971), p. 59.
[8] *Poems of Today* (London: Sidgwick & Jackson, 1930), pp. 311–12.
[9] R. Watson (ed.), *The Poetry of Scotland* (Edinburgh: Edinburgh University Press, 1995), pp. 632–3.
[10] George Sutherland Fraser, 'Meditation of a Patriot', *Poems*, p. 37: my italics.
[11] George Sutherland Fraser, 'For Hugh MacDiarmid', *Poems*, pp. 37–8.
[12] George Sutherland Fraser, 'Monologue for a Cairo Evening', *Poems*, pp. 111–14.

Art and War

Review of: M. R. D Foot, *Art and War: Twentieth Century Warfare as Depicted by War Artists* (London: Headline, 1990); Ken McCormick and Hamilton Derby Parry (eds), *Images of War: The Artist's Vision of the Second World War* (London: Cassell, 1991).

One of the ancient functions of art was to depict war, and some of the most important European paintings do this. Uccello's *Rout of San Romano* (c.1450) exemplifies the discovery of perspective. In his *Surrender of Breda* (1634) Velasquez showed that the old function of flattering power could be combined with the psychological realism of modern portrait painting. Benjamin West's *Death of Wolfe* (1771), despite or because of its wild historical inaccuracy, established that prints of battle pictures could be firm favourites with the UK paying public. Hence the very odd career of Elizabeth Thompson (1846–1933). In her twenties she watched some army manoeuvres, was smitten, and painted *The Roll Call*, an image of soldiers after Crimean battle. It was exhibited at the Royal Academy in 1874 to such effect that it had to be specially protected from the sweating multitudes pushing to see it. Three years later she married a Major Butler, whose eventual knighthood made her Lady Butler. Virtually all her subjects, including *Scotland for Ever!* (1881), were military. She tickled Ruskin's nasty imperialism, and he described one of her not-quite-accurate reconstructions of the Napoleonic Wars as 'the first fine pre-Raphaelite picture of battle that we have had'.

Goya's etchings of *The Disasters of War* (1810–13) can perhaps be seen as the start of an oppositional tradition. But by Lady Butler's day the camera, with its democratic veracity, had shown – for instance, with corpses after Gettysburg – the evil banality of slaughter. Wilfred Owen, before his own premature death, was collecting, in the trenches, not oil paintings or prints, but photographs, such as could bring home the horror of his own 'Great War' to British civilians. The Second World War was the first great conflict of which a substantial photographic archive would exist in colour, but even so its most famous celluloid images are monochrome. (The wartime England of Powell's colour film *Colonel Blimp* looks at first like Walt Disney fantasy because we are used to seeing Austerity Britain as grey.)

Given that photographs were not quite up to the mark yet, it is not at all odd that the era of nationalism and mass society produced a new class of state-patronized daubers: 'Official War Artists'. In the Second World War many combatant countries had them. The motives of those who authorized them to roam about carnage with sketch pads were mixed. Like the makers of Babylonian mosaics or Roman columns, artists were expected to produce suitably dignified images of victory and heroic death. But the idea that art had autonomous spiritual value and that artists were special people with 'vision' meant that officials in bourgeois democracies could use strange and even scary images to prove that they were still 'civilized'.

It was a Liberal, C. F. G. Masterman, who, as director of propaganda, launched in 1916 Britain's official war artists. The noble aim of generating large canvasses to be hung in a hall of remembrance cycled in tandem with more immediate propagandist purposes. Nevertheless, Augustus John was commissioned as major to paint the Canadian Expeditionary Force, was allowed to retain his beard despite King's Regulations, and was rescued from a court martial after he knocked down a staff officer in a fight. He abandoned plans of turning his vast cartoon of life on the Western Front into a mighty oil, and it languishes unseen in an archive in Ottawa.

Or so M. R. D. Foot tells us. His *Art and War* is a very useful introduction to official British war art and to the holdings of the Imperial War Museum (IWM), from which all its thirty-one colour plates and 241 black-and-white illustrations are drawn. The museum was established partly as a repository for some 4,000 products of Masterman's project and housed from 1936 in the old Bethlehem Hospital, also known as Bedlam madhouse, in the Lambeth Road. Kenneth Clark (later Lord Clark of *Civilisation*), as director of the National Gallery, London, helped to set up the Second World War official scheme and played God with its results afterwards. He went through the pictures dividing them into two broad categories: 'art' and 'record'. 'Art' went 'either to the Tate Gallery or to such galleries as Clark thought suitable in the provinces or the Commonwealth; the "record" pictures went to the IWM'.

Such lordly dispensations gang aft agley. The paradoxical effect of Clark's last judgement was that the best-known images by painters of Britain's Second World War are mostly found in the IWM. The museum sells lots of postcards. It is a convenient first port of call for picture researchers and TV companies. Clark's literally fatuous efforts mean, for instance, that Stanley Spencer's amazing murals of Clydeside shipyard workers and very powerful images from both world wars by the brothers Nash can be inspected in the same building as Bill Brandt's photographs of blitz shelterers and your actual planes, tanks etcetera. When I was last there, on an ordinary weekday afternoon in winter, business was terrific. And folk queuing to be shuggled up in a simulated war flight or deafened by the realistically pongy 'Blitz Experience' must in some cases have had their eyes drawn to distinguished artworks.

Foot is a renowned historian of the Second World War whose interest in such art goes back, he tells us, to a visit to the Venice Biennale of 1938 where three pavilions (Italian, German and Franco-ite) were 'crammed with fascist-realist depictions of Aryan heroes and of machines, mostly aircraft, in violent action'. (By contrast, the oils by Spencer and Matthew Smith in the British pavilion provided a 'haven of peace and joy'.) He is well informed about art and artists, but writes as if drawn to the value of images as 'record' (in Clark's terms) over and above 'art'. He correctly notes that Paul Nash's remarkable paintings of air war are 'schematic rather than abstract' but even so tries to read veracious detail from them or into them. He recognizes that Nash's *Whitleys Over Berlin* is a product of 'keen' imagination, then goes on to say that while S. B. Jones in his drawing of an RAF raid on Cologne is 'well behind Nash in artistic skill' he does 'at least' provide 'more topographic detail'. Presumably Jones derived this either from an aerial photograph (in which case, as 'record' his work was superfluous) or from the exercise of imagination over a guidebook which would make him, in effect, as 'schematic' as Nash. Or perhaps Jones actually flew on this raid? Foot cannot, or does not, tell us this but some war artists certainly did such things. Same difference. It is either instant record which supplies 'topographic detail', or memory controlling imagination. The former, unless photographic is a fallible as the latter.

The problems arising from Foot's tendency to literal-mindedness are exposed by his statement that Edward Ardizzone 'simply painted what he saw'. Ardizzone, as his ties with the left-wing members of the Artists' International Association both before and after the war suggest, should not be automatically dismissed as an amiable young fogey good at book illustrations. Foot outlines a rather interesting war record. Plucked from the Royal Artillery to serve as an official war artist, he was with the British Expeditionary Forces in France before Dunkirk and the Desert Rats in Africa and Italy. One day in Sicily he walked into Taormina with a film photographer. They found they had outstripped their own army, but managed to persuade the Italian colonel in charge of 400 troops in the town to surrender . . .

However, Ardizzone's bent as an artist was for humour. His desert rats are not heroic patriots, they are round-faced, round-shouldered, mild-looking chaps who potter about as if absent-minded or bewildered. It clearly pleased Ardizzone to find children in Italy turning an abandoned tank into a toy. The irony here is genial, not grim. But *On the Road to Tripoli*, the image of three young soldiers in the desert pausing for a cuppa behind the still-open graves of the dead men they are burying, is either validly bitter or horribly misconceived. It could seem tasteless because Ardizzone is domesticating the brutalities of warfare: the horrors of the Blitz in London had been so often dissolved, as it were, in the warm tea of humorous Cockney community – or so the wartime newspapers told you. But one might read restrained rage in Ardizzone's picture: decent young men have to do this, and seem inured to it. In either case, Ardizzone is not 'simply' drawing 'what he sees'.

Leonard Rosoman was serving as a fireman in the Blitz when the wall of a burning building fell on his crew. He survived to paint, as official war artist, an unforgettable, 'schematized' and distanced image of the episode. A 'record' gathered by Frank Tibbs, one of a pair of constables employed by the City of London police to photograph bomb damage as an aid to future rebuilding, shows the Salvation Army collapsing into Queen Victoria Street in May 1941. Tibbs just happened to be there. Shock waves pushed him backwards as he took his picture – hence its disturbed focus and strong immediacy. Its detail 'proves', if you like, that Rosoman (who probably never saw it) was not inaccurate about how walls fall. But while Tibbs's 'record', in which no person stands under the falling wall, reminds us of bad things safely in the past, Rosoman's painting interbreeds with our nightmares. By his own entirely suspect criteria, Kenneth Clark was daft to leave it in the IWM.

Foot's book is unexciting. Its small black-and-white reproductions are inadequate to convey even the details he wants us to notice, let alone any sure sense of artistic quality. But it is a valuable work of reference, full of accurate information.

Images of War, by contrast, is desirable, spectacular, engrossing – and utterly unreliable. Two elderly American publishers, with 'a team of researchers', have drawn from over a score of collections of 'war art' works by some two hundred artists from a dozen countries. The reproductions are large and vivid, the range of styles exemplified is fascinating. Here are 'Fascist realism', 'socialist realism', their Japanese equivalent and our own dear Royal Academy realism, all producing eerily similar results. Here too are some strange misapplications. Can Tatyana Nazarenko have been serious when she painted the bringing-down of a Soviet partisan hanged by the Germans in the manner of a deposition by Pietro Lorenzetti? The USSR Ministry of Culture clearly thought she was, since that is where the picture can be seen.

Competent artists from all countries put sights 'on record'. Though photographs might have done his job just as well, or even better, one must pay tribute to Anthony Gross, whose role as war artist replicated that of a star frontline newspaper correspondent. He was there when British commandos raided Norway in March 1941; in North Africa a few weeks later when exhausted survivors arrived from Crete; went on to sketch the 'forgotten army' in Burma; got to Paris to catch liberation day in pen and wash; and produced something rather more worked up, a 'history painting', as Benjamin West would have understood the term, of the meeting of Allied and Soviet armies at Torgau in Germany on 26 April 1945.

Equivalent figures to Gross, artistically more ambitious, were the German Wilhelm Wessel, who documented Rommel's Africa Korps, and the industrious Mitchell Jamieson, with the US marines in the Pacific. Examples of such could be multiplied: artists producing work in which the interest of dateable, placeable subject matter overrides, though it does not preclude 'artistic' effect. As it happens, Wessel's picture of a Berlin street bombed by the RAF in 1943 transcends both documentary and fascist realism and is one of the most imposing *Images of War*. Dame Laura Knight's bold draughtspersonship and no-nonsense way with composition made her images 'for the record' of British women at war very strong indeed: Daphne Pearson, for instance, a WAAF awarded the George Cross for bravery, and that much-reproduced image of a female crew hauling up a barrage balloon over Coventry.

And Tom Wood's paintings of the lives of Canadian sailors are the work of a grittily individual talent. I had never, to my shame, heard of him before I opened this book, nor of another Canadian artist, Lawren P. Harris, whose paintings from the 1943 Italian campaign, held by the Canadian War Museum, seem quite extraordinary. Unless reproduction flatters him, he matches Paul Nash in brilliant use of colour. Up to a point, he is as 'schematic' as Nash – one is aware that what was seen has been rearranged and simplified for artistic reasons. But Nash does not usually include people; Harris does. His quasi-surrealist picture of Canadian tanks shrouded in camouflage mats so that they look like moving haystacks or whiskery monsters driving through a storm of golden dust towards Rome (or, rather, towards us) and his image of a battlefield near Ortona, dead horse and tree stumps in the foreground, burning town in the distance, are for my money important pictures. Both have something in common with Katsuda Totsu's *Divine Soldiers Descend on Menado* from Japan's Malayan campaign of 1941–2. The reality of parachutists dropping outstripped surrealist imagination. Several artists found them captivating. Katsuda Totsu's dreamlike image seems to be 'documentary' in purpose and detail, but draws to haunting effect on Japanese traditions of schematization.

So *Images of War* is full of artistic discoveries. Its text, alas, is appalling. This consists of 'chapters' made out of chips and clips from first-hand witnesses and historians without adequate editorial comment – a kind of do-it-yourself (or perhaps pointillist?) approach to history – and also of lengthy captions to the pictures. One can forgive the occasional slip such as 'Landcaster' (Lancaster) bomber. But what is one to do with this caption: 'Sevastopol, USSR, 1942. Until December 1941, heroic stands by Soviet fighting men – and women – became by necessity a frequent art theme. Aleksandr Deineka, in his painting "The Defence of Sevastopol", 1942, depicts a Soviet Navy shore detachment driving back German infantry' . . .? The scale and technique of the picture above are such that it is likely that it was not completed even in 1942, but polished up, perhaps from sketches, long after, since the writer of another caption tells us that this was common Soviet practice. Any competent publisher's editor should have dispelled the chronological miasma here.

The 'chapters' are full of similar infelicities. Nicholas Harman, the post-war historian who wrote *Dunkirk: The Necessary Myth* will be as gobsmacked to see himself referred to as a 'correspondent' on the evacuation beaches as that amiable poet, the late James Reeves, would have been by the description 'historian'. Through an unbelievable blunder it is implied that Hong Kong fell to the Japanese (December 1941) before the London Blitz (May 1941). I touch only on matters where my own limited knowledge counts and shudder to think how many howlers an expert on military history and hardware might spot. This beautiful volume needs a sticker on its cover: WARNING: DOUBLE CHECK EVERYTHING YOU READ IN THIS BOOK.

1991

The New Zimbabwe Writing
and Chimurenga

In this essay I will discuss the three most famous novels produced by Black Zimbabweans since independence in 1980. (Incidentally, there is, of course, no old Zimbabwe writing.) I can offer no profound new thoughts about the Chimurenga war, or second Chimurenga war, in which African guerrillas liberated Zimbabwe within fifteen years of Ian Smith's declaration of UDI for Rhodesia in 1965. What that war 'meant' is very much under discussion. It is highly controversial because it raises 'academic' issues about the understanding of Zimbabwean African communities and their histories, and because it raises 'political' issues about the conduct of affairs not only by Ian Smith but by Robert Mugabe's government.

However, black writing from Zimbabwe is not an arcane subject at all. It could be said that the literary 'balance of power' in Anglophone black Africa south of the Sahara but, in Shiva Naipaul's phrase, 'North of South', held initially in the 1950s by Nigeria, then contested by east Africa in the 1960s, has latterly swung to central Africa. Malawian poets have prestige out of all proportion to their land's small population. The larger, but quite sparsely populated, nation of Zimbabwe has in recent years established almost a monopoly of major literary prizes, primarily, though not solely, through fiction.

The three novels with which I shall deal chiefly are all by writers in what could be called the 'second wave' of black writers from Zimbabwe. The first emerged before independence, with two or three precocious writers of fiction. Charles Mungoshi's short stories in *Coming of the Dry Season* (1972), published when the author was only twenty-five, were banned by the Smith regime a few years later. His novel, *Waiting for the Rain*, came out in the Heinemann African Writers series in 1975. He won the 1992 Noma Award for a book published in Africa with stories rendered from his mother tongue, Shona. Dambudzo Marachera, born in 1952, dead of drink and AIDS in 1985, established the prize-winning precedent with his collection of stories *The House of Hunger* (1978). When it won the *Guardian* fiction prize, its young author turned up to receive this bizarrely dressed and literally smashed up the party, throwing saucers at the chandeliers. I shall refer in passing to him and to Mungoshi and shall try to incorporate their work into my concluding remarks. I will just add now that I much regret that I have no time for Stanley Nyamfukudza, born in 1951, whose novel, or novella, *A Non-Believer's Journey* (1980), ironically narrates the last days of a Salisbury teacher, drunk and cynical, who travels to his rival homeland on family business, is sucked into the Chimurenga struggle, and dies. Like his volume of short stories, *Aftermaths* (1983), it is the work of a writer of Chekhovian subtlety.

However, Nyamfukudza does not have the international fame of Chenjerai Hove whose novel *Bones* won the Noma Prize in 1989. Hove, born in 1952, emerged only after independence and has now tallied several books of verse as well as a second novel *Shadows* (1991). Shimmer Chinodya is five years younger. *Harvest of Thorns* (1989), was his fourth novel and was acclaimed by the Commonwealth Prize jury. Like Hove's his book initially appeared from Baobab Press, a Harare firm, and was then taken up by Heinemann. Tsitsi Dangarembga's *Nervous Conditions* (1988) did not appeal to Zimbabwean publishers, but caused a sensation here when it came out from the feminist Women's Press in London in 1988. I propose to use it as a foil to the novels of Hove and Chinodya which are obviously, and centrally, about the Chimurenga war. What is striking in this connection about *Nervous Conditions*, dealing with the same period, is its lack of direct reference to the war.

I have mentioned publishers rather more than 'in passing'. May I crudely now sketch a view of African writing in English in general in relation to its conditions of production, and reinforce the obvious point that African fiction does not in any simple way 'reflect' historical 'reality', or 'document' African life.

'Literary' writing by black Africans arises historically in two ways from the processes of imperialism. One could be called 'spontaneous'. African consciousness – or rather, the consciousness of Africans educated to perform subordinate roles under white masters – arrives at the point represented, famously or notoriously, by Joyce Cary's *Mister Johnson*. The use of imperfect English, like that of Babu English in India, is embraced by Africans as conferring prestige – they read avidly in magazines and pulp fiction. In Chinodya's *Harvest of Thorns*, the hero's father, a messenger and tea boy under the white district officer of a small town, woos his mother in terms derived from such reading:

'I was surprise you do not replying my letter,' he wrote. 'Everyday I come back from job expecting letter under my door and is not even a little emvlope and I take off my jackit and sits in my sofa thinking why are you not writing. Please please please write to me. My life depending on you, Shamiso. Every nights I woke up thinking about you and everybody at work says what's wrong Clopas are you ill or has eneone died at your home or you brather or you sister is not well? but I can't talk because I want to make sure first. My heart is swolling and paining with love for you. I can't even do job propery because of you and Baas is scolding every day. Please seve my life and my job by marry me. I love you better than myself. Please please please reply. Please Shamiso. Yours in saspence, for bitter or worse. Clopas Wandai J Tichafa. P.S. Greetings to your sister's baby son and if only you say yes then I can say Maiguru to her please.' (p. 35)

This is in the 1950s. At about the same point in chronology, the fictions of Amos Tutuola, from Nigeria, were captivating English intellectuals with such 'bad English' applied with gusto to Yoruba folk material; and the so-called Onitsha Market school was publishing home-made pulp fiction in English. Cyprian Ekwensi was establishing himself as a Nigerian novelist competing for the same market – directly, that is, with popular English and American paperback writers. A few brave souls elsewhere have since tried the same thing – that is, they have sought to provide for African readers fictions by Africans which might be as successful with them as those of Barbara Cartland, James Hadley Chase and so on. The odds are stacked up against them, but I am happy to report that David Maillu, whose self-published so-called pornography sold quite literally like newspapers on the pavements of Nairobi in the 1970s, is still trying every which way to become a national and international best-seller and in 1991 brought out *Broken Drum*, the longest novel ever written by a black African (1,112 pages).

Writers like Ekwensi and Maillu, one might say, are into import substitution. Identifying a market for popular fiction in English among black Africans, they seek to provide a home-made equivalent. The aim of the most famous African writers, though, has been conditioned by very different preoccupations. In conjunction with London-based multinationals or with local publishers they have sought to reconstruct the perceptions of new generations of Africans through the textbook market. Achebe and Ngugi are not 'best-sellers' as Alastair Maclean was or Jeffrey Archer is a 'best-seller'. The seven-figure sales of their novels represent the penetration of a vast – almost infinite – market for African fictions at various levels in the education systems of newly independent African countries: not just their own countries. Their aims are appropriately didactic. They are teachers to a continent, and its representatives in school and university syllabuses in other continents.

Typically, such writers emerged from universities conceded by the British as independence loomed. They allied themselves with publishers who foresaw, correctly, huge textbook sales. They campaigned for the replacement of works in the set-book canon by their own works and those of other African nationalities. If the writing of Ekwensi and Maillu was unashamedly oriented towards the actual literary tastes and – nationalists would say – debased, colonial mentality of English-reading clerical workers, that of Achebe, Ngugi and others was professedly 'literary'. Literature was conceived as a noble art. Criticism was written, by blacks and whites, to prove that *Things Fall Apart* was a great novel fully suitable to replace, say, *David Copperfield*. This educational and commercial offensive, launched primarily through Heinemann's African Writers Series, was momentously successful. More than a decade after Ngugi exiled himself from Kenya for political reasons, his novels are still freely on display in Nairobi bookshops. You find them in the textbook section.

Let us call the two types of writers I have discussed 'hacks' and 'dons'. Either class could be seen as comprised of liberators, working with nation-builders in other fields. You beat Hadley Chase at his own game, you oust Buchan and Rider Haggard from schools. But an irony will not have escaped you. These writers, using English as a medium, operating within markets and institutions inherited from the colonial period, are helping to complete the destruction of native African cultures. Confronted with this contradiction, Achebe argued that English was the indispensable lingua franca of Nigeria and he would use it without shame. Ngugi, midway through his career, renounced English as a medium of fiction and insisted that Africans should write in their mother tongues, reaching users of other mother tongues through translation.

Zimbabwe was by many years the last Anglophone African country 'North of South' to be rid of white rule. Its pre-independence writers emerged under peculiar constraints. They could not freely treat themes of liberation struggle in books which could be freely read in their homeland. For publication, they had to rely on Heinemann's expectation that there would, when liberation came, be a large market for their work, primarily educational. Curiously, as it may seem, the educational policies of the white regime, which as in South Africa favoured 'authentic' and 'tribal' expressions as part of an ideology emphasizing the separateness of blacks and whites, meant that publishing in African languages was a real option, so long, again, as dangerous subject matter was avoided. Meanwhile, according to precedent established in west and east Africa, UK publishers would expect, after independence, to sell African titles through local firms headed by black Africans. The pre-independence work of Mungoshi, Marachera and Nyamfukudza is accordingly found in Harare today in editions using Heinemann's print and design but published by Zimbabwe Publishing House. On the other hand, Baobab aim to sell books published on their own initiative to Heinemann for worldwide distribution.

Let me summarize at this point the conditions under which the novels I deal with were written and published:

(1) With precedents well established, a work of literary ambition could expect large sales through the educational system.

(2) The writers themselves could expect a great deal of support as required from universities, not only at home but in Europe and North America, as writers in residence or lecturers in African literature. To that extent their work was intrinsically 'academic', contributing, as it were, to their CVs.

(3) But the independence of the writer, as a witness in independent Zimbabwe, was strongly predicated. First, the spectacular career of Marachera involved flamboyant and widely admired gestures of revolt against Mugabe's new government. Second, this new government set itself standards of free speech to contrast both with the overt repression of the south and with the creeping censorship of capitalist Kenya. Third, the UDI regime had left behind a relatively strong infrastructure of local publishing. The prospect existed of being both educational and oppositional, both widely sold in the education system and free to criticize the government.

(4) Most importantly, the dilemma regarding language which had faced writers elsewhere, in the generations of Achebe and Ngugi, did not exist so acutely in Zimbabwe. This is because the preponderance of Zimbabweans speak either Shona or Ndebele and education goes forward to the highest levels in both languages. Mungoshi, moving from English to Shona, does not, unlike Ngugi, have to create his own market. Chirikure, another Noma laureate, sees his pioneering volume of poetry in Shona taken at once into the educational syllabus. Hove, like other writers uses both English and Shona. His use in his fiction of English, heavily modified by Shona idioms and orature, cannot be explained by the

impossibility of using Shona itself – it must represent a free turning outwards towards the world audience for books in English.

On the other hand, the broader issue of the viability of native African cultures in the contemporary world is far from settled. From the ironies and contradictions involved in literary production we should now turn to contradictions within the liberation struggle which so much post-independence literature has felt compelled to address. We may discuss these under the headings of race, religion, class and gender, after briefly recalling salient facts.

Before Ian Smith's declaration of Rhodesian independence in 1965 the African nationalist movement had split between ZANU and ZAPU. Both organizations infiltrated guerrillas and the first large-scale combat occurred in the so-called 'Battle of Sinoia' in April 1966. But the liberation struggle began to build up from 1970 as ZANLA (ZANU) guerrillas entered north-eastern Rhodesia from Mozambique. Fighting began there in December 1972. ZANLA activity greatly expanded after a *coup d'état* in Lisbon ended Portuguese rule in Mozambique in 1974. Meanwhile ZIPRA (ZAPU guerrillas) operated out of Zambia. African political leaders who continued to operate in Rhodesia itself were increasingly disunited, and in April 1975 Robert Mugabe left for Mozambique, where he gradually became the prime leader of ZANU. Joshua Nkomo was ZAPU's equivalent. In 1977, the chief leaders still in Rhodesia, Muzorewa and Sithole, began negotiations with Smith. But concessions to them did not end the war. Agreement on new elections was reached at a conference in London in December 1979. Next year, ZANU under Mugabe won a smashing victory and in April the party formed a new government with the coming of independence recognized by Britain and other foreign powers. Before this, the war had affected every section of Rhodesia. Hit by international sanctions and conscripted into a bloody war against the guerrillas, many whites had left the country. Nevertheless, whites still dominated the agricultural economy after independence. The Marxist rhetoric of ZANU was worn threadbare by 1991 when an Economic Structural Adjustment Programme, imposed by international finance, confirmed the country's capitalist direction. ZANU and ZAPU had been reconciled with Nkomo's joining the government as vice-president. But in 1992 hideous evidence began to emerge of the extreme violence used by ZANU government forces in crushing former ZIPRA guerrillas in their Ndebele baseland after independence. Avoiding the grossly tribalist politics of certain other African countries, Zimbabwe nevertheless retained potential for ethnic tension between the Shona-speaking majority, old ZANU, and the Ndebele-speaking minority centred on Bulawayo, formerly identified with ZAPU.

The word *Chimurenga* applied to the liberation struggle, is Shona, and harks back to African reaction against white invasion by Rhodes's British South Africa Company in the 1890s. In 1896 and 1897 there were armed risings against the whites. Shona in the south fought on the side of Rhodes's men against the Ndebele, seen as their greater enemy. So did some of the central and eastern Shona. But many Shona defied white capitalist rule, and traditions of that Chimurenga were extremely alive for their descendants after UDI. This was an important factor in the success of the guerrillas. For instance, when a band penetrated Dande, on the north-eastern border near Mozambique, early in 1971, they contacted an ancient spirit medium. Her name was Kunzawara. The name of her spirit was Nehanda. She represented a venerated *mhondoro*, one of the ancestral owners of the land. Her *mhondoro* was much invoked in story and song by the guerrillas. A previous medium of Nehanda had been captured and executed by the British in the Chimurenga of the 1890s. Through Kunzawura and other spirit mediums, the guerrillas established their status as representatives of the land's right owners and of authentic traditions of resistance to white expropriation. Such mediums rejected all European things – even petrol fumes were potentially fatal to them. The ideological construction, Chimurenga, in the 1970s – and after independence – involved gluing revolutionary liberation struggle to ancient authoritarian traditions and to a fierce attachment to land properly owned by ancestors.

But this was in potential contradiction with the Marxist ideology of ZANU. To quote David Lan, whose remarkable book *Guns and Rain: Guerrillas and Spirit Mediums in Zimbabwe* (1985) explores the matters just mentioned very richly:

> There is . . . no doubt of the great success the guerrillas achieved in communicating one central aspect of ZANU's conception of the nature and goal of the struggle. It was clearly explained and understood that the return of the land could only be achieved by the victory of one class rather than of one ethnic group over another. The enemy was defined as racism and the structures of exploitation, rather than as individual members of the white population.[1]

One feature of the Chimurenga novels of Hove and Chinodya is implicit tension between affirmation of the bond joining Shona and land and accommodation of the values attached to this with the multi-ethnic character and proletarianized and urbanized population structure of the new Zimbabwe. These writers, in effect, seem to me to claim for their own generation, that of the young guerrillas, a relationship with the ancestors which leapfrogs back over that of their parents and grandparents. They implicitly claim the right to incorporate tradition on their own terms into a vision of society which is 'modern', which is informed by the humanist values presupposed and generated by what is called 'literature', and can therefore be 'universalized'.

However, Chinodya, Hove and others of their generation may surprise non-African readers by their sympathetic attitude to beliefs of the kind which both Christians and Marxists have dismissed as superstitions. In its broadest sense, Chimurenga was, and still is, a cultural concept, involving affirmation of African tradition, in adaptation to the new culture of novels, printed poems, commercial sculpture and rock music. Great as their fame has become, the new Zimbabwean writers probably count for less in the image of their country as a culturally vibrant one than the Shona stone sculptors whose work commands admiration and high prices in Europe and North America, or the musicians, above all Thomas Mapfumo, who are renowned amongst lovers of World Music. Mapfumo's admitted influences include classic US rock and roll, Zairean or Congolese 'jazz' and Caribbean reggae. Nevertheless, in 1973 he began to sing in Shona. He became involved with ZANU guerrillas while working in Mutare (Umtali) in 1975 and began to be seriously political. In 1977 he was detained for three months without trial. He is the prime exponent of modern 'mbira' music, along with his closest rival, Oliver Mutukudzi. The *mbira* or 'finger piano' is a traditional Shona instrument closely associated with the ancestors who can be heard speaking through Mapfumo and his band. Mapfumo modestly denies that he is actually a spirit medium, but his significance for his home audience has not been merely secular.

His association with Chimurenga raises the question of what the ideological content of the liberation struggle effectively was, and this in turn relates to the problem of its class basis. In his important and controversial book, *Peasant Consciousness and Guerrilla War in Zimbabwe* (1985), Terence Ranger argues from a point generally agreed – that Zimbabwean Africans attempted from the 1890s to relate to the new capitalist economy as peasants rather than as wage workers – to a debatable one – that peasant class-consciousness was the basis of the guerrillas' success in the Chimurenga war:

. . . peasants had a long tradition of understanding what had been done to them. They knew that their land had been taken in order to establish white commercial farming and ranching; they knew that the Rhodesian state had discriminated in favour of white agriculture and had intervened in their own production in intolerable ways. Locally they fought during the guerrilla war for the recovery of their lost lands; nationally they desired a transformed state – a state that would back black farming against white rather than the other way round . . . During the war the guerrillas encouraged this type of consciousness. They intensified the sense of resentment over the lost lands; generalized it by showing how land alienation had affected everyone in the whole country; and promised that when a ZANU/PF government had come to power the lost lands would be returned. But they did not seek to transform peasant consciousness so far as land or agricultural production was concerned.

They did not, it seems, advocate collective or even cooperative farming. Their message was acceptable to the peasants, and to the spirit mediums who, Ranger argues, were crucial in peasant radical consciousness even before guerrillas entered the countryside, and vital in securing the acceptance of young outsiders with guns by the old men who expressed that peasant consciousness.

Unlike the position in Kenya in the 1950s, where the colonialists had strong support from successful African entrepreneur-farmers who provided a Home Guard against the Mau Mau and were able to hijack the nationalist banner, Rhodesian white settlerdom had striven rather effectively to prevent the emergence of a prosperous African bourgeoisie. The educated children of better-off rural and urban Africans were not automatic allies of the Smith regime. To quote Ranger again:

Teachers and secondary school students had essentially the same choices as purchase farmers and businessmen – they might bid for a privileged role by means of an alliance with the administration; they might bid for leadership of a populist nationalism . . . they might throw in their lot with radical peasant nationalism.[2]

'It is clear', Ranger further observes, that

it was especially dangerous to be a businessman or a teacher in the rural areas during the war, but it is far from clear that they were marked out as petty-bourgeois class-enemies by the guerrillas. If they were prepared to cooperate . . . indeed, they were regarded as valuable allies.[3]

Class divisions in the countryside were not salient as they had been in
Kenya. But on the other hand middle-class elements did not control the
struggle or its ideology.

Can Chimurenga, therefore, be seen as a movement bringing
together, potentially if not actually, all African elements in Rhodesia
behind a peasant ideology consecrated by a potent religion of the
ancestors? Not if Norma Kriger's controversial conclusions from her
work in north-eastern Zimbabwe are sound. She identifies several areas
in which internal conflicts within peasant communities gave them
remarkable power to challenge their elders. Poorer people likewise used
the revolt as a way of revenging themselves against better-off Africans.
What about women? In Shona society, where wives knelt before their
husbands when serving food and in other ways were expected to show
obeisance, their daughters, through the institution of bride price, were
an important source of potential wealth. Now rural women, Kriger
says, turned to the guerrillas as potential allies. For a brief period,
wives acquired control over their husbands. The guerrillas beat men
who beat their wives. Girls as well as boys served as *mujibas*. Young
women served in the guerrilla army. In the end, male guerrilla leaders,
confronted by a backlash from married men and fathers, backed away
and patriarchalism prevailed. But Chimurenga destabilized gender
relations along with social hierarchy in general.[4] There are two ways of
looking at the sexual intercourse between guerrillas and village girls,
which took place despite the orders of both commanders and spirit
mediums enjoining celibacy. One is that young male fighters abused the
power given them by their rifles to seduce and rape unfortunate young
women. The other is that young women had a chance to express sexual
preference denied them by the patriarchal constraints of bride price.
Both views are presented in Chinodya's novel, *Harvest of Thorns*.

Chinodya was born in the substantial provincial town of Gweru and
educated during the Chimurenga period at Goromonzi High School
and the University of Zimbabwe. He did not fight with the guerrillas.
Harvest of Thorns involves vivid imagining, probably informed by
knowledge of the surveys which historians and social scientists such as
Ranger, Lan and Kriger had undertaken in north-east Zimbabwe.
Chinodya began the novel in 1984 and it was published five years later.
It was partly written, like other African books before it, at the famous
Writer's Workshop in the University of Iowa. It displays the technical
finesse of a writer thoroughly at home in Anglo-American and
European traditions of fiction. Any reader of novels anywhere should
find it a compelling 'easy read'. I do not say this dismissively, just to

make the point that Chinodya's 'universal' medium implies that there are 'universal' messages in his book which his readers can decode in terms of their own different backgrounds.

'Universalized', it has to be a tale of generational conflict. Its hero, Benjamin Tichafa, aged only twenty at the novel's conclusion, has re-emerged from the ranks of the guerrillas in newly independent Zimbabwe in a mood to confront his parents and dominate his family. The first section presents his homecoming. It ends with a furious row with his mother. 'This whole family is damned by all the blood on your hands,' she rages. 'That's all you can think of,' he says. We'd have killed traitors like you during the war' (p. 24).

The second section, largely, is leisurely and humorous. It details Benjamin's family background and early years. His mother, a naive country girl of eighteen, is wooed and won, in the mid-1950s, by a smart young government messenger, Clopas Tichafa. We see her kneel to serve him when he first visits her home, we hear her bride price arranged at a meeting between him and her male relatives. They live together in an African location, neither well nor badly off, but increasingly worried by her failure to produce children. They try a western clinic, then a traditional African doctor who prescribes nauseous medicines. But nothing works till proselytizers for the African Church of the Holy Spirit persuade them to come to a service and they are converted.

They bring up the three children now given to them as strict puritans, forbidden dance and music, make-up, drink and politics. The family's abstention from politics means that Benjamin is taunted at school with being a 'sell out'. In reaction, he helps burn down a government-owned beerhall and gets a caution and a police record. He is further accused, unjustly, of cutting off his younger brother's leg with an axe. This is in fact an accident, but people in his parents' church attribute it to his possession by a demon. Sent to a Catholic boarding school (for respectable black Rhodesians, it seems, the imperative to educate one's son prevails over the strongest doctrinal inhibitions) he takes part with schoolfellows in a demonstration against the call-up of blacks to fight the guerrillas, and flees to the border when police intervene. Trained in camp in Mozambique, he serves in the Zimbabwe bush during the last phase of the struggles: combat and relations with villagers are described in vivid detail. Benjamin sees three of his comrades die. He brings home after it is over a girl *mujiba* he has met in a village destroyed by Selous Scouts, looking for her murdered parents. He has no job, thinks of joining the new united army, and regards the liberated nation cynically:

I see the same old house, the same old street and the same old faces struggling to survive. We won the war, yes, but it's foolish to start talking about victory. All this talk about free schools and free medical treatment and minimum wages is just a start. The real battle will take a long, long time; it may never even begin. (p. 272)

But he is well placed to confront his parents with their hypocrisy and failure – his mother who failed to respond when her husband started an affair with a widowed neighbour, his father who left the church, but is still a sycophantic conformist: now, of course, a ZANU member. But at least his homecoming brings the family back together. They are all there when his wife gives birth to his son and the novel ends with Benjamin picking up the tiny child in his white bundle:

'Zvenyika will use his head and hands and grow up to be somebody,' he says.
He's only twenty and he has no job or house of his own yet but he tells himself he'll do all he can to raise the little bundle of humanity in the cot. He'll do all he can, even though all he has is a pair of chapped hands.
He tells himself he'll do it. (p. 277)

The book's title refers to the 'harvest of thorns' reaped by the Shona after the best land had been stolen. But Benjamin, as a centre of consciousness in the novel, is relatively detached. It is revolt against his petty-bourgeois upbringing, and resulting fear of punishment, which drives him to the frontier, not love of particular land, or even of Zimbabwe in general. He reaps, as we have seen, his own 'harvest of thorns' – no job and no great hopes. But he represents young honesty, youthful activism. Though his guerrilla comrades are not idealized, the reader is never allowed to suppose that their cause is unjust. Indeed, as readers, it must be our cause. (Contrast another Chimurenga novel published by Baobab Press in 1992 – Charles Samipindi's *Pawns* which presents many murderous and brutalizing episodes in the struggle negatively.)

The omniscient, humorous first-person narrator of Chinodya's first quarter gives way, suddenly, in Chapter 11, as Benjamin becomes conscious of the world around him, to a particular 'we':

For those of us who saw the traumas of our country from the doors of township houses, peeking through restraining skirts of our mothers like young Benjamin, the sixties are a special period. Every generation has its sentimentalities, its nostalgias; for us the sixties were both an end and a beginning . . . Those were the days when – to keep pools of rainwater from washing away our houses – we went with our mothers in the dark to steal whitewash from the hills municipal trucks dumped at the road sites . . . We yelled furious obscenities at couples we caught in a delirious tangle among the thorn bushes and when our voices cracked or we were hissed away or threatened we went to sit at the edge of the road counting and claiming for ourselves the Zephyr Zodiacs, Morris Oxfords and Fords from the traffic that streamed past. (p. 77)

Chinodya here associates himself with the urbanized children of Ben's generation, some of whom, like Ben, became 'The Children', as the guerrillas were known to older people. In Chapter 17, with Benjamin training in the camp, this section of 'we' becomes 'you' – still implying strong association between the authorial voice and the protagonist's situation:

And then you ran off, through the darkened tents to the clearing where the others sat having the political discussion session, and you found a place on the grass and sat down carefully so as not to raise too much dust and you folded back your legs and clasped them at the ankles so you didn't toe the back in front of you and you sat there and listened, your fist raised over your head, stabbing the air, chanting slogans and you heard about capitalism and socialism and democracy and equitable distribution of wealth and racism and discrimination and equal rights and injustice and justice and the Land Apportionment Act and segregation and exploitation and neo-colonialism and many other words you had never heard before . . . (p. 129)

In Chenjerai Hove's *Bones*, Chisaga is cook to the baas Manyepo, total tyrant over the lives of all who work on his estate. People dispossessed of land or compelled to earn wages to pay tax have to work for the big white farmer. Chisaga is a specially privileged house servant, almost a friend of this white man whose wife has left him:

Baas drinks until he cannot say my name properly, all in my own eyes. Did he not once send me away before he started drinking? Then what happened? Manyepo started asking me to remain for the night so that I could fetch him the drinks. He drank the beer that burns the lungs until he could not walk, until his legs were made of water, then walking became as difficult as lifting an elephant. Very difficult. And I lifted him with my own arms and put him into his bed like a child. I did it, with my own arms. From that time, he scolds me with a smile on his face, he does not scold me too much about my drinking and singing in the farm compound. He just jokes about it, calls my mother a few names and asks for his food. (p. 32)

Marita, the novel's heroine, calls Chisaga 'a good man'. And, when guerrillas arrive and question her about Manyepo's treatment of his workers, she saves the white man's life by lying for him:

'Marita, [Janifa asks,] did I not see Manyepo kick you in the back as if you were a football? Did I not hear him curse at you, calling you all the bad things that the tongue can still mention and not rot? Marita, your heart surprises me.'

'But Marita, why did you save Manyepo's life by lying like that?' I ask. 'Child, what do you think his mother will say when she hears that another woman sent her son to his death?'

'But Marita, did you not say that a tongue that lies will die a shameful death?'

'Yes, child, but it is better to let that tongue kill itself than to help it kill itself. The white man thinks we are children, that is why his tongue is loose. The day he learns that we are also grown-ups, he will learn to tighten his tongue. He was brought up like that. You do not expect him to think differently from what his mother told him. Do you think all of us here went to school where the white man is called baas: we were brought up like that. So it is not our fault. One day we will learn that the white man is like us, if you prick him with a thorn in his buttocks, he will cry for his mother like anybody else.' (p. 63)

Hove goes further than Chinodya in the direction of quasi-Christian, universalist forgiveness.

Yet this seems to be in tension *with,* if not contradiction *to,* the very form of his fiction. It is not like any of the kinds of novel which most fiction-readers in English seek out in libraries or buy from bookstalls. It is closest to such extreme Modernist experiments in fiction as Joyce's *Ulysses* or Faulkner's *As I Lay Dying*. It tells a story, but cryptically and opaquely, from several different unmediated points of view and with severe disruptions of chronology. What it attempts to suggest, throughout, is the thought processes of Shona-speakers, using Shona proverbs, Shona rhetorical forms to bring educated readers up against the fact that African peasants think and react differently from themselves. Paradoxically, as with Edward Kamau Brathwaite's use of 'Nation Language' in *Mother Poem*, the writer's identification with uneducated consciousness produces 'difficult' effects like those characteristic of

Modernist works by avowed elitists. Though only 112 pages long, *Bones* can, as I found, take days to read.

Chapter 7, central to the book, has no personally named narrator. It is headed 'The Spirits Speak: 1897 My Bones Fall'. Ancestral voices of prophecy speak in defeat. The novel's title is explained:

> Bones spread like rough mats on the banks of the rivers and in the water. But the fish would not eat them. Rising bones. They spoke in many languages which I understood all. Tongues full of fire, not ashes. Clouds of bones rose from the scenes of many battles and engulfed the skies like many rain birds coming to greet the season. There were so many bones I could not count them . . . Right across the land of the rivers that flooded all the time: they heaved on the chest of the land until they formed one huge flood which trampled on the toes of armed strangers. Armed strangers who shot all the time for many days as if they were now hunting for ever. They shot into the hearts of the bones and kept on firing until they could not be seen in the smoke of their own gunpowder. (p. 64)

Janifa, who has, as it were, adopted Marita as her mother, rejects passionately her physical mother, who she sees as conniving in Chisaga's rape of her. On the last page of the book she angrily tells her to go and live with Chisaga. *Bones* is a fiction which fiercely opposes not only white colonialist oppression, but also the patriarchal obsessions of Shona society in 'the parent's' generation. The Children, the guerrilla fighters who have broken away from society in order to return and save it, and who are represented by Marita's son, themselves represent the possible reconstitution of the spirit of the ancestors in a new social order.

Cryptically, tragically, *Bones* presents Chimurenga as a communal struggle on behalf of a new community in which human relationships, including those between the sexes, must be on a new basis. Tsitsi Dangarembga's *Nervous Conditions* rejects the values of the parent's generation in much greater detail and with equal passion. It too shows how these values can drive a young woman mad. Its first-person narrator is a young woman who has escaped both madness and patriarchal oppression. What differentiates Dangarembga's conclusion from Hove's, and from Chinodya's, is that her heroine conceives escape and health in personal rather than communal terms. She leaves her cousin Nyasha, whose revolt had an explicitly political content, in a clinic. She accepts her own peasant mother's diagnosis that it is the 'Englishness' which Nyasha has imbibed during education in England which is responsible for her breakdown – 'you couldn't expect the ancestors to stomach so much Englishness' (p. 203). In the book's last paragraph, Tambu, its heroine, tells us she has taken this aboard, confronted it, and overcome it in a 'long and painful process'. This process appears to have ended in personal triumph over forces assimilating her to 'Englishness': there is no hint as to how it positions her vis-à-vis her black Zimbabwean relatives and the society in which they move.

Dangarembga's narrative begins in 1968, when Tambu is thirteen years old. It goes on to span years in which the guerrillas infiltrated north-eastern Rhodesia, where the novel is set. (Tambu lives in the communal lands surrounding the town then called Umtali, now Mutare, which became a prime centre of struggle.) Guerrillas, however, do not appear in the novel.

It centres on one extended family: village community and urban social life do not feature. Tambu's family has two poles. Her parents are poor farmers, living squalidly. Her father's elder brother, usually called Babamukuru, is a schoolteacher who has spent two years studying in England, has a wife with a postgraduate degree, and lives in middle-class comfort. Tambudzai's older brother Nhamo, a bright, snobbish lad, goes to the mission school where Babamukuru is head-master. She herself has raised the money to pay for her own school fees (in town selling maize to pay for them she is given £10 by a rude but charitable white woman). When her brother suddenly dies, she replaces him at the mission boarding school, and stays during term time in her uncle's modern house. Here she is close to her cousin Nyasha.

Educated in England to the point where she could not speak Shona, Nyasha has also learnt there at first hand lessons about oppression and discrimination. Socially unable to mix freely with normal African children, she is intellectually an egalitarian revolutionary. *Nervous Conditions* is immensely acute about the web of contradictions in which Nyasha and her bourgeoisified family struggle. Her father wants her brother to stay at his own all-black mission school 'to counteract the unAfrican exposure he had been subjected to in England' (p. 106). But a white colleague at the school arranges for him to sit the exam for the elite multiracial school to which he sends his own sons:

> Not surprisingly, since Whites were indulgent towards promising young black boys in those days, provided that the promise was a peaceful promise, a grateful promise to accept whatever was handed out to them and not to expect more, Chido was offered a place at the school and a scholarship to go with it. Nyasha was sure that Mr Baker had had a hand in that scholarship.

To ease his conscience, she said. 'A word with the headmasters' she told me when Nyasadzo was not present. 'You know how it is, bwana to bwana: The boy needs the cash, old man!'; 'He's a good boy, what. Pity to waste him. We'll see what we can do.' So Chido gets his scholarship and Mr Baker feels better about sending his sons there in the first place. 'Really! The things they get up to to pull the wool over our eyes. Really!' Nyasha's analysis made sense because Babamukuru did not approve of European habits, easy options or unnecessary expenditure. Without the scholarship Chido certainly would not have gone to that school and Mr Baker would have had his sons' superior education nibbling away at his conscience. The upshot of all this was that Chido did go to this boarding school and by the time I went to the mission he had adapted remarkably well to private school life. He had acquired the usual courteous, self-indulgent, private-school habits and was firm friends with the Baker boys . . .

Nyasha, as the headmaster's daughter, did not really have to worry about being screened out of school. She could afford to fail as long as she did not do it too badly. Even with the vicious competition for the strategically small number of Form Three places the Government gave us, the headmaster would have been able to find a place somewhere for his daughter. And if she did fail dismally, he would probably have been able to use his influence to allow her to repeat the exam. The authorities thought Babamukuru was a good African. And it was generally believed that good Africans bred good African children who also thought about nothing except serving their communities. So Nyasha really didn't have to worry.

Nyasha found a lot to be amused about in that situation. Practising such nepotistic ways of getting advantages would mean that Babamukuru would no longer qualify as good, and though he valued, if not his children, then at least their education, he valued being honourable even more. Maliciously, Nyasha threatened to fail her exams to observe the conflict or, as she put it, to see what her father would do. But everybody except Nyasha knew that fail was one thing she could not do. She was working much harder than I had ever seen her work before. (pp. 106–7)

Dangarembga's analysis of Babmukuru's position – of the position, that is, of a highly placed African under UDI in the Chimurenga years – is sympathetic but devastating. However, the novel's declared pre-occupation is with the women in Tambudzai's life – her mother and her aunt Lucia, oppressed by lazy husbands, her aunt with her M.Phil. degree who does a job and runs a home and defers to Babamukuru, and Nyasha, who argues furiously with her father, becomes anorexic and breaks down. All are in conflict with what Tambudzai calls 'the patriarchy'. Babamukuru, chief in the family's patriarchy, is identified with Smith's regime, and so rates outwardly submissive Tambudzai above his own rebellious daughter:

Beside Nyasha I was a paragon of feminine decorum, principally because I hardly ever talked unless spoken to, and then only to answer with the utmost respect whatever question had been asked. Above all, I did not question things. It did not matter to me why things should be done this way rather than that way. I simply accepted that this was so. I did not think that my reading was more important than washing the dishes, and I understood that panties should not be hung to dry in the bathroom where everybody could see them. (p. 155)

Tambudzai simply cannot bring herself to participate in the expensive charade foisted by Babamukuru on her parents when he arranges for them to have a Christian wedding after so many years of life together. Her uncle punishes Tambu with a beating and chores for not attending the wedding. When her lively aunt Lucia finds out about it, she defies Babamukuru to his face. The latter's reaction prompts Maiguru to quarrel with him and leave his house – when she returns five days later her behaviour is less deferential – 'most of her baby-talk had disappeared' (p. 175).

Despite launching this domestic Chimurenga, Tambudzai continues to triumph in educational conformity, winning a scholarship to an elite multiracial school. Nyasha warns her against taking it. She will be assimilated, brainwashed. But she goes. This leaves Nyasha exposed – at odds with her father, at odds with herself, intellectually superior to anyone in the family, at least in terms of political consciousness, but trapped in her situation: she is 'evil', not a 'good' girl. She does not want to be good, yet she hates being evil.

'Can I get into bed with you, Tambu?' she whispered, but when I rolled over to make room for her to climb in she shook her head and smiled. 'It's all right,' she said. 'I just wanted to see if you would let me.' Then she sat on her bed and looked at me out of her sunken eyes, her bony knees pressed together so that her nightdress fell through the space where her thighs had been, agitated and nervous and picking her skin. 'I don't want to do it, Tambu, really I don't, but it's coming, I feel it coming.' Her eyes dilated. 'They've done it to me,' she accused, whispering still. 'Really, they have.' And then she became stern. 'It's not their fault. They did it to them too. You know they did,' she whispered. 'To both of them, but especially to him. They put him through it all. But it's not his fault, he's good.' Her voice took on a Rhodesian accent. 'He's a good boy, a good munt. A bloody good kaffir,' she informed in sneering sarcastic tones. Then she was whispering again. 'Why do they do it, Tambu,' she hissed bitterly, her face contorting with rage, 'to me and to you and to him? Do you see what they've done?

They've taken us away. Lucia. Takesure. All of us. They've deprived you of you, him of him, ourselves of each other. We're grovelling. Lucia for a job, Jeremiah for money. Daddy grovels to them. We grovel to him.' She began to rock, her body quivering tensely. 'I won't grovel. Oh no, I won't. I'm not a good girl. I'm evil. I'm not a good girl.' I touched her to comfort her and that was the trigger. 'I won't grovel, I won't die,' she raged and crouched like a cat ready to spring. (p. 200)

Tambudzai, moving onwards, will make her own accommodation with the ancestors. Like Hove and Chinodya, Dangarembga seems to affirm that the young must and can do this, that the generations between 1897 and 1965 have failed. Colonial values, paradoxically, can only be ousted by those who have grown up in, are at home with, motor cars, the English language, western ideas. The three novelists I have discussed rework a theme established in the writings of Mungoshi and Marachera in the 1970s – generational conflict, young versus old. They do so with the later knowledge that a military and political victory has been won over colonialism – by the young, by the children – but that basic problems – men over women, rich versus poor – have not been solved. Nor, of course, has the problem of how a distinctively African culture can be created which preserves positive elements of a pre-colonial culture while suppressing negative, patriarchal ones.

1995

Notes

1 David Lan, *Guns and Rain: Guerillas and Spirit Mediums in Zimbabwe* (London, Harare: Currey, 1985), p. 129.
2 Terence Ranger, *Peasant Consciousness and Guerilla War in Zimbabwe* (London, Harare: Currey, 1985), pp. 177–8.
3 Ibid., pp. 245 and 272.
4 Norma Kriger, 'Popular Struggles in Zimbabwe's War of National Liberation', in Preben Kaarsholm (ed.), *Cultural Struggle and Development in Southern Africa* (London/Harare: Currey, 1991), pp. 125–48.

References

Chinodya, Shimmer, *Harvest of Thorns* (London: Heinemann, 1989).
Dangarembga, Titsi, *Nervous Conditions* (London: The Women's Press, 1988).
Hove, Chenjerai, *Bones* (London: Heinemann, 1990).
—, *Shadows* (Harare: Baobab Books, 1991).

Marachera, Dambudzo, *The House of Hunger* (London: Heinemann, 1978).

Mungoshi, Charles, *Coming of the Dry Season* (Oxford: Oxford University Press, 1972).

—, *Waiting for the Rain* (London: Heinemann African Writers Series (AWS), 1975).

Nyamfukudza, Stanley, *A Non-Believer's Journey* (London: Heinemann AWS, 1980).

—, *Aftermath* (Harare: The College Press, 1983).

Verse and Bosnia

Review of *In the Heart of Europe: Poems for Bosnia*, edited by John Price and Chris Agee, with original prints by Alfonso Lopez Monreal (Belfast: Rushlight Editions, 1998); *Scar on the Stone: Contemporary Poetry from Bosnia*, edited by Chris Agee (Newcastle: Bloodaxe, 1998); Colin Mackay, *Cold Night Lullaby* (Edinburgh: Chapman, 1998).

On 11 July 1995, the town of Srebrenica, ineffectually and hypocritically declared a 'safe area' by the UN, was taken by Bosnian Serbs whose forces had invested it for three years. In the next few days, upwards of 7,000 Bosnian males were massacred, including elderly men and boys. The remaining non-Serb population were driven out. This monstrous act of 'ethnic cleansing' did speed the international action which made Bosnia a fraught, but 'peaceful', ethnically divided UN protectorate. But the Bosnian Serb leaders, Radovan Karadzić and General Ratko Mladić indicted for genocide by the International Tribunal for War Crimes at the Hague, remained at large. The Yugoslav state dominated by Serbs, which had supported these men, went on to perpetrate further 'ethnic cleansing' against the overwhelmingly Albanian population of the province of Kosovo.

In the Heart of Europe, a booklet published in Belfast in which four poems by distinguished hands stand beside striking prints by a Mexican artist with an Irish base, is a strong artistic response to the Balkan crisis. Proceeds go to Amnesty International, the Irish Section of which clearly believes that the organization's primary commitment to exposing the unjust behaviour of states towards their home populations and the plight of prisoners of conscience can be extended to wider concerns. Alfonso Lopez Monreal's images evoking the ordeal of Sarajevo are named *Desastres*, after Goya's *Disasters of War*, that unprecedented response by a major European artist to the horrors of the Napoleonic era. Civilian sufferers represented by Monreal are stripped of their skin. Nuala Ní Dhomhnail's poem in Irish Gaelic, 'Dubh' , is a direct response to the fall of Srebrenica. Translated as 'Black' by Paul Muldoon, it reads magnificently. The event eclipses everything:

The spuds are black.
The turnips are black.
Every last leaf of cabbage in the pot is black.

Echoes of Northern Ireland's three decades of crisis are present, as they are bound to be. They resound in 'Fleur-de-Lis' (named after Bosnia's national emblem), by the booklet's co-editor Chris Agee, an American poet long domiciled in Belfast. Harry Clifton's 'The Literal Version' is dedicated to Ranko Sladojević, a Bosnian writer whom he has translated, and explores the problem of rendering into an alien language another's experience of the world. I will come back to these poems, but concentrate a while on the implications of the last poem, 'Reassurance', by Bernard O'Donoghue. It is accomplished, but what it says worries me.

It begins with a wife assuring her dying husband that Heaven certainly exists, and goes on:

> Personally, I hope not. Because, if Hell and Heaven
> Are assorted by the just God we learnt of,
> We can have little prospect of salvation:
> We who have turned on the sports news,
> Leaving the hanged girl from Srebrenica
> On the front page, just as before we watched
> Without a protest while the skeleton soldier
> Burned by the steering wheel on the road to Basra:
> We too who are so sure about the frailties
> Of those who failed to do anything about
> The Famine, or who'd turn up the volume
> To drown the clanking of the cattle trucks
> That pulled away eastward in black and white.

This seems to me to demonstrate why poets should leave certain kinds of statement about certain issues to journalists, photographers, film-makers, pamphleteers, historians and theologians. Ní Dhomnaill's forceful personal reaction, politically highly charged, shows what poetry, as itself, can do. It is of the same order as Neruda's acclaim for the International Brigade in 'The Battle of the Jarama River'. Such direct and passionate responses beg no questions, and do not pretend to answer any. O'Donoghue refers, rather inexactly, to a famous, controversial picture of an Iraqi soldier in the Gulf War reduced to a cinder. Whether factual or sincerely faked, that, too, made a direct statement, and I do not believe that it failed to stir 'us', the public confronted by it on the front page of a newspaper, with its reiteration of Wilfred Owen's truth that it is not sweet and decorous to die in war. The Irish Famine was both accidental – no human agency caused potato blight – and exacerbated by social and ideological factors which historians unravel with difficulty. The response of the Young Ireland movement was to attempt an insurrection to throw off English rule. This abortive rising – comic, had the context not been so fearful – did no immediate good, unlike the actions of doctors and philanthropists who risked death from disease to help the suffering, and were not 'frail' at all in a situation where strong minds and acute consciences offered no clear overall solution. As for the German massacre of European Jewry, arguments will go on forever about the culpability of German gentiles who did or did not know what was happening, of Jews who might have at least resisted their extermination, as thousands did in Warsaw, and of Allied governments which might have bombed the death camps (though it is unclear how this would have saved Jewish lives). In fact, the world's media, and many of its people, did recognize what was happening in Bosnia, did condemn it, and supported airstrikes against the Serbs.

Though well intended, O'Donoghue's suggestion that if Heaven exists we would not deserve to enter it because we have not responded to Srebrenica by cancelling out the rest of life in favour of total commitment to action relating to this one event is sociologically preposterous and theologically frivolous, and on both counts rhetorically unpersuasive. Careful readers of the *Economist* and the *Observer* – even watchers of BBC News and ITN – will have registered that during a decade of Balkan conflict, terrible massacres have resulted from political breakdown, the machinations of corporations and arms-dealers, fundamentalist zealotry and ethnic rivalries in various parts of Africa, in Indonesia and in Algeria. The Russians have savaged Chechnya without international intervention. Mass murderers have remained at large in Cambodia. Those who share my belief that the Serbia of Milosević, his eggers-on and his accomplices had to be beaten by international action must accept, as I fully do, that there many other monsters deserving chastisement, but this is no reason for not attacking these particular monsters. If God exists and sits in judgement on us, He or She would presumably see in reasoned support for action on this front cause for mercy, but not be hard on those who continue to change nappies, holiday in the sun and play football while appalling events take place elsewhere. Precisely because of its immense scale, and cold-blooded organization, the Holocaust should not be freely invoked. There is no wholly comparable event in history.

I think that O'Donoghue does not believe in God or Heaven. 'Thou shalt respond at once and completely to all suffering' would be a perverse commandment anyway. Someone who spent all her or his time agonizing over distant atrocities would be useless to family, friends, associates and compassionate bystanders. People besieged in Sarajevo yearned for precisely the daily pleasures and little decencies enjoyed by denizens of peaceful places. Goodness attaches to taking children cheerfully to school and cooking pleasant meals for friends. As in Ní Dhomnaill's 'Black', shock and outrage may for a time overshadow such considerations completely. But 'life goes on'. And within it racism persists without reaching its logical extreme, and avoidable evils kill decent people. We should not stop concerning ourselves about cases where we can act directly, or argue to immediate effect.

As for verse, perhaps its most ancient subject is war. Ironically, the South Slav arena, in which the recitation from memory of ancient epics has been in modern times a communal custom, has provided models for scholars studying the origins and transmission of the poems eventually written down as the *Iliad* and the *Odyssey*. Epic, following 'Homer's' formulae, was until quite recently regarded as without question the most serious and important sort of poetry. For people still attracted to that view, the bad news is that epic may have fed Serbian racism. In the twentieth century, huge wars have been fought by conscript armies. The mind-boggling casualties (ten times the present population of Scotland dead as a result of the Second World War alone) have included many civilians. Epic treatment of war has become impossible. 'War poetry' has emerged, a genre reserved for men at arms and civilians directly caught up in conflict. 'Anti-war' poetry is another new genre, a species of committed verse. Christopher Logue's versions of parts of the *Iliad,* which 'deconstruct' Greek heroism, are in effect 'anti-war poems'.

'Committed' or 'protest' poetry has proliferated. The stripped 'simplicity' of Brecht has usually been a disastrous model, but Neruda has been followed to effect (for instance, by George Gunn). The women's movement has engendered (forgive me my pun) much verse which its adherents value. Powerful black power voices arose in the USA in the 1960s, and black people resident in Britain have produced much effective poetry about racism and its effects. But this, often delivered in performance, raises, at its less-than-best, a critical problem which I associate above all with verse by black South Africans. One of the ironies of the apartheid era was that white publishers were allowed to print masses of protest poetry by black, 'coloured' and white writers.

That the authorities permitted this showed, firstly, their concern to assure their open and tacit supporters in the USA and Britain that 'freedom of the press' still prevailed in their republic, and, secondly, their judgement that poems (and such plays as those of Athol Fugard) would not damage their regime. As W. H. Auden had famously put it in his 'In Memoriam W. B. Yeats', poetry 'makes nothing happen'. Brecht could not bring down Hitler, nor could Neruda save Allende.

South African protest poetry went over and over the themes of white oppression and violence, of black suffering and the need for resistance; Mongane Wally Serote, who showed that major poetry could be based on these themes, was forced into exile. Lesser writers remained free in South Africa. It is possible that their verse, read aloud at public meetings, or circulating among intelligent young people, did have a directly useful effect, because it said what it said over and over again, and did so openly. Much of it, to an outsider, seemed to be mediocre or bad verse, judged as verse. And it is surely a general rule that the topicalities and current concerns handled in most 'committed' poetry would be better served by well-written rapportage, articles and pamphlets. Good prose, whether inspired or merely efficient, is normally the best medium for topical comment and effective political advocacy. The distinction of the best 'political' poetry is not that it has immediate results, but that people remember it decades later. Yeats's 'Easter 1916' may have helped in some smallish way to rally opinion in favour of Irish independence, but its long-term, more important effect was to assist the mythologization of the rising's leaders. American corporations producing fruit in Latin America have recently bared their claws in the US tariff war against EU preference for smaller Caribbean banana growers. This means that Neruda's 'United Fruit Co' is still as topical as ever, half a century after publication – precisely because what it willed to 'happen', the overthrow of exploitation, has manifestly not happened. It 'survives', to continue Auden's point, 'in the valley of its making'. The best articles and pamphlets are usually out of date in weeks, months or years. Wilfred Owen's 'war poetry' featured again and again in 1998, in public commemoration of the eightieth anniversary of the end of the First World War. It was odd to imagine that Owen, killed a few days before the Armistice, might just otherwise have been among the centenarian veterans who appeared on TV or even took part in ceremonials.

'War poetry' emerged as a distinct mode or genre in the twentieth century, with the 'soldier poets', including Owen, of the Western Front. They provided ironic comment on the epic tradition, deployed satire,

254   Representations of War

and developed the devices of 'nature poetry' and the pathos of 'love poetry'. They had self-conscious successors in the Second World War. Numerous anthologies of war writing, some of them bringing in the Holocaust, tend to communicate the idea that adequate response to the worst events of the first half of the twentieth century, even now, in long retrospect, represent a moral peak in poetry, scaled also by later writers confronting Auschwitz, approaching the Irish Troubles, or, perhaps, responding to Bosnia. God, for most writers, no longer counts. In His absence, war has become the most august theme of verse, as it was for Homer, or rather for those who wrote the Greek epics down and chose to attribute them to a sole author. In the 1960s, Ted Hughes seemed to some of us much more important than Larkin because he wrote about violence, while the latter inspected the miseries of diurnal suburban existence. I do not now think that criterion was a sound one. But whereas Larkin stupidly professed to despise foreign poets, Hughes was an internationalist, who encouraged translation of European verse and himself translated the disturbing Yugoslav poet, Vasko Popa.

One of Hughes's last tasks before he died in 1998 was to translate six poems by Abdulah Sidran for Chris Agee's anthology Scar on the Stone: Contemporary Poetry from Bosnia. This impressive and very readable book gets several things right where they might have gone badly wrong. It is not just that the translators include well-known poets in English – Charles Simic, Harry Clifton, Ruth Padel, Ken Smith, John Hartley Williams, Kathleen Jamie, as well as Nuala Ní Dhomnaill and Agee himself, while others, Francis Jones and Ammiel Alcalay, are distinguished scholars. Agee has wisely compiled a selection of recent Bosnian poems – not just 'war poems' and 'anti-war poems' – only half of which were written after the break-up of Yugoslavia began in June 1991. 'The sole criterion for the inclusion of the twenty-two poets has been artistic distinction.' Eight are 'New Voices', the oldest born in 1954, the rest since 1968. Most boldly, Agee recognizes that poetry from an unfamiliar context cannot, or at least need not, 'work single-handledly'. He includes prose, some of it, about Sarajevo during the years of siege, by the poet Semezdin Mehmedinović, who was there; impressive extracts from Miljenko Jergović's collection Sarajevo Marlboro; 'before' and 'after' accounts of visits to the city by Francis R. Jones and Agee himself, both very well written, a fictionalized memoir from the death camps by Reszak Hukanović – not so well written – and two striking pieces by distinguished dead outsiders. The great Serbo-Croat writer Danilo Kiš (a Jew from Vojvodina, Yugoslavia's multi-ethnic northern province) wrote fiercely against nationalism in 1973, as 'first and foremost paranoia'. The southern Irish essayist of Protestant background, Hubert Butler, whose reputation has escalated since his death in 1991, lived in the former Yugoslavia for three years in the 1930s, and wrote frequently about the country. In two pages from 1956, he distinguishes geographically based nationalism of the Young Ireland variety from the racism which gripped Europe after 1919, when 'The old view that men should enjoy equal rights in the land of their birth began to seem hopelessly out of date.' He quotes with sombre irony an Exiles' Charter published on behalf of 7.5 million Germans driven out of their homes in eastern Europe after Hitler's defeat in 1945. 'God placed men in their homes.' We should not forget (though most people have) that the recent European precedent for Serbian 'cleansing' in Croatia, Bosnia and Kosovo was the rape, murder and expulsion meted out to *Volk-deutscher* in places where their families had been settled for centuries. The brutalities of Nazi occupation explain but can never condone these.

'Those to whom evil is done / Do evil in return.' This further quotation from Auden – his 'Shield of Achilles' – is horribly apt in regard to the Balkans. Serbians trace their Orthodox Christian state back to the ninth century. Defeat at Kosovo in 1389 by the Turks preluded the conversion of many Slavs to Islam, and the total eclipse of the Serbian kingdom under Ottoman rule from the early sixteenth century. Serbia regained independence in 1878. In 1908, Austria's annexation of Bosnia-Herzegovina, over which it had previously had a mandate, provoked a major international crisis. Two 'Balkan Wars' followed as the Turkish Empire continued to crumble, Kosovo was reconquered, then a Serbian assassin set off war throughout Europe by shooting the heir to the Austrian throne in Sarajevo. Serbians fought on the side of the western Allies against South Slavs in the Austro-Hungarian service. Post-war diplomacy united their country with Slovenia, Croatia, Bosnia, Montenegro and Macedonia, as 'Yugoslavia'. Orthodox Christians outnumbered northern Catholics; in the centre and south there were substantial Muslim minorities, Bosnian Slavs and non-Slavic Albanians, totalling 11.2 per cent in the 1931 census.

This unstable conglomeration suffered appallingly in 1941–5, when the Nazis occupied the whole country and created a puppet Croatian state under Fascist leaders whose treatment of Serbs and others in concentration camps shocked even hardened SS men. The pattern of sectarian massacre and counter-massacre was occluded by the triumph of a secular, multi-ethnic guerrilla movement under the leadership of Tito, a Croatian Communist, who ruled the country as a federation till his death in 1980. About 1,700,000 Yugoslavs died as a result of war from 1941 to 1945, well over a tenth of the population. Inter-ethnic fighting accounted for many of these. Serbs in particular had scores against Croats. Just because they were paranoid, it did not mean that no one had tried to get them. Serb spokesmen will declare that Albanians took over Serb land in Kosovo in the 1940s.

Yet in Sarajevo, Croats, Serbs and Muslims lived peacefully side by side after 1945. The rate of intermarriage was the highest in the federation. When the government of Bosnia defied Serbian attempts to take over the whole of Yugoslavia in 1991, the new state resulting had no one distinctive religion, and almost all of its inhabitants spoke Serbo-Croat. Sarajevo under siege stood for tolerance. Serbs who remained there did so in solidarity with Muslim friends and neighbours against the sudden eruption of Serbian irredentism. Republican Spain in 1936–9 had not been ruled or populated by saints, but its struggle for survival seemed to many outsiders to represent the battle of democracy against Fascism. Chris Agee declares that 'Bosnia was the Spanish Civil War of our time.' Based in Northern Ireland, he has had more immediate reason than most of the intellectuals who identified strongly with Sarajevo to hail its cause as that of the inclusive, secular, multi-cultural ideal of civic republicanism, against the dark forces of ethnic self-assertion and religious intolerance. Agee has sought poets who express 'not the Chorus of identity, but the suppleness of the single sensibility'. Of the first fourteen poets, he can state that eight are of Muslim background, four of Orthodox, two of Catholic. 'As for the New Voices section,' he writes, 'I never bothered checking up on backgrounds, and a guess based on names is unreliable.' There is a Bosnian version of Serbo-Croat and Agee remarks in his biographical note on Husein Tahmiščić (born 1931) that 'many of his poems, are written (unusually for a Bosnian) in the "ekavski" or Serbian version of the language.'

It is clear that Sarajevo has been a city of rich artistic culture, publishing books and magazines even under siege. Keeping that culture going was a 'happening' of significance, and the great majority of Agee's contributors stayed in Bosnia throughout the war, carrying on the work of distinguished forerunners, alert as before to writing in English, French, German . . .

Another thing Agee gets right is to begin with Mak Dizdar (1917–71), though he died two decades before the Bosnian War. Dizdar, from Herzegovina, fought in Tito's Resistance during the Second World War. His last, and, we are told, most important book is *Stone Sleeper* (1966). It is 'rooted in the mystery of the schismatic Bosnian Church of the Middle Ages and its resistance to the heretic-killers of the established church – a mystery crucial to our understanding of modern Bosnia's strengths and tribulations.' It can only be 'crucial', it strikes me, if people in Sarajevo have identified strongly with what Dizdar wrote – otherwise that statement is as dodgy as the old racist rubbish which sought to explain our modern Scottish psychology by reference to the peculiarities of Celtic Christendom in the Dark Ages.

Medieval Balkan dualism 'saw mortals as fallen angels, expelled from heaven and imprisoned in human bodies. Nor did they return to heaven when they died, their souls stayed with their bodies until the Last Judgement.' One implication of this is that burial grounds, as in many cultures, must have tremendous significance for the living. To 'cleanse' communities rooted for centuries, in such a perspective, becomes especially abhorrent. In a wonderful poem, 'Text about the hunt', Dizdar takes on the voice of Master Grubač, a fifteenth-century tombstone sculptor who is buried in the necropolis of Boljuni, where in life he carved an elaborate hunting scene. This will remind us of Keats's 'Grecian Urn'. Its vision of life is equally poignant, more disturbing:

> A tall horseman masters seething spaces of unrest
> Handsome Dumb with deep desire Blind
> without a sound he tramps behind
> the baying and howling of hounds
> panting thirsty straining for the blood of future
> battlegrounds

Whatever gets lost in this translation it is not, *pace* Robert Frost, 'poetry' – Francis R. Jones's English is wholly convincing. I am less convinced by the language of three other poems, out of fifteen, which Jones translates with Middle English diction and spelling, though the risk was worth taking, and the effects, rather 'twee' on first encounter, may grow on me. I want to own his translation of the whole of *Stone Sleeper*, if and when available. The last poem he renders, 'A text about the five', dates from 1941, when the Nazis and their Croat *Ustasa* collaborators descended on Bosnia. To prevent their reading it, Dizdar wrote it out in the Arabic-based *alhamiya* script, to make it look like a religious text, since this had been the main script used for the Bosnian

Slavic language throughout the Turkish occupation from the early fifteenth to late nineteenth centuries.

> One man counted bound and led
> One man whom the four men dread.

A theme of *Scar on the Stone* is the threat perceived by others in the Balkans in Bosnia's *haeccitas,* its unorthodox and non-Orthodox differentness.

Thus, differently, Abdulah Sidran (born 1944) has written screenplays for the highly original Serbian film director Emir Kusturica, who is now working abroad – see the latter's brilliant *Black Cat, White Cat* (France/Germany, 1996) – whereas Sidran stayed in Sarajevo throughout the siege. Two of the poems which Ted Hughes translated, using cribs by Antonela Glavinić, with his usual, admirable effacement of his own powerful verse personality in the interests of presenting a foreign writer, evoke violence from the past. 'Gavrilo' appropriates, sympathetically, the voice of Gavrilo Princep, assassin of the Austrian archduke in 1914. – 'Hurry, my heart, let's get the weapons.' 'The Partisan Cemetery' recalls Tito's multi-ethnic, multicultural band of dourly committed heroes and heroines:

> ... The dead
> Are here simply to set our sufferings
> In perspective. So now let's go – slowly
> As after a feast, a wholly Slavonic
> Feast in a graveyard, souls intoxicated.
> Let the bone walk, the flesh
> Walk. The books, little sister, are open –
> The history is being written
> The Martyrology is open. What remains
> For us
> Is to remember our names, and never to forget them,
> Never, never again, to forget them.

Not, as in Yeats's 'Easter 1916' 'to murmur name upon name' of heroes who died for us, but to write our own history of struggle. Sarajevo's people were not passive victims. They fought or supported fighters. This is neither a 'war poem' nor an 'anti-war' poem. Like Dizdar's evocation of long-dead heretics, it is poetry about history: a force in the present.

Izet Sarajlić (born 1930) was wounded by a shell in Sarajevo during the siege. Clearly an awkward customer, he became president of the

Writer's Union of Bosnia-Herzegovina in 1971, was dismissed after seventeen days and later expelled from the Communist Party. But apparently his clear, precise verse remained very popular. His translators have included Brodsky, Enzensberger and Yevtushenko – hard to think of three other names as high in international profile – and now, in this anthology, the very distinguished Yugoslav-American poet Charles Simic. (I cannot remember just now who it was once told me on an Edinburgh bus that Simic was his, or her, favourite contemporary poet.) Saraljlić is one of the rare beings who can make something out of Brechtian 'simplicity':

> If that Tuesday I had died in Berlin
> *Neues Deutschland* would announce that a Yugoslav
> writer of the middle generation
> suddenly died of a heart attack, while I – and this is
>   not just idle talk –
> need to croak on my native soil.
>
> You see how good it is that I didn't die
>   and that I'm once again among you?
> You can whistle, you can applaud.
> You see how good it is that I didn't die,
> and that I'm once again among you all.

Again, this is not a 'war poem' – it is an incident in the ongoing relationship of a writer with his known public, cherishable in its cocky understatement of feeling which might be called 'patriotic' but escapes the dodgier definitions of that word.

Writers who follow them in this anthology do not suffer from comparison with the three big hitters I have just discussed. Simic also translates Dara Sekulić (born 1931), whom he compares (astronomically) with Emily Dickinson and Paul Celan. Agee himself, from cribs by Glavinić, renders the magnificent Marko Vešović (born 1945). 'White Hawthorn in Pape' says nothing about war, but presents themes of beauty and endurance in nature and human history which echo in what we read of Bosnia's crisis. Ilija Ladin (born 1929), translated by Ken Smith, is completely different, 'highly influential among the "rock" generation of poets that emerged in the early eighties'. Nuala Ní Dhomnaill translates into both English and Irish Gaelic a poem by Ferida Duraković (born 1957), whose popular bookshop in Sarajevo was burnt down during the siege. It is called 'Georg Trakl on the Battlefield Revisited, 1993'.

On high, above the planes, dwells God, the beloved
eyes gleaming gold above the Sarajevo gloom.
Fruit-blossom and mortar shells both fall beyond my window.
Madness and me. Alone. We are alone. So alone.

Trakl (1887–1914) died young as a result of the First World War – he
overdosed after a nervous breakdown in uniform on the Eastern Front –
but cannot be called a 'war poet'. His last poems are the response of a
remarkable Expressionist and Modernist poet to horrors of war which
extended his perception of the general crisis of bourgeois Europe. The
aloneness evoked by Duraković is a state of human consciousness
which isn't confined to battlefield situations. The next poem by her in
this book bitterly counterposes direct experience of the siege with the
witterings about 'history' and 'Europe' of a famous postmodernist
thinker arrived from Paris to lecture in Sarajevo, and ends with a
cryptic reference to Edvard Munch – the poet's aloneness relates to
Munch's famous peacetime image of *The Scream*.

My copy of *Scar on the Stone* now has pages inscribed 'with love
Vojka' and 'Thanks for listening Igor Klikovac.' In April 1999 I heard
them perform, with Chris Agee and Ken Smith, who read from other
writers in the anthology, at the Cúirt International Festival of
Literature in Galway. Agee teased Vojka Djikić for her recklessness in
front of the Irish traffic (living in Sarajevo, as she did throughout the
siege and still does, she is not used to people driving on the left). She
said, 'I'd like to die here, in Galway.' Later, over fish, her preferred food,
she repeated that she wanted to die. Was this a joke? She talked with
zest about cooking – apparently she is terrific in the kitchen. I have
heard other people approaching old age (Vojka was born in 1932) say
that they wanted to die. Her five poems in the anthology are not
directly about the siege. 'We must bid farewell to the words / which
have betrayed us' is a statement about life passing which is applicable
anywhere. But she is clearly haunted by unhappy memories of the siege.
Igor, nearly four decades younger, got out of Sarajevo in 1993 and now
works as a freelance writer in London. His four poems in the book,
translated by Ken Smith, come directly from the siege. A bag is packed
for a 'trip' as the mortars thunder. A boy throws paper planes from a
balcony as sirens wail, and the poet thinks of the 'childlike absent-
mindedness' on the faces of Serb killers. In a football stadium 'The
souls of the dead are taking the best seats.' This handsome and charm-
ing young man, striking new poet, has still barely started his career,
which he may sustain in permanent exile. Will the siege have only a

small role in his work, like that verse about Europe after D-Day written out of war service by Kingsley Amis? Or will nightmares haunt him as they did Robert Graves? The anthology's title quotes from a poem by Fahrudin Zilkić, 'Ricochet':

> It's when you hear the shot,
> and while you're lying flat on your
> face you're splattered with gravel.
>
> Ricochet –
> it's when a year later
> you recognise the scar on the stone
> where your life went on again.

I guess these two people I met, not visibly scarred, may suffer ricochets writing about anything. Their late twentieth-century outward normalcy, whatever 'timeless' themes they may handle, has been marked by intersection with the siege.

Colin Mackay's extraordinary sequence of sixty-eight poems, *Cold Night Lullaby,* presents an intersection between wartime Bosnia and everyday Edinburgh. It attracted press attention unusual for a 'slim volume' of verse, and a whiff of controversy. Did the events described 'really happen'? Except by those stupid enough to believe that poems only possess authority if they approximate to the things we call 'historical documents', the issue can be ignored as irrelevant. Walcott's verse narrative of childhood and youth, *Another Life,* which is manifestly 'autobiographical', leaves out the large fact that the author has a gifted twin brother. Like most vivid prose memoirs, Graves's *Goodbye to All That,* which we all think contains a 'truthful' account of the Western Front in the First World War, has many passages of description and dialogue which must blend memory and imagination. Try writing down an account of any interesting experience immediately after it has happened, and you will discover that the process involves leaving out lots of remembered information for which there is too little space, and improvising other information on the basis of probability. The question we have to ask of writings of the kinds we call 'literary' is not 'are they exactly factual?', but 'do they ring true?'

Mackay does ring true. His eloquent Foreword evokes the experience of someone inspired to drive from Edinburgh to Bosnia as an aid worker, part of a new 'International Brigade without self-righteousness'. Some of them died, and the death of a man whom he calls

'Johnny' is the subject of an especially powerful poem. Johnny's real name, he suggests, was 'Everyman', and Bosnia – both very like Scotland and like Napthali in the Bible, 'lovely and a land lost in darkness' – was truly 'Everywhere'. Mackay's convoy reached a village, recently 'cleansed' by its Muslim inhabitants of Serbian families domiciled there for generations. Just one Serb woman had been allowed to remain, because her Muslim husband had died fighting for Bosnian independence. While Mackay was away in Sarajevo to arrange a flight out for Svetlana and her two children, Serbian fighters crossed the river and hit the village. 'When we returned that afternoon, it was a place of corpses.' Everyone had been killed. 'Svetlana had been butchered. Ludmilla, six years old, was dead beside her with her brains blown out. Ahmad had disappeared.'

In the poem-sequence, though not in the Foreword, Mackay himself has a passionate love affair with Svetlana. It has to be said that the lyricism of the poems which evoke this is not as convincing as the terseness of other sections:

> and my weaker half cried to you, Svetlana
> shield me, shield me
> between your serene breasts
> with the calm of your woman's strength,
> with the calm of your river
> and your village, and its ancient hearth
> when day explodes around us
> in all the plains of the sun.

Earth Mother or Muse of all the Ages, she does not seem to belong with the vivid mundane entities of a war-torn land which Mackay presents elsewhere so well. 'Serene breasts' is not quite a cliché, but sounds like one. Yet in context this discrepancy is moving in itself – an attempt to assert the timeless against bad time. And the writing remains careful.

What is evident, and immensely impressive, throughout *Cold Night Lullaby,* is effort towards precision. This is not 'protest poetry' pressing for such-and-such a political reaction. It lives through as-if-observed detail. To repeat that crucial point, the details may not be patterned exactly as in this or that particular experience, but one feels that they derive from experience:

> In the burnt-out cafe
> stray pigs from a nearby farm feed
> on Ivan the chef and his two pretty waitresses.

> Somewhere
> the thud of mortars
> somewhere the splatter of shots,
> the scream of an incoming shell,
> but beyond the blackened hole
> where the window used to be
> under the still-functioning Coca-Cola sign
> the pigs feed on.

The Coca-Cola sign is crucial to the power of this passage. It verifies, so to speak, this implausible horror. The narrator, overpowered with hysteria, is given a jab by a medic and falls asleep to dream of Scotland, where:

> the office will be having its coffee break
> about now and the Number 27 bus
> will be halfway up Dundas Street
> and no one will believe that
> any of these things are happening
> in the same world as the office
> and the 27 bus.

The flat free verse here is characteristic of much of the book, though from time to time Mackay heightens or tightens his rhythms, or enriches his language. It is a general truth that poets should beware of assuming that such verse, charged with powerful subject matter or thoughts, can thereby create durable poetry. But Mackay's successful use of it here verifies horror as a more attention-seeking discourse could not. Again, the 27 bus, by being so extremely particular, enforces the very important point that our everyday coexists with horror. Mackay states fact. He does not say that people at home are morally deficient for not screaming about Bosnia all the time, merely that they cannot imagine such things. Until he tells them. Now, he can lift the verse towards a more 'poetic' conclusion, worked for, earned, very impressive:

> But the pigs are still feeding on
> Natasha's breasts and Ivan's buttocks
> done to a nicety and crisp round the edges,

and the morning sky
is blue as the robe of glory
and warm as my love,
so glad to be alive
to make these ashes speak.

'Love' . . .? Proleptically, at this stage of the book, love of Svetlana? Or a wider love of humanity? The effect here is complex, but I cannot help thinking of Owen's determination to 'speak for' his dead, loved comrades. The whole poem, 'Pigs', makes the macabre mundane, then turns back with bitter irony, but also with warmth, to validate, in a sense, the burnt and eaten dead. So this is 'war poetry', by a civilian, spanning like Graves's prose narrative from peace across war to haunted peace.

Much more could be said about this remarkable book, and, I think, will be. Meanwhile, to return to *In the Heart of Europe*. In Chris Agee's complex poem, 'Fleur-de-Lys', memories and talk of Bosnia tumble together with references to Ireland, to Achilles, to Moses in the bullrushes, to Herod, to the US Cavalry's massacre of Nez Perce Indians – 'The same old story, males on the rampage.'

Our tendency to attribute the horrors of Bosnia (Rwanda, Algeria, Congo, Sierra Leone . . . on and on the list might go) to some 'Evil in the heart of humankind' makes sense in terms of traditional Christian theology and its doctrine of the Fall. But we can get along without this explanation, and Agee points to another one. From ancient times and in many, perhaps most, places males from puberty to young manhood have 'proved themselves' by aggressive behaviour. Young African or Melanesian warriors were programmed to steal cattle or pigs, to provoke little wars of a ritual nature. In medieval Ireland a young chief had to establish his prowess by rustling. To be a man, the Bornean Dayak must bring home a head. The Capulets and Jets of Shakespeare's Verona and Bernstein's New York and the razor gangs of old Glasgow are extreme instances of the same phenomenon as sends Hibs and Hearts supporters reeling through the streets of Edinburgh at week-ends. Young males account for the preponderance of violent crime in lowland Scotland. Then, just as the Igbo warrior settled down to farm yams, they marry, have children, become peaceable citizens.

The murderous young males of Northern Ireland over the last three decades have been given causes by their elders' bigoted interpretations of history. This seems to have been the case also in the former Yugoslavia, where the hideous circumstances of two world wars must have provided every gangable youth with a real or imaginary grievance against this or that group of neighbours. The vast conscript armies of modern Europe have enlisted the violence of young males and made its exercise respectable. But no one should be surprised that the Russians who entered Germany in 1945 were minded to rape every woman in sight, just as young Germans had zestfully slaughtered the Jews whom the Nazis had told them were their mortal enemies. The atrocities committed by Canadians in Somalia, where they were part of a UN peacekeeping force, are a recent example of what young men can get up to.

Prose fiction and drama, I would suggest, can cope with this area of human experience when poetry, as a rule, cannot – if it sets out in some old-fashioned way to be 'epic' it will alienate all decent readers. Contemporary verse commonly teases us to enter the undramatic persistences of life, the enigmas of unofficial personalities outside what Agee, as quoted before here, calls the 'Chorus of identity'. I think Harry Clifton's 'The Literal Version', in *In the Heart of Europe,* deals finely with the problem which we often have, with approaching not only a foreign poet in prose translation, but one of our own in a brand new book – 'where is this guy at?':

> On Sundays at least, 'her lips' –
> I am quoting from various texts –
> 'Ice-cold, pressed against my cheeks'
> And his weekends, snowed in
> By a blizzard of football games
> On changing screens, or given over
> To cemetery visits, godlessness,
> Bleak honesty. For the dead
> Are everywhere – there has been war,
> There will be again . . .

And that is the only reference to war in a lengthy poem about a Bosnian poet whose work, Clifton concludes, displays 'a sense of solitude / And a longing to connect'.

Is that what all the writing I have discussed is primarily *about* – connection? Connections are random, unpredictable. The German infantryman on the Eastern Front remembers Goethe as he moves in to destroy a village. The RAF bomb-aimer over Berlin suddenly recalls lines of Blake. After gang rape, a Russian thinks of *Onegin.* The expansions of imagination and empathy and conscience which we believe poetry provides are no guarantee against barbarous behaviour. But to keep writing verse in besieged Sarajevo is to affirm the faith that the connections which might be made could be worthwhile, as well as to strive to leave something behind to represent whatever oneself had been, or might have been.

1999

Just a Nasty Kid

Review of Peter Sellars, *The Persians*.

Early in what might be called 'the last movement' of Peter Sellars's extraordinary *Persians*, sections of the Edinburgh Festival first-night audience began to laugh.

What they had seen was grim: enactment in words, mime and dance of the destruction of Iraqi forces in the Gulf War. Now Xerxes, a figure borrowed from a very old play (the oldest surviving European drama) in order to represent Saddam Hussein, had made his way back through the dead and dying to his court. He was wearing soiled battledress. His mother urged him to go and change his clothes.

Up in the Grand Circle (probably not the best part of the Lyceum from which to view the production), I reacted to the audience's laughter three ways in succession. First, I was dismayed: the spell that Sellars's remarkably skilful company had worked to cast had been violated. Then I remembered how Africans laugh during tragic plays and how this reaction can be justified. Shakespeare's groundlings may well have hooted at Ophelia's madness, and thousands of ancient Greeks, enjoying high festival, quite conceivably rocked with hilarity when Oedipus came back blind. But my third thought was that others were disconcerted, as I was, by the play's switch of mode.

Eugene O'Neill's *Long Day's Journey* is invoked by Sellars himself in the programme. That is a very great tragic drama. Unfortunately, Robert Auletta, who scripted *Persians*, is not O'Neill. The pup Xerxes, splendidly played though he is by John Ortiz, irresistibly suggests a bad boy in some soap opera. His Mom, Atossa, has already accused the ghost of Pop, also known as Darius, of denying him affection. Now look how he has turned out! Destructive, callous delinquent . . . What have we done to our young people in America?

Sellars, setting up the first version of his *Persians* in an aircraft hangar in Salzburg, was allured by Aeschylus' daring in presenting to the Athenians in 472 BC – just eight years after the battle of Salamis – the grief of the defeated Asian enemy. He is a very intelligent man. He has read Edward Said and Martin Bernal's *Black Athena* (which argues that the culture of the Greeks, as they said themselves, derived from Africa). Aeschylus' play is the first projection that we have of the non-European Other, the 'Orient', which defines the 'West' by its difference, and so is the first attempt that we know of to insist, across a constructed 'racial' divide, that 'they, too, are human'.

Sellars is honestly committed. He was properly outraged by US media coverage of the Gulf War that excluded Iraqis, dead or alive. He sees theatre as 'a kind of alternative public information system . . . able partially to humanise the denatured results of our vaunted and costly objectivity . . . television permits you to be spectator, but theatre makes you a participant.'

But then we, the participants, laugh out of turn. I do not blame the Edinburgh audience. Their laughter served to expose the fact that, in setting out to denounce the arrogance of the US superpower, to confirm, with a 'multicultural' cast, the human stature of the Other, Sellars has Americanized both Aeschylus' Persians and contemporary Iraq. A drama presenting the defeat of one cultural system by another is adapted as the text for a sermon about how parents need to get closer to their children, to this younger generation, whose presumed nihilism clearly obsesses Sellars.

The 'gulf' between young and old is not a trivial issue, Indeed, the ancient Greeks had quite a lot to say about it, and *King Lear*, even more than *Long Day's Journey*, is the cardinal text in our tradition that deals with it.

Aeschylus' text gives Sellars and Auletta their cue. Darius ruled the world, and 'all called him king'. His ghost denounces Xerxes: 'He's raw . . . No mind for what I taught him.' But, like everything else in the Greek, this primal tragic situation is contorted by Sellars's adaption. If Xerxes is Saddam Hussein, the Other whom we must understand and not demonize, who, then, is the Other's father? Darius, memorably played by Howie Seago, a deaf actor, is Pop, O'Neill Pop, Soap Pop, American Pop. The Other is America's bad son. But Iraq was, in fact, part of the British Empire, not a great world power, when Saddam was a nasty kid. There was no Iraqi Darius.

Mom (a Puerto Rican, Cordelia Gonzalez, is hauntingly fine as Atossa) could have been, as in Aeschylus' script, the emblem of majestic, resigned, cultural continuity. Through her, Persia survives. In the Greek drama, Atossa does not confront Xerxes after she has left the stage to find fresh royal robes for her son, who has returned from the war in rags. But in Sellars's version, she is a sad old rich girl who has depended on men all her life and whose final embrace of Xerxes, after a family row, represents only the continuity of mutual psychological parasitism. The range of reference that her part evokes includes not only Jackie Kennedy, but Imelda Marcos: Atossa's bad dream of two sisters, one dressed in Persian style, one in Greek, in which the latter refuses to be yoked to Xerxes' chariot, is transferred to a fashion show.

And of course such audacity is compelling. Sellars's *Persians* is full of wonderful theatrical skills. The transfer of much of the chorus, all Darius' speeches, and fierce military sound effects, to loudspeakers thickly spread under the Lyceum's seats works very powerfully. The use of mikes attached to the chorus of two is a thrilling substitute for Greek tragic masks, and it is impossible to praise too highly the majestic speaking of an African-American, Ben Halley Jr, and a Palestinian-American, Joseph Haj. The music provided live by a Nubian lute player, Hamza El Din, is fresh and sharp. Best of all, Martinus Miroto, trained in the Javanese tradition of court dance, who performs wordlessly the role of Messenger, expresses with magnetic finesse the sufferings of unknown soldiers.

But this 'multiculturalism', however splendid its incidental results, poses further ethical and political problems. Not just the Iraqi Other, but all conceivable Others are melted into Sellars's new world pot. Compared with Peter Brook's, *The Mahabharata*, the absence of condescension is commendable. But if one contrasts the electrifying Ninigawa *Macbeth* and *Medea*, seen in Edinburgh a few years back, the Japanese appropriation of European classics bridged cultures by artistic means, but left both east and west intact: Sellars's version of humanity hamburgerizes every kebab it touches.

In the US, this production might work valuably with its natural audience. No resident of that country has ever cowered, at home, in an air-raid shelter: British audiences still contain people who, like myself, were actually 'bombed out', and remembered that when we heard of missiles striking Baghdad. Sellars, for us, is laying on the evocation of life under bombardment unnecessarily thick (though it is masterfully done, with a handheld lamp, searchlight and hurricane lamp in one, moving around the ruins as the ghost of Darius and his widow express their horror). In America, perhaps, this piling of Pelion on Ossa is necessary. And I must stress that Sellars's *Persians*, whatever embarrassment it caused me, is ambitious, intelligent, deeply serious theatre, not just a show: it is something important.

1993

Coda: Christa Wolf's Cassandra and the Future of Epic

It was here. This is where she stood. These stone lions looked at her; now they no longer have heads. This fortress – once impregnable, now a pile of stones – was the last thing she saw.

So Christa Wolf begins her novel *Cassandra*, with a paragraph setting herself (her authorial persona) in the present-day ruins of Mycenae. The second paragraph has just one sentence: 'Keeping step with the story, I make my way into death.' From now on, the author will be Cassandra. What follows is her surge and recoil of memory, as she waits outside the palace of Agamemnon, conqueror of her native Troy, who has brought her here as his slave and presumed concubine (though this Cassandra allowed him no sex). Now he has entered the palace where as Cassandra, the seer, knows, his wife Clytemnestra will butcher him as he washes travel away in a bath. Then she will kill Cassandra, who has to accept the fate she foresees: 'Nothing, nothing I could have done or not done, willed or thought, could have led me to a different goal.'[1]

Wolf understands her doomed seer through two of the fundamental works of Western literature, the *Iliad* and *Agamemnon*, the first of Aeschylus' Oresteian trilogy of tragic dramas. Cassandra also appears in Book 2 of Virgil's *Aeneid*, where the hero recalls for Dido, Queen of Carthage, the fall of Troy – Priam's most interesting daughter is dragged captive by Greeks who have spilled from the wooden horse. Wolf makes Aeneas the joy of Cassandra's life. Her last thoughts before she goes in to death are of him.

Most unusually, Wolf's US publishers printed with her short novel four items which she calls 'Conditions of a Narrative' which together exceed it in length – two Grecian travelogues, a diary, and a long letter to a friend, all delivered as 'Lectures in Poetics' at the University of Frankfurt in May 1982. Her fifth 'lecture' was a draft of the novel. 'Fiction' and 'Conditions' appeared in different volumes in German. So we have in English translation a hybridized work – a narrative followed by the considerations and research which preceded its finalization. This might suggest witty, anarchic 'Postmodernism' but in fact Wolf, exploring her self-identification with Cassandra, is earnestly engaged, as a Marxist, in an attempt, first, to understand the ancient origins of war and tyranny, and, second, to apply such understanding to the Cold War crisis of the Reagan era. 'I am a European woman', she writes in her diary for 8 July 1980.

> Europe cannot be defended against an atomic war. Either it will survive in one piece or be destroyed in one piece . . . I conclude that the sensible course may be the one which holds out absolutely no hope: unilateral disarmament . . . By choosing this course, we place the other side under the moral pressure of the world public; we render superfluous the USSR's extortionary policy of arming itself to death; we renounce the atomic first-strike capability, and we devote all our efforts to the most effective defence measures.[2]

Is she really saying that 'we Europeans' can and must withdraw simultaneously from NATO and the Warsaw Pact? Those who find this preposterous must be told how desperately dangerous the world seemed in 1982 with Reagan in the White House. In any case, it is not a London litterateuse or Cambridge academic who writes this. It is East Germany's most famous woman writer, a lifelong member of the ruling party of the German Democratic Republic (DDR), who ventures criticism of the USSR to an audience on the western side of the Iron Curtain . . .

Wolf had, before and after *Cassandra*, moments of high celebrity in the West. She was initially admired and honoured as the most interesting woman writer in Communist Eastern Europe. In 1987, her novel *Accident*, a reflection on the Chernobyl nuclear disaster, was in the best-seller lists in West Germany for twenty-nine weeks. Then, after the fall of the Berlin Wall in November 1989, came a horrendous reversal. She published a novella, *What Remains*, which was vilified by leading West German critics. It presents a day in the life of a writer under surveillance by the Stasi secret police, and is based on Wolf's own situation for a period in 1979. Hypocrisy and worse were alleged against the author, who had admitted to having herself collaborated with the Stasi in 1959–62. The charge was that, rather than risking expulsion or even imprisonment and torture, like a true, brave dissident, she had accepted the privileges of a writer honoured by the DDR.

In retrospect, the 'Christa Wolf Affair' seems to have been a spasm in the transition from divided to reunited Germany. Intellectual right-wingers in the West reacted against the aura of moral superiority which had gathered round the long-dead Brecht, who had preferred the 'pregnant whore' in the East to the 'syphilitic whore' of the West, round Stefan Heym, who had spent the war years in the US Army but preferred the DDR to Eisenhower's America, and round Wolf and other quietly dissident writers who had stayed East for their own various reasons, operating in the surprisingly large interstices of a regime which tolerated much more artistic freedom than Western Cold Warriors liked to think.[3]

Two points are worth making about *Cassandra* in this connection. First, no unprejudiced reader of the book could see its author as anyone but a woman of painful, tentative honesty, deeply concerned at once with the intimate texture of personal relationships and the geopolitics of the nuclear age. Further – she offers, in her account of the corruption of Trojan politics and social life by a war which the city has brought upon itself, a powerfully imagined prototype of the totalitarian state, in which Cassandra herself, daughter of King Priam and priestess of Apollo, is thrown into especially vile confinement for her intolerable nonconformity.

'The Troy I have in mind is not a description of bygone days but a model for a kind of Utopia.'[4] Wolf is, and is not, concerned about the historicity of the Trojan War. As a Marxist she sees a material cause for such a conflict. Troy controlled the Hellespont, to which the Achaeans wanted free access. The abduction of Helen, had it occurred, would have been catalyst or pretext. 'The Trojans would have been massacred no matter what . . . is this precisely what Cassandra is lamenting, that her people have no alternative?'[5] But economic necessity as conceived by Marxists need not, perhaps, have brought doom to Troy at that particular juncture? The Trojans could perhaps have stopped war just then by giving Helen back? Wolf importantly departs from Homer by adopting the legend of 'Egyptian Helen'.

According to this ancient variation of Helen's story, which itself exists in several variations, Helen never reached Troy. Wolf has Paris attempt her abduction, only to lose her to the king of Egypt on his way home. A heavily veiled woman comes off board and is said to be Helen.

Cassandra is the last person in the palace to recognize that there is no beautiful Helen in Troy. The political corruption of Trojan Utopia begins thus: for reasons of face it cannot be admitted to the Greeks that there is no Helen to give back. And since war against the Greeks is now thought both necessary and winnable, the name of Helen must serve as a rallying cry for the common soldiery, raising them 'beyond themselves'.

At the point where Paris says to Cassandra, 'Wake up, Sister. Ye gods: She doesn't exist', Cassandra has a seizure, exclaims, 'Woe, we are lost' and is grabbed by the palace guard, whose commander Eumelos (a Beria, a Himmler) is now beginning to control Troy so completely that 'The Eumelos inside me', Cassandra thinks, forbids her to shriek out, 'Trojans, there is no Helen.' She tries to reason with her beloved father Priam, but he is past reason. War will come, Priam says. 'They want our gold. And free access to the Dardanelles.' And he wants war because Troy's military leaders are telling him that Troy will win.[6] One might think of Hitler madly and almost gratuitously declaring war on the USA in December 1941 . . .

But her powerlessness has another explanation. Wolf cannot discard entirely the basic postulate in all traditional accounts of Cassandra. She desired to be priestess of Apollo, and seer. The god came to her and promised her the gift of prophecy in return for her sexual favours. She accepted the gift, then repelled the god. His retort was to ordain that no one would believe her true prophecies. Wolf's Cassandra herself becomes a sceptic. Though she functions as his priestess, Apollo exists for her only as an evil dream. The literal intervention of supernatural beings in human affairs which is inseparably part of both *Iliad* and *Aeneid* is not compatible with Wolf's vision of Troy. Yet the gods are a live issue for Wolf and her Cassandra, in terms prefigured by Aeschylus' Oresteian Trilogy, where the Eumenides, 'kindly ones', primordial feminist potencies who hound Orestes after he kills his mother in revenge for her murder of Agamemnon, are finally tamed and accommodated, as subordinates, in the brave new Athens where Apollo and the unwomanly goddess Athene have taken charge. Motherly divinities held sway on earth before the usurpation of power by Zeus and his gang of Olympians.

The most striking and most questionable invention of Wolf in her *Cassandra* is the idea that alongside Troy, towards Mount Ida, exists a community which provides refuge and succour for the victims of war and wicked power. Here the rites of the ousted Mother Goddess are still practised. We are offered a prototypical hippie commune where the delightful wise Anchises, father of Aeneas, works benevolent magic by carving in wood and Arisbe, mother by Priam of Cassandra's beloved half-brother Aisakos, a massive woman with a trumpet-like voice, commands the rituals of Cybele, a name attached heuristically to a shadowy stone figure on the wall of a cave, focus of solace for all regardless of class and ethnicity.

Crucial to Wolf's trajectory of argument is a debate, at 'Anchises's place', between Arisbe and Penthesilea, leader of the warrior Amazons who have come to fight for Troy:

> All the women I knew were there [remembers Cassandra]. They said they wanted to get to know each other.
>
> It turned out that in many ways they were at one. I say 'they,' for I held back at first. That part of the inhabited world which we knew had turned against us ever more cruelly, ever more swiftly. 'Against us women,' said Penthesilea. 'Against us people,' Arisbe replied.

PENTHESILEA:	The men are getting what they paid for.
ARISBE:	You call that getting what they paid for when they are reduced to the level of butchers?
PENTHESILEA:	They are butchers. So they are doing what they enjoy.
ARISBE:	And what about us? What if we became butchers, too?
PENTHESILEA:	Then we are doing what we have to do. But we don't enjoy it.
ARISBE:	We should do what they do in order to show that we are different?
PENTHESILEA:	Yes.
OENONE:	But one can't live that way.
PENTHESILEA:	Not live? You can die all right.
HECUBA:	Child, you want everything to come to a stop.
PENTHESILEA:	That is what I want. Because I don't know any other way to make the men stop.

> Then the young slave woman from the Greek camp came over to her, knelt down before her, and laid Penthesilea's hands against her face. She said: 'Penthesilea. Come join us.' 'Join you? What does that mean?' 'Come to the mountains. The forest. The caves along the Scamander. Between killing and dying there is a third alternative: living.'[7]

What Wolf has conceived here is an ancient, 'Utopian', prototype of the European women's movement c.1980 where it is an issue whether women to oppose male aggression and dominance should or should not, à la Thatcher, become aggressively domineering themselves. Does this, in detail, now seem dated? The issues raised will not go away.

Wolf's Troy is not the centre of basic wealth and heroic values found in Homer, nor is it like Aeschylus' more complex Mycenae, where the voice of the people is raised ineffectually against a usurping tyrant. It is a sophisticated polity with civil-servant scribes, professional security forces, far-flung trade and an important market. In such a place, relationships between men and women (Priam's very numerous sons and daughters, for instance) can be permutated and modulated many ways. It can provide features reminiscent of the Nazi Germany of Wolf's childhood and her present-day Cold War world. And alongside this place, Wolf can imagine a free community of women – plus Anchises –

> grateful that we were the ones granted the highest privilege there is: to slip a narrow strip of future into the grim present, which occupies all of time . . . Anchises, I believe, loved our life in the caves wholeheartedly, loved it without reservation, sadness, and scruple. He was fulfilling a dream of his and was teaching us younger ones how to dream with both feet on the ground.[8]

The punchline, as it were, of *Cassandra* involves Anchises' son Aeneas. In the *Iliad,* he is a sturdy, not very characterful, Trojan hero. In Virgil's epic, of course, he is the brave leader dogged by 'reservation, sadness, and scruple', who escapes from burning Troy with a few score followers and sails west, eventually to settle in Italy, where his descendants are destined to found Rome. For Wolf's Cassandra, he is the decent man, her one soulmate amongst those she beds. As Troy's fall impends, she quarrels with him. He urges her to join him in flight, 'to found a new Troy somewhere else'. She refuses:

> Aeneas. Dear one. You understood long before you would admit it. It was obvious. The new masters would dictate their law to all the survivors. The earth was not large enough to escape them. You, Aeneas, had no choice. You had to snatch a couple of hundred people from death. You were their leader. 'Soon, very soon, you will have to become a hero.'

> 'Yes!' you cried. 'And so?' I saw by your eyes that you had understood me. I cannot love a hero. I do not want to see you being transformed into a statue.[9]

Wolf-Cassandra's rejection of the hero comes, I now suggest, at the end of a phase extending over four centuries in which 'Western Man' has applied to the interpretation of warfare Homeric and Virgilian paradigms. At the start of this phase, there was Shakespeare's eminently sensible treatment of the Trojan War in *Troilus and Cressida,* where Ulysses is a crook and Achilles – here Wolf concurs completely – is a graceless brute. But as Virgil and Homer were captured by Dryden and Pope within the genteel rationality of the 'heroic couplet', as the reconciliation of the classics with revisionist Christianity proceeded, models of heroism and mourning, pathos and expiation, were provide for all military eventualities, affecting obituary and statuary, 'history painting', music and memorial. Andromache's parting from doomed Hector has expressed the loyal heart of every soldier's wife, Aeneas' indecision before he despatches Turnus the soldier's recoil, which must be reversed, from necessary killing. War was a business for 'heroes', as it still is for British tabloid newspapers, which during the Iraq War of 2003 extended the accolade of 'heroism' even to unfortunate 'other ranks' dead by 'friendly fire'.

To return to the matter of historicity – that always controversial study, *The World of Odysseus* (1954, revised 1977) could not settle matters which M. I. Finley addressed there about whether and when there was actually a Trojan War and which if any archaeological layer in the Turkish site of Hissarlik, first excavated by Schliemann in the 1970s, might or might not be Priam's Troy. Indeed, Finley's demolition of wishful scholars implied that the snark was a boojum, and that conclusive evidence will never be found either way. What he could establish, with great force and elegance, is that the texts of the Homeric epics themselves may yield genuine historical evidence about a society which Finley dates not to the time of the presumed Trojan War – believed by ancient Greek scholars to have occurred between 1350 and 1100 BCE, dated usually by modern experts in the early thirteenth century BCE, during the period of 'Mycenaean' civilization – but to the Greece of the tenth and ninth centuries BCE. Bringing legends together, bards in that society homogenized them with the social forms around them. Essentially the picture offered by the poems of the society and its system of values is a coherent one.

Its coherence provides no space for such a woman as Christa Wolf's Cassandra. Aristocratic households and kinships, in which women are essentially subordinate, domineer completely over needful craftsmen, slaves, and rightless agricultural labourers. Merchants are despised. When goods change hands between person and person, territory and territory, it is ideally through lordly gifts to retainers or other lords, or via heroic pillage. According to the values of this world, Finley says, ' "Warrior" and "hero" are synonyms, and the main theme of a warrior culture is constructed on two notes – prowess and honour. The one is the hero's essential attribute, the other his essential aim. Every judgement, every action, all skills and talents have the function of

defining honour or realising it . . . Even life must surrender to honour.'
So Achilles and Hector go their deaths 'without flinching and without
questioning'.[10]

Remarkably, the gods who are in charge of this world are entirely
human. 'God was created in man's image with a skill and a genius that
must be ranked with man's greatest intellectual feats.' (Finley should
perhaps have added here that the power attributed to goddesses and
their forceful politicking around Zeus mitigate mightily the overall
male chauvinism of the epics.) Homer's gods behave petulantly,
treacherously, brutally. But they cannot be seen as wicked. Homer's
gods were 'essentially devoid of any ethical quality whatsoever'.[11] For
humans, ethics are subsumed under heroism. Achilles is a hero, so his
brutality is heroic.

To an astonishing extent, benevolent eighteenth-century moralists
and seriously Christian nineteenth-century statesmen and scholars
were able to accept that heroic standard. Admiration of Napoleon
depended on a parallel suspension of normal ethical considerations.
When heroism could be harnessed to another force beyond ethics –
history – the cult of Napoleon, and later those of Lenin and Stalin,
might acquire ineluctable power over many.

The Homeric epics set aside Demeter, goddess of fertility, a major
force in Greek religion, closely related to the Cybele of Wolf's novel.

> Demeter-worship was carried on outside the formal Olympian religion, for
> its founders had place neither for her nor for mystery rites altogether.
> Homer knew all about Demeter (she is mentioned six times in the *Iliad* and
> *Odyssey*); and that is just the point. He deliberately turned his back on her
> and everything she represented.[12]

The 'world of Aeneas', as Virgil imagines it, is very different. Aeneas
is servant not master of fate, or what we could call history. His destiny –
to prepare the way for the great World Empire of Rome and what the
poet clearly hoped would be lasting peace – compels him to desert Dido,
a woman with fine human qualities whom he sincerely loves. He has to
fight to get a foothold for his Trojans in Italy, and this entails detestable
griefs and losses. His heroic efficiency in slaughter is a means, not an
end, and cannot preclude guilt, or at least strong compunction.
Countless readers over more than two millennia have been deeply moved
by a particular episode which concludes Book X of Virgil's epic.

Mezentius is a mighty warrior but a very bad man – a ruler in Etruria
deposed by subjects sick of his tortures and repression, now fighting as

a renegade against fellow Etruscans. He stands to await Achilles and promises his son Lausus that he will slay the Trojan hero. But as Aeneas begins to batter him, Lausus bravely rushes in to parry a fatal blow aimed at his father, who escapes. Aeneas now pleads with Lausus to stand aside: 'Why rush upon death like this? You're too rash, fighting out of your class.' But the youth continues to defy him. In rage, Aeneas slays him. Then in pity he sighs over Lausus. Rather than stripping his corpse of arms, he personally hands it over to the boy's comrades for due rites. Then, of course, he goes after Mezentius. As he stands over this vanquished hero, Mezentius croaks:

> Harsh foe, you need not rail, or waste words on your deadly purpose.
> No crime in killing: I never supposed there was, when I made war.
> Mercy is not in the bond my Lausus made between us.
> I ask but one thing – if the conquered has any right to a favour –
> Allow my body interment. I know I'm beset by my people's
> Bitter hatred. I ask you, protect my remains from their fury,
> And let me rest in the same sepulchre as my son.
> He spoke, and deliberately offered his throat to the sword, and received it.
> His life went out in waves of blood all over his armour.[13]

This pre-echoes Aeneas' despatch of the reckless Turnus at the very end of the epic. It is as if the mission of Virgil's hero is to defeat the kind of hero who sees 'no crime in killing'.

Eighteenth- and nineteenth-century readers of Homer must surely have tended to see his heroes through a Virgilian filter (though it has to be admitted that materials are there in the *Iliad* from which Achilles and Hector can wishfully be reconstructed as moral beings). The Homeric spell has been broken not only by the ousting of classics from the centre of educational curricula, but by the horrendously anti-heroic character of mechanized warfare since 1914.

While working towards a conclusion of this essay, and with it of this book, I was privileged to attend, with a few dozen others, a rehearsed reading at the Traverse Theatre, Edinburgh, of Peter Arnott's latest play, *The Wire Garden*.[14] Watching this I realized for the first time that nowadays Western humankind arranges its musings and judgements of war not in relation to the Trojan cycle of legends or the Arthurian Matter of Britain, but to information about two world wars and Vietnam. The Homerization of commanders – Napoleon, Wellington, Robert E. Lee – with a rare exception such as Rommel proving the rule, became an unworkable trick in the face of mechanized carnage.

Generals were executants for engineers and playthings for politicians. Officers executed orders from generals with merciless machines. To render the common soldier Christlike as Wilfred Owen did was an unrepeatable feat. We think now of action in warfare in terms of blocs, divisions and specialist arms – Eighth Army, Luftwaffe, Green Berets, SAS . . .

Arnott achieved renown as a very young writer in the mid-1980s with a startling play, *White Rose,* about a Soviet woman flyer over Stalingrad. Now, it seems to me, bombed London and Dresden, besieged Stalingrad, falling Berlin, have replaced Troy as we try to think about new conflicts – Kosovo, Afghanistan, Iraq, where next . . .?

A particular modulation of epic has been an admitted influence on Peter Arnott – Vasily Grossman's huge novel *Life and Fate,* finished in Russia in 1960, banned from publication, smuggled out to the West, eventually published in Switzerland in 1980, sixteen years after the author's death . . .[15] It centres on Stalingrad in 1942, but spreads out to represent the entire Soviet system, and also projects, with intimate detail, the Final Solution. Grossman's model was Tolstoy's *War and Peace* – that his book is technically conservative may explain why it has not been in fashion with critics. Tolstoy's prose epic demystifies and resacralizes war. The great commander is not Napoleon, absurdly trying to impose his will on nations and battlefields, but old Kutuzov who holds back and lets events take their natural course. The true heroes are ordinary Russians of all classes defending their country instinctively. Grossman presses the second point just as strongly. Stalin will appear to have won a victory because apolitical – and in some cases even oppositional – soldiers obey the patriotic momentum which encircles and destroys Paulus's German Sixth Army.

That process – tragic almost in the Greek sense for Paulus himself – is present throughout offstage in *The Wire Garden,* as are the death camps of Poland. The action in front of us primarily concerns the fate of Jacob Djugashvilli, Stalin's son by his first wife, rejected by the dictator for marrying a Jewess. He is now in Sachsenhausen prison camp near Berlin, receiving the obsessive attention of Major Echtlinger of the Security Service. This arrogant madman is a polished aristocrat who studied in England and Russia and believes he can use Jacob's witness against his father to end a war which he considers crazy. Jacob, with no reason to love his father, whose appearance to him in hallucinations is a powerful feature of the play, nevertheless will not consent to treachery. His eventual death under duress will be reported as suicide.

Before this, early in 1943, Echtlinger arrives triumphant in the room in the prison which Jacob has shared with a highly connected Soviet officer, Harbin, who has just been battered to death by their captors:

ECHTLINGER: You're going home. In a few weeks. You're going to be exchanged. We have a Field Marshal . . . called Von Paulus . . . who got himself . . . stuck in Stalingrad. Surrendered to save his men. Hitler wants him back. To throttle him personally on the radio I should imagine. In any case . . . I've pulled a string here . . . a string there . . . and word has already been sent to both your families.
JACOB: He's dead, Major.

Jacob, most movingly, represents the anti-heroic new model of heroism prefigured in E. E. Cummings's affirmation, 'There is some shit I will not eat', and Orwell's advice against submission to any domineering ideology. He has just whispered to the dying Harbin:

> You mustn't talk. That's what matters. It only takes a word. They can take a hold of ONE WORD in your mouth and they can pull you inside out by your tongue. Tell me NOTHING.

I think that Arnott's play is a recension of Grossman's recension of Tolstoy's recension of epic, and that it resonates with Christa Wolf's ultimately uncompromising *Cassandra*, who refuses to be part of Aeneas' heroic project and hopes against hope that from the commune of Arisbe and Anchises, memories will be handed on, that a 'narrow strip of future' has been slipped into 'the grim present which occupies all of time'.

Arnott's play, 'epic' in the Brechtian sense itself, with eighteen sharply differentiated characters, German, Russian, British, Irish, will eventually, one hopes, receive the prominent staging which it deserves. Meanwhile, the drip, drip, drip of TV documentaries about the world wars continues – at least one new one, it seems, every weekend. The good thing about this obsession is that most documentaries do not mask the cruelty, horror and chaos of the events to which they refer. Less good, at first sight, is the inherent marginality of women in the story-cycle which includes the Somme and Stalingrad. Picking a Soviet woman flyer as the protagonist of his early play, Peter Arnott mined a rare seam. The participation of countless ferocious women in many front line roles in the Red Army had counterparts elsewhere only in resistance movements. But perhaps a beneficial effect of the sidelining thus of half the human race will be to reinforce antipathy to war as such, to broaden Wolf's 'narrow strip of future' – if humankind has much future at all.

2003

References

[1] Christa Wolf, *Cassandra: A Novel and Four Essays,* tr. Jan van Heurck (New York: Farrar Strauss Giroux, 1984).

[2] Ibid., pp. 229–30.

[3] I write here from the experience of several visits to the DDR in the 1980s. If free-thinking intellectuals such as I met there were indeed, in a sense, 'privileged', this itself was a sign that repression was not 'total'. The immense prestige of Brecht, for instance, licensed politically awkward experiments in theatre. Karen McPherson kindly supplied me with a file of cuttings from the British press about the Christa Wolf affair of 1990. A review by Natasha Walter of *What Remains* on its appearance in English (*Independent,* 24 April 1993) is especially judicious in Wolf's defence.

[4] Wolf, *Cassandra,* p. 224.

[5] Ibid., p. 255.

[6] Ibid., pp. 66–70.

[7] Ibid., pp. 117–19.

[8] Ibid., pp. 134–5.

[9] Ibid., pp. 137–8.

[10] M. I. Finley, *The World of Odysseus* (London: Chatto & Windus, 1977), p. 113.

[11] Ibid., pp. 132, 137.

[12] Ibid., pp. 136–7.

[13] Virgil, *Aeneid,* tr. C. Day Lewis (Oxford: Oxford University Press, 1986), pp. 315–21.

[14] My thanks to Peter Arnott for giving me a copy of his play marked up for rehearsed reading. I should stress that my quotations are from a text not yet finalized.

[15] Now available in English, tr. Robert Chandler (London: Harvill Press, 1985, paperback, 1995).

Peter Millington
2 October 2013
£15·81 Amazon